# Clinical Graphs Using SAS®

## Sanjay Matange

support.sas.com/bookstore

# Contents

# About This Book

## Purpose

SAS users in the Health and Life Sciences industry need to create complex graphs so that biostatisticians and clinicians can use them for analysis of the data. The graphs are also used for submissions to FDA for drug approvals. These graphs have specific requirements and must be designed to deliver the data accurately and clearly without distractions. Many users do not have the skills with SAS graphics tools such as Statistical Graphics (SG) procedures and the Graph Template Language (GTL) to create such graphs. This book provides the know-how and the code to create the graphs that are commonly used in this industry.

## Is This Book for You?

This book is for the SAS graphics programmer who is responsible for creating sophisticated graphs for the analysis of clinical trials data. Most of these graphs are not automatically created by some analytical procedure, and must be custom built. However, many of these graphs are commonly used in the Health and Life Sciences industry, and there is an effort in the industry to standardize. This book describes how to create such graphs for intermediate and advanced graph programmers.

## Prerequisites

Some knowledge of SAS DATA step programming may be required to get the data into the shape needed for the graphs. Knowledge of SG procedures and GTL will be helpful, but is not required.

## Scope of This Book

This book includes detailed instructions about how to create some of the standard, commonly used graphs for analysis of data in the Health and Life Sciences industry. The book provides some introductory information on the use of SG procedures and GTL.

However, this book does not cover the features of SG procedures or of GTL in depth. Such comprehensive information is beyond the scope of this book.

# About the Examples

## Software Used to Develop the Book's Content

All the graphs shown in this book are generated using SAS 9.4 or SAS 9.3.

## Example Code and Data

To access the book's example code and data, visit the author's page at
http://support.sas.com/publishing/authors. Select the name of the author. Then, look for the book
cover and select Example Code and Data.

If you are unable to access the code through the website, send email to saspress@sas.com.

## SAS University Edition

If you are using SAS University Edition to access data and run your programs, ensure that the
software contains the product or products that you need to run the code:
http://support.sas.com/software/products/university-edition/index.html.

## Output and Graphics Used in This Book

All the graphs included in the book are created using the program code shown in the chapters.
Some appearance options in the code might have been trimmed to fit the space available on the
page. The full programs including the data generation and procedure code are available.

# Additional Help

Although this book illustrates many analyses regularly performed in businesses across industries,
questions specific to your aims and issues may arise. To fully support you, SAS Institute and SAS
Press offer you the following help resources:

- For questions about topics covered in this book, contact the author through SAS Press:
  - Send questions by email to saspress@sas.com; include the book title in your
    correspondence.
  - Submit feedback on the author's page at http://support.sas.com/author_feedback.
- For questions about topics in or beyond the scope of this book, post queries to the relevant
  SAS Support Communities at https://communities.sas.com/welcome.
- SAS Institute maintains a comprehensive website with up-to-date information. One page that
  is particularly useful to both the novice and the seasoned SAS user is the Knowledge Base.
  Search for relevant notes in the "Samples and SAS Notes" section of the Knowledge Base at
  http://support.sas.com/resources.
- Registered SAS users or their organizations can access SAS Customer Support at
  http://support.sas.com. Here you can pose specific questions to SAS Customer Support; under
  *Support*, click *Submit a Problem*. You will need to provide an email address to which replies

can be sent, identify your organization, and provide a customer site number or license information. This information can be found in your SAS logs.

## Keep in Touch

We look forward to hearing from you. We invite questions, comments, and concerns. If you want to contact us about a specific book, please include the book title in your correspondence.

### Contact the Author through SAS Press

- Visit the author's page at http://support.sas.com/author_feedback.
- Send comments by email to saspress@sas.com

### Purchase SAS Books

- Visit sas.com/store/books.
- Phone 1-800-727-0025
- Email: sasbook@sas.com

### Subscribe to the SAS Learning Report

Receive up-to-date information about SAS training, certification, and publications via email by subscribing to the SAS Learning Report monthly eNewsletter. Read the archives and subscribe today at http://support.sas.com/community/newsletters/training!

## Publish with SAS

SAS is recruiting authors! Are you interested in writing a book? Visit http://support.sas.com/saspress for more information.

# About The Author

 Sanjay Matange is an R & D Director in the Data Visualization Division at SAS, responsible for the development and support of ODS Graphics. This includes the Graph Template Language (GTL), Statistical Graphics (SG) procedures, ODS Graphics Designer, and other related graphics applications. Sanjay has extensive experience in building complex graphs for all domains including Health and Life Sciences. Sanjay has been with SAS for over 25 years and is coauthor of two patents and the author of three SAS Press books.

Learn more about this author by visiting his author page at http://support.sas.com/matange. There you can download free book excerpts, access example code and data, read the latest reviews, get updates, and more.

# Acknowledgments

I wish to express my gratitude to my editor, Brenna Leath, for her steady support, to Susan Schwartz and Wei Cheng for sharing freely their expertise in clinical graphs, Philip Holland for his insights into SAS programming, and Jeanette Bottitta and Steve England for their thorough technical review of the contents.

I thank Caroline Brickley for her copyedit, Denise Jones for production, and Robert Harris for the excellent art work for the cover. I thank Armistead Sapp for helping convince everyone that this book deserves to be published in color.

# Preface

Clinical data is easier to understand when presented in a visual format. The human brain allocates a large percentage of its resources to take in and process visual information rapidly. Pattern recognition is key to human survival, and we can rapidly and accurately make sense of complex visual information to make decisions. We can make judgments on visual data even when we are not focused on the task explicitly.

In comparison to this remarkable ability developed through sheer necessity for survival, the remembering and processing of numeric data in raw tabular firm requires the explicit and intentional involvement of the cerebral cortex. The human brain is relatively slow in absorbing pure numbers, and remarkably poor in remembering more than a handful at a time. Furthermore, making evaluation of relative magnitude between such numeric data is slow.

Graphical views of the data allows quick processing and evaluation that can help in planning the analysis phase of the project. Results of the analysis are easier to understand when they are delivered in a graphical form. Graphical representation of the data along with the derived statistical information can be a key factor in understanding of the results.

Presenting the data as a simple bar chart or a scatter plot can help in its understanding. In some cases, sophisticated graphs with complex layouts help to understand the trends and see the associations in the data. These include graphs with raw data along with derived statistics and tabular information, classification panels by multiple class variables, scatter plot matrices of multiple measures and ad-hoc layout of dissimilar graphs necessary to display the information using multiple representations of data, often on a uniform scale.

To create such graphs you need a language to systematically describe the complex layouts and the relationships between the different parts of the graph. Individual graphs could be created using extensive annotate functionality, but such graphs are difficult to adapt to different situations, hard to build and hard to maintain. The new graphics software included in Base SAS® such as the Graph Template Language (GTL), the Statistical Graphics (SG) Procedures, and the ODS Graphics Designer provide you with the tools you need to create complex clinical graphs.

GTL is a comprehensive syntax to define the structure of a graph. GTL has a structured and logical syntax, necessary to build complex graphical layouts, with a large set of features. With a high level of features comes some complexity, so GTL has a significant learning curve. Often you just need a simple graph quickly. For such situations we can use the Statistical Graphics (SG) procedures, which provide an easy to use procedure like syntax to the GTL functionality.

GTL was first released with SAS 9.2, and was initially motivated by the needs of the SAS statisticians and procedure writers to create the graphs that are automatically created by the SAS analytical procedures. SG procedures provide a simplified, value added syntax to create graphs using GTL under the covers.

With SAS 9.3, significant new features were added to make the building of complex clinical graphs possible. This set of features was further expanded with SAS 9.4 and the maintenance releases to make clinical graphs easy. While most types of graphs can be made using the SAS 9.3 feature set, they are much easier to make using the SAS 9.4 features, many of which were developed expressly for such use cases.

In this book, I have described how to create many clinical graphs using SAS 9.3 in Chapters 3 and 7. Many new plot types and features have been added with SAS 9.40M3 making clinical graphs much easier to create. So, the recommended way to create clinical graphs is with the SAS 9.40M3 release as shown in Chapters 4 and 8.

Often, the SG procedures are all you need to create a large percentage of the graphs that are commonly used in the HLS domain. The SGPLOT procedure is designed to create "Single-Cell" graphs. These graphs comprise a very large proportion of the graphs in use that display all the data related information in one graphical data display area. Other items necessary to decode and convey the information such as legends, statistics tables, titles and footnotes are also included in the graph. The SGPANEL procedure makes it easy to create classification panels for one or more class variables.

Often, a complex, multi cell layout is necessary to create graphs that that contain a lot of information. The data in each cell has to be displayed on a uniform scale with other data and tabular information. Such graphs need a bit more structure and functionality and are best created using GTL.

In this book, I will organize the graphs in two categories based on complexity. Graphs we can create using SG procedures and complex graphs that require use of GTL. For each case, I will show you how to make the graph using SAS 9.3 features and also SAS 9.4. SAS 9.4 provides you with many new features that will make the task much easier.

Clinical graphs have their own aesthetic requirements which are based on industry standard usage and requirements of scholarly journals for publications or for submissions to regulatory authorities. Such appropriate visual aesthetics are built in by default and you have to do little to get the right graph "out-of-the-box". The graphics system is designed with the principles of effective graphics in mind to convey the information with maximum clarity and minimum clutter. However, extensive customizations can be done to meet your specific requirements.

This book shows you how to create the required clinical graph given the data. Often, the data I use is simulated using mathematical functions and random number generators. The graphs themselves attempt to duplicate the presentation of data as proposed by experts in the clinical domain. My goal here is not to invent new graphical displays for clinical use, but to show you how to create displays commonly used in the industry, and how certain aspects of the displays may be better from the point of view of effectiveness of the graph. Techniques for modeling and analysis of the data itself are beyond the scope of this book.

# Chapter 1: Introduction to ODS Graphics

There has been a sea change in SAS graphics capabilities over the past few years. The advent of ODS Graphics has made it possible for many SAS analytical procedures to create graphs as part of the procedure output. This is of great convenience to users, as many standard graphs are created automatically, providing a consistency that was absent before. All users now get a set of graphs that are carefully designed by the procedure writers for each specific procedure.

These standard graphs are created by use of the Graph Template Language (GTL). GTL provides a flexible and structured syntax to define many types of graphs into StatGraph templates using the TEMPLATE procedure. These templates can range from the simplest scatter plot to complex diagnostics panels. These templates are then associated with data from within the analytical procedure to create the graphs. The same template can be used with different compatible data to create graphs for different use cases.

Other tools, such as the Statistical Graphics (SG) procedures and ODS Graphics Designer, are made available that provide an easy-to-use interface to the commonly used features of GTL. You can use GTL yourself to define your own graph template and render it using the SGRENDER procedure. Or, you can use the SG procedures or Designer to create your own custom graphs. Now you have a choice of different tools.

## 1.1 A Brief History of ODS Graphics

Prior to SAS 9.2, only a few analytical procedures created graphs automatically as part of the procedure output. The normal process for creating graphs from the procedure output often required post-processing of the data. First, it was necessary to run the procedure step to compute and save the data. Then, users had to use the SAS/GRAPH procedures to create custom plots from this data.

This process had some drawbacks.

- There was no standard set of graphs that were available to all users of a procedure.
- All users had to create their own graphs from the data.
- Each user had to become proficient in SAS/GRAPH code, diverting precious resources away from the analysis task itself.
- Important analysis data computed during the procedure step was lost once the procedure terminated.

In light of these issues, there was a strong desire that the analytical procedures create the appropriate graphical output automatically as part of the procedure step. However, visual presentation of the output from analytical procedures requires sophisticated graphs, as each procedure has its own unique requirements. To achieve this, it was necessary to develop a new structured graphics language that would allow for the definition of complex, sophisticated graphs in a systematic way. This led to the development of ODS Graphics software and the Graph Template Language.

The ODS Graphics software released with SAS 9.2 has made it easier for you to obtain high quality graphs with little or no effort in the following ways:

- You can get automatic graphs from SAS analytical procedures.
- You can create custom graphs using the Graph Template Language (GTL).
- You can create custom graphs using the Statistical Graphics (SG) procedures.
- You can create custom graphs using the ODS Graphics Designer application.

Let us review the benefits and audience for each of the above methods.

## 1.2 Automatic Graphs from SAS Analytical Procedures

Many Base SAS, SAS/STAT, SAS/QC, SAS/ETS, and SAS High-Performance Forecasting procedures create high quality graphs automatically. Below, we have enabled ODS Graphics software and then run the LIFETEST procedure.

```
ods graphics on;
proc lifetest data=BMT plots=survival(atrisk=0 to 2500 by 500);
   time T * Status(0);
   strata Group / test=logrank adjust=sidak;
   run;
```

**Figure 1.2 – The Product-Limit Survival Estimates Graph1**

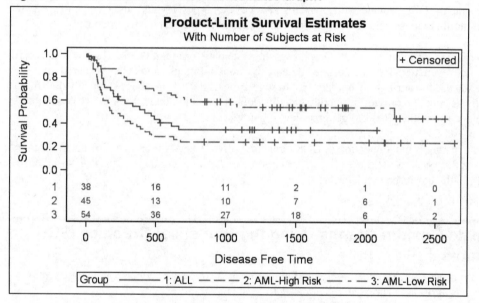

To obtain automatic graphs, all you have to do is turn on ODS Graphics.

- With SAS 9.3, ODS Graphics is on by default in DMS (windowing) mode, and the default output destination is HTML.

- In SAS 9.2 for both line and DMS modes, ODS Graphics is off by default and graphics are not created automatically. The default open destination is LISTING. ODS Graphics can be turned on by using the following statement.

  ```
  ods graphics on / < options >;
  ```

Over 100 analytical procedures create statistical graphs as part of the analysis process. You do not need to know anything about ODS Graphics to have graphs created for you that are relevant to the analysis. The audience for such graphs is the analyst or statistician.

## 1.3 Create Custom Graphs Using the Graph Template Language (GTL)

GTL was originally designed to create complex graphs for the SAS analytical procedures. Just as with tabular data, there was a need to display the data in a graphical form for easier understanding by the user. With SAS 9.2, the Output Delivery System (ODS) was extended to support graphics in a way similar to tabular data. The TEMPLATE procedure was extended to create StatGraph templates. These templates are defined using the GTL syntax. SAS procedures use such predefined templates along with data generated during the procedure step to produce the graphs. These can vary from simple scatter plots to complex panels of fit diagnostics data.

You can use the TEMPLATE procedure and GTL to create the StatGraph templates for your own custom graphs. GTL provides you an extensive set of plot types, layouts, and other statements for legends, attribute maps, and so on, that you can use to define the graphs that you need.

Another important feature of ODS Graphics is the systematic usage of ODS styles for graphs. Each ODS destination has an associated default style, and all graphs and tables rendered to a destination use the attributes from the style to render themselves. The styles shipped with SAS are carefully designed to provide aesthetic output by default. You no longer have to tweak color and marker settings in the graphs to get great-looking graphs.

The GTL syntax is the foundation of ODS Graphics software and is used to define the structure of a graph. In this book, we will use GTL to create some of the more complex graphs. The audience for GTL is the advanced graph programmer.

## 1.4 Create Custom Graphs Using the Statistical Graphics (SG) Procedures

The SG procedures create commonly used graphs using a simple and concise procedure syntax. These procedures use GTL behind the scenes to create the graphs:

- the SGPLOT procedure for single-cell graphs
- the SGPANEL procedure for classification panel graphs
- the SGSCATTER procedure for comparative scatter plots and matrices

In this book we will primarily use the SGPLOT procedure to create most of the commonly used clinical graphs and the SGPANEL procedure to create classification panels. The SG procedures would be the tool of choice for programmers comfortable with using procedure syntax for creating graphs. The audience for the SG procedures is the graph programmer.

## 1.5 Create Custom Graphs Using the ODS Graphics Designer Application

The easiest, pain-free, and fastest way to create a custom graph is by using the ODS Graphics Designer, referred to in this book as *Designer*. The interactive Designer application is the tool of choice for you if you fit the following profile:

- You want to create a graph quickly using an interactive application.
- You are not familiar with graph syntax, and have no desire to learn it.
- You export your data to third-party software just to create graphs.

Designer can help you create graphs with zero programming. Here are some key features:

- Designer is an interactive GUI application.
- You can begin your graph from a gallery of commonly used graphs.
- You can customize your graph by adding more plots and insets.
- You can create single-call graphs, classification panels, and ad hoc layouts.
- You can view the GTL code generated for you while creating the graph.
- You can save your custom graphs to the graph gallery for quick access.
- You can save your graph as a .sgd file to the file system.
- You can run a Designer graph in batch using the SGDESIGN procedure and send the graph to the open ODS destinations with the same or different data.

Designer is not only a great interactive tool to create your graph, but it is also a great learning tool for GTL. You can see how the GTL is put together every time you make a change to the graph. You can copy the GTL code from the code window into the SAS program window and run the code. The audience for the ODS Graphics Designer is the data analyst or statistician. It can also be used by programmers for rapid prototyping or as a learning tool for GTL.

## 1.6 Data Sets and ODS Styles

Some of the examples in this book use the data sets available in the SASHELP library. These include CARS, HEART, and a few others. However, for creating clinical graphs we often need unique data sets that are not available in the SASHELP library. In this case, data is simulated using trigonometric and random number generator functions to create data appropriate for such graphs.

Custom styles are sometimes used to render the graphs in this book. Primarily, these are necessary to reduce the font sizes to help fit the graphs into the small space available. This is especially true for examples of multi-cell graphs.

## 1.7 Color and Grayscale Graphs

The graphs are created using the active style of the open destination. Often, these styles are optimized for full color output. This works well when the graph is also viewed in a color medium.

However, when color graphs are printed in grayscale, there is a significant loss of fidelity in the representation of distinct categories in the graph. For example, a graph with two series plots, one for Drug A and one for Drug B, can be well represented in color with use of two distinct colors such as red and blue. These colors are often designed to have equal weight to avoid unintentional bias.

When such a graph is printed in grayscale, these two series plots can look very similar unless they have other distinguishing features such as line patterns and marker shapes. Bar charts can benefit from use of fill patterns to facilitate discrimination between classifiers.

This book is printed in full color, so you can see the full impact of the graph. However, if you need to submit the graphs to a journal in grayscale, care should be taken to ensure that the different group classifications are easy to differentiate using marker symbols, line patterns, or fill patterns.

## 1.8 Summary

Starting with SAS 9.2, ODS Graphics software provides flexible ways to create graphs for multiple audiences.

- As an analyst or a statistician, you can get statistical graphs automatically from the analytical procedures. These graphs are relevant to the analysis and do not require any extra effort on your part to create.
- As an advanced graph programmer, you can use the GTL directly to create the complex graphs that you need. You can also create flexible graph templates that can be used with different data to create graphs.
- As a graph programmer, you can use the Statistical Graphics procedures to create most of the commonly used graphs in most domains.
- You can use the ODS Graphics Designer to quickly create graphs using a point-and-click method, without writing a single line of graph code. You can also use this tool to quickly prototype the graph you or your analyst might want, or you can generate graphs in bulk, based on the variables selected from a data set. You can also use Designer as a learning tool to learn GTL.

Starting with SAS 9.3, ODS Graphics is included with Base SAS. With SAS 9.3 and SAS 9.4, new features and plot types have been added to the software to make creating graphs truly easy. These tools enable you to layer multiple plot types in myriad ways to create the custom graph that you want. Annotation is supported starting with SAS 9.3, and can be used to add custom features that are otherwise hard to add using plot layers.

For clinical graphs, SAS 9.4 has introduced the new axis table statements. These statements make it a breeze to add axis aligned statistics to be displayed in any graph. All in all, you will find that one of the tools mentioned above will provide you the way to create the graph that you need.

# Chapter 2: A Brief Overview of the SG Procedures

In this chapter, we introduce the key concepts for the SG procedures, and their general syntax. Describing all the features of these procedures in detail is beyond the scope of this book. Here, we will review the methodology to create graphs; the details will be evident through the usage.

The SG procedures provide a simple interface to creating commonly used graphs. The SGPLOT and SGPANEL procedure syntax enables you to build up graphs by layering one or more plot statements in combination with other statements. The SGPLOT procedure creates single-cell graphs, and the SGPANEL procedure creates graphs that are classified by one or more class variables.

The SGPLOT and SGPANEL procedures use similar concepts of plot layering to create complex graphs from combinations of multiple plot statements.

The SGSCATTER procedure does not use plot layering concepts and instead uses three distinct statements: PLOT, COMPARE, and MATRIX. This procedure is a good way to get a quick view of your data prior to the analytics phase of your project. We will not be using the SGSCATTER procedure much in this book. Suffice it to say that you can use this procedure to create comparative scatter plots or matrices.

## 2.1  Single-Cell Graph Using the SGPLOT Procedure

The SGPLOT procedure creates single cell graphs. The graph in Figure 2.1 displays the data in the "data area", bounded by the axes. Two plot statements are used to overlay a line chart on a bar chart by year. A legend is displayed in the graph, with a title at the top as labeled in the figure.

**Figure 2.1 – Single-Cell Graph**

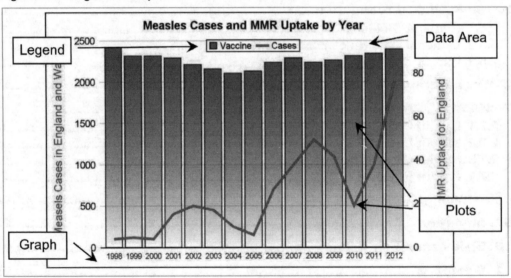

A typical single-cell graph has the following components:

- Zero or more titles appear at the top of the graph.
- Zero or more footnotes appear at the bottom of the graph.
- One region in the middle displays the data.
- One or more plots are used to display the data.
- Zero or more legends or insets can be placed inside the data area or outside.

We refer to every statement as a "plot", regardless of whether it is a series plot or histogram. The SGPLOT procedure supports many plot statements that can be used individually, or in combination with other plot statements. Compatible plot statements can be layered together to create more complex graphs. As we begin, let us explain several key terms.

**Graph:** Refers to the individual output that is created by the procedure. In most of the common use cases, each execution of the procedure creates one graph output file. Often these procedures produce multiple output files (for BY variable usage, or paging of large panels), each of which is referred to as a "Graph".

**Cell:** Each graph can have one or more data areas to display the data as shown in Figure 2.2. Each one of these is referred to as a "Cell". A cell might or might not have axes.

**Plot statements:** Each plot statement is responsible for drawing only its own data representation. The container tells the plot where the data is to be drawn, and how to scale the data appropriately.

**Axes:** The X and Y axes are shared by all the plots in the graph. The data range for each axis is determined by the plots in the data area. Each cell can have a second set of axes, called X2 (at the top) and Y2 (on the right). Each plot can specify which axes to use.

**Legends and Insets**: A graph can have zero or more legends or insets, and each can be placed in any part of the graph. Each legend can specify the information to be displayed in it.

## 2.2  Multi-Cell Classification Panels Using the SGPANEL Procedure

The SGPANEL procedure creates classification panels. These are multi-cell graphs as shown in Figure 2.2. A classification panel is very useful to visualize the distribution of data classified by one or more class variables in one display. Both graphs in Figure 2.2 display the association between Systolic blood pressure and Cholesterol by Sex and Weight_Status.

**Figure 2.2 – Classification Panel with Panel and Lattice Layouts**

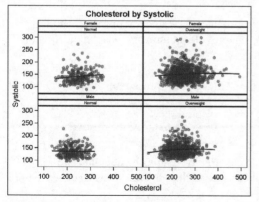 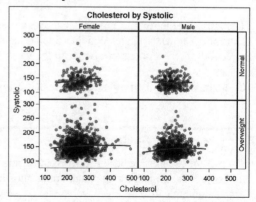

The graph on the left in Figure 2.2 displays a classification panel with a "Panel" layout, which supports multiple class variables. Each cell has multiple headers, one for each class variable.

The graph on the right in Figure 2.2 displays a classification panel with a "Lattice" layout, which supports two class variables, one for Row and one for Column. Each row and column has a header that displays the value of the classification variables.

Multiple, compatible plot statements can be combined to create more complex graphs.

## 2.3 Multi-Cell Comparative Scatter Plots Using the SGCATTER Procedure

Although classification panels provide a convenient way to compare the same data across classifiers, it is often desirable to view side-by-side comparative scatter plots of different variables.

**Figure 2.3 – Comparative Scatter Plot and a Scatter Plot Matrix**

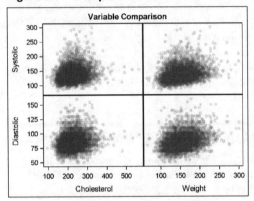 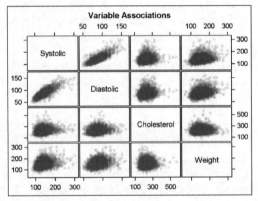

The graph on the left in Figure 2.3 displays a comparative graph for Systolic and Diastolic blood pressure by Cholesterol and Weight. This graph has common axes for comparison of the values.

The graph on the right in Figure 2.3 shows a scatter plot matrix for four variables – Systolic, Diastolic, Cholesterol, and Weight. Such a matrix can provide preliminary visual indication of direct or inverse associations between the variables.

Comparative and matrix graphs are created using the SGSCATTER procedure.

## 2.4 Automatic Features

The SG procedures are designed to create aesthetic and effective graphs by default. The procedures examine the syntax and apply built-in heuristics such as the following to enhance the graph automatically.

- Add a legend when appropriate for multiple overlays and classifiers.
- Create custom legend labels as needed for certain plot types.

- Assign different visual attributes to overlaid plot statements.
- Paginate large classification panels automatically.

If the results of the built-in heuristics are not desirable, they can be turned off for a custom appearance.

## 2.5 The SGPLOT Procedure

The SGPLOT procedure enables you to create a wide variety of single-cell graphs by combining compatible statements in creative ways. The procedure supports over 30 different plot statements, along with statements for customization of legends, axes, and insets. For the full details about the features of the SGPLOT procedure, see the software documentation.

Here is the syntax for the SGPLOT procedure:

1.  PROC SGPLOT < DATA= *data-set* > < *options* >;

2.     *plot-statement(s)  required-parameters* < / *options* >;

     < *styleattrs statement(s)* >;

     < *refline-statement(s)* >;

3.     < *inset-statement(s)* >;

     < *axis-statement(s)* >;

     < *keylegend-statement(s)* >;

     RUN;

1.  The procedure statement supports multiple options. Use of these options will be demonstrated in the examples shown in later chapters.

2.  One or more plot statements can be used to represent the data. Each plot statement has its own set of required data roles and options. These options will become evident as we create multiple clinical graphs in Chapter 3 and 4. Many plot statements are supported, and can be grouped as shown below.

    a.  Basic Plots such as scatter, series, and so on.
    b.  Fit and Confidence Plots such as regression and loess plots.
    c.  Distribution Plots such as histograms and box plots.
    d.  Categorization Plots such as bar charts and dot plots.

3.  Supporting statements can be used to customize the graph.

    a.  STYLEATTRS, SYMBOLCHAR, and SYMBOLIMAGE statements.
    b.  Reference lines and drop lines.
    c.  Insets.
    d.  Axes.
    e.  Legends.

### 2.5.1 Required Roles

Each plot statement has required roles needed to render the plot. Data set variables must be assigned to the required roles to produce a graph. Some required roles can take scalar value. Here are some examples:

    SCATTER X=<var-name> Y=<var-name>;
    SERIES  X=<var-name> Y=<var-name>;

Sometimes there is no specified role name, but a variable name still needs to be provided as shown below.

    HISTOGRAM <var-name>;
    VBOX <var-name>;

### 2.5.2 Optional Data Roles

Optional data roles can be provided for each statement that go after the "/". These are assigned variable names from the data set for rendering features that are data dependent, such as group classification or color by response.

    SCATTER X=<var-name> Y=<var-name> / GROUP=<var-name>;
    VBAR  <var-name> / RESPONSE=<var-name> COLORRESPONSE=<num-var-name>;

### 2.5.3 Plot Options

Plot options can be used to change the behavior of the plot or to assign attributes for different parts of the plot. Each plot can have custom options that control the plot behavior and have names that are specific to the plot, such as MARKERCHAR for scatter plot or MU and SIGMA for density plot.

Plot options are used to customize the behavior or appearance of the plot, such as placement of the group values or to set the color of the line or shape of the marker symbol.

    VBAR  <var-name> / RESPONSE=<var-name> GROUP=<var-name>
                    GROUPDISPLAY=CLUSTER;
    SCATTER X=<var-name> Y=<var-name> / MARKERATTRS=(SYMBOL=plus);

## 2.6  Plot Layering

A key feature of the SGPLOT procedure is the ability to layer compatible plot statements to create more complex and intricate graphs. The SGPLOT procedure supports over 30 plot statements that are grouped in four groups as mentioned above. The plots in the "Basic Plots" group can be combined with each other or with statements in the "Fit and Confidence Plots". Plots in other groups can be combined with other plots in the same group. All plots can be combined with the "supporting statements" like REFLINE and DROPLINE. See the table in Section 2.8 for plot combinations that are allowed.

One or more AXIS, KEYLEGEND, and INSET statements can be used to customize the graph. The STYLEATTRS statement can be used to set group attributes in the syntax. New marker shapes can be defined using the SYMBOLCHAR and SYMBOLIMAGE statements.

Figure 2.6.1 shows the layering feature of the SGPLOT procedure. This graph is created by layering three plot statements. The statements are rendered in the order in which they are specified as shown in the program listing on the left in Figure 2.6.1.

**Figure 2.6.1 – Plot Layering**

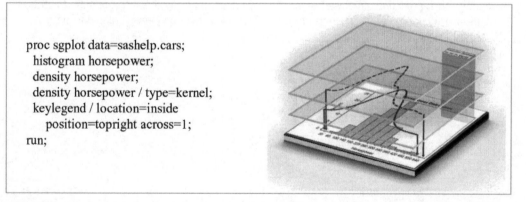

```
proc sgplot data=sashelp.cars;
  histogram horsepower;
  density horsepower;
  density horsepower / type=kernel;
  keylegend / location=inside
    position=topright across=1;
run;
```

Let us use the process above to create a distribution plot for Cholesterol from sashelp.heart data set. The code is shown on the left in Figure 2.6.2, and the resulting graph is shown on the right. This graph uses the HTMLBlue style that has an ATTRPRIORITY of COLOR. This attribute priority uses only color to differentiate the different plots or groups, as far as possible.

**Figure 2.6.2 – Distribution of Cholesterol**

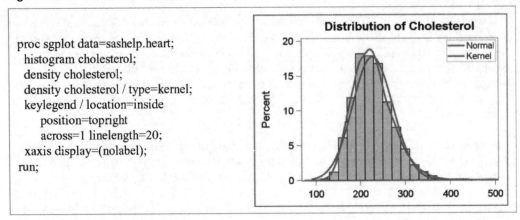

```
proc sgplot data=sashelp.heart;
  histogram cholesterol;
  density cholesterol;
  density cholesterol / type=kernel;
  keylegend / location=inside
      position=topright
      across=1 linelength=20;
  xaxis display=(nolabel);
run;
```

## 2.7  SGPANEL Procedure

The SGPANEL procedure creates classification panel graphs using one or more classification variables. The graphs shown earlier in Figure 2.2 are classification panels created using the SGPANEL procedure.

Here is the syntax for the SGPANEL procedure:

1.  PROC SGPANEL < DATA= *data-set* > < *options* >;

2.  PANELBY *classvar1* < *classvar2* ... <*classvarN* > < */ options* >;

3.  < *plot-statement(s)* >;

4.  < *styleattrs statement*(s)>;

   < *refline-statement(s)* >;

   < *inset-statement(s)* >;

   < *axis-statement(s)* >;

   < *keylegend-statement(s)* >;

   RUN;

1. The procedure statement supports multiple options, some of which will be used in the examples shown in later chapters.

2. The PANELBY statement is required and must be placed before of any of the plot, refline, inset, axis, or legend statements. This statement is used to set the layout type and other options that control the overall paneling of the cells. The following layouts are supported:

   a. PANEL – the default.
   b. LATTICE – creates a panel with rows and columns.
   c. COLUMNLATTICE– creates a lattice of columns (one row).
   d. ROWLATTICE – creates a lattice of rows (one column).

3. One or more plot statements are used to represent data. Each plot statement has its own set of data roles and options. This procedure supports many of the same plot statements as the SGPLOT Procedure.

4. Supporting statements can be used to customize the graph.

   a. STYLEATTRS, SYMBOLCHAR, and SYMBOLIMAGE statements.
   b. Reference lines and drop lines.
   c. Insets.
   d. Axes.
   e. Legends.

## 2.7.1 Layout PANEL

This is the default layout type. This layout supports one or more class variables. A cell is created for each crossing of the unique values of all the class variables. Figure 2.7.1 shows a program on the left using the SGPANEL procedure to create the 2x2 panel graph shown on the right.

**Figure 2.7.1 – Classification Panel**

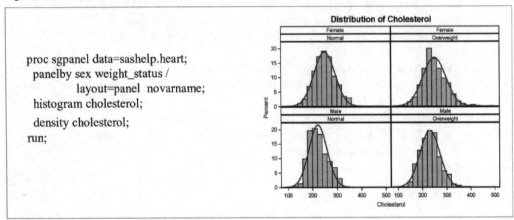

```
proc sgpanel data=sashelp.heart;
  panelby sex weight_status /
          layout=panel  novarname;
  histogram cholesterol;

  density cholesterol;
run;
```

The graph in Figure 2.7.1 has the following features:

- The layout can have N classifiers. In this case, we have two classifiers, Sex and Weight_Status.
- The layout creates one cell for each crossing of the panel variables.
- Each cell has N cell headers, one for each class variable, displaying the value for each cell.
- Each cell displays the plot statements that are defined for the subset of the data.
- Only the cells that have data are displayed. Cells without any data are dropped from the graph. An option can be used to display all cells.
- The procedure automatically decides the number of rows and columns for the grid. The procedure automatically breaks up the graph into multiple "pages", to prevent the cells from getting too small.
- Common external row and column axes are used.
- Options are available to allow control of most of the automatic settings for the graph.

## 2.7.2 Layout LATTICE

The SGPANEL procedure also supports the LATTICE layout. This layout supports two class variables, the first one used for columns and the second for rows. A cell is created for each crossing of the unique values of both class variables. Figure 2.7.2 shows the program on the left, uses the SGPANEL procedure to create the graph shown on the right.

**Figure 2.7.2 – Classification Lattice**

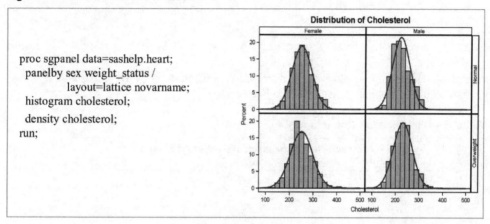

```
proc sgpanel data=sashelp.heart;
  panelby sex weight_status /
          layout=lattice novarname;
  histogram cholesterol;

  density cholesterol;
run;
```

- The LATTICE layout must have two classifiers, one for columns and one for rows.
- A grid of cells is created for all crossings of the unique values of the two classifiers.
- Each unique value of the first classifier (Sex in the example) creates a column in the grid.
- Each unique value of the second classifier (Weight_Status) creates a row in the grid.
- Empty cells are retained.
- Each column gets a column header, by default at the top.
- Each row gets a row header, by default on the right.
- Each cell displays the plot statements defined for the subset of the data.
- Common external row and column axes are used.

### 2.7.3 Layout COLUMNLATTICE

This is a special case of the LATTICE layout, where only one variable is provided in the list of class variables. This layout produces a panel of columns in one row. Each cell has a column header and displays the specified plots in each cell for the subset of the data.

```
proc sgpanel data=sashelp.heart noautolegend;
   panelby weight_status / layout=columnlattice onepanel novarname;
   histogram cholesterol;
   density cholesterol;
   density cholesterol / type=kernel;
run;
```

A program to create a column lattice of the distribution of Cholesterol by Weight_Status is shown above. The resulting graph is shown below in Figure 2.7.3.

**Figure 2.7.3 – Classification ColumnLattice**

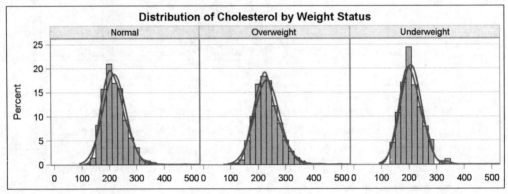

## 2.7.4  Layout ROWLATTICE

This is a special case of the LATTICE layout, in which only one variable is provided in the list of class variables.  This layout produces a panel of rows stacked in one column.  Each cell has a row header and displays the specified plots in each cell for the subset of the data.

A program to create a row lattice of the distribution of Cholesterol by Sex is shown on the left in Figure 2.7.4.  The resulting graph is shown on the right.

**Figure 2.7.4 – Classification RowLattice**

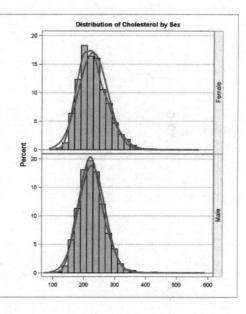

```
proc sgpanel data=sashelp.heart;
 panelby sex / layout=rowlattice
          onepanel novarname;
 histogram cholesterol;
 density cholesterol;
 density cholesterol /  type=kernel;
run;
```

## 2.8  Combining Statements

The table in Figure 2.8 below shows the plot combinations that are allowed with SAS 9.4.  An 'x' for a crossing means that it is allowed.  Most of this is also applicable for SAS 9.3, except that some combinations of VBOX or HBOX with Basic Plots are not allowed.

**Figure 2.8 – Table of Plot Combinations**

| | SCATTER | SERIES | STEP | BAND | NEEDLE | VECTOR | VBARPARM | HBARPARM | BUBBLE | HIGHLOW | REFLINE | LINEPARM | REG | LOESS | PBSPLINE | ELLIPSE * | HISTOGRAM | DENSITY | VBOX | HBOX | VBAR | VLINE | HBAR | HLINE | DOT |
|---|---|---|---|---|---|---|---|---|---|---|---|---|---|---|---|---|---|---|---|---|---|---|---|---|---|
| **Basic Plots** | | | | | | | | | | | | | | | | | | | | | | | | | |
| SCATTER | X | X | X | X | X | X | X | X | X | X | X | X | X | X | X | X | | | | | | | | | |
| SERIES | X | X | X | X | X | X | X | X | X | X | X | X | X | X | X | X | | | | | | | | | |
| STEP | X | X | X | X | X | X | X | X | X | X | X | X | X | X | X | X | | | | | | | | | |
| BAND | X | X | X | X | X | X | X | X | X | X | X | X | X | X | X | X | | | | | | | | | |
| NEEDLE | X | X | X | X | X | X | X | X | X | X | X | X | X | X | X | X | | | | | | | | | |
| VECTOR | X | X | X | X | X | X | X | X | X | X | X | X | X | X | X | X | | | | | | | | | |
| VBARPARM | X | X | X | X | X | X | X | | X | X | X | X | | | | | | | | | | | | | |
| HBARPARM | X | X | X | X | X | X | | | X | X | X | X | | | | | | | | | | | | | |
| BUBBLE | X | X | X | X | X | X | X | X | X | X | X | X | X | X | X | X | | | | | | | | | |
| HIGHLOW | X | X | X | X | X | X | X | X | X | X | X | X | X | X | X | X | | | | | | | | | |
| REFLINE | X | X | X | X | X | X | X | X | X | X | X | X | X | X | X | X | X | X | X | X | X | X | X | X | X |
| DROPLINE | X | X | X | X | X | X | X | X | X | X | X | X | X | X | X | X | X | X | X | X | X | X | X | X | X |
| LINEPARM | X | X | X | X | X | X | X | X | X | X | X | X | X | X | X | X | | | | | | | | | |
| **Fit and Confidence Plots** | | | | | | | | | | | | | | | | | | | | | | | | | |
| REG | X | X | X | X | X | X | | | X | X | X | X | X | X | X | X | | | | | | | | | |
| LOESS | X | X | X | X | X | X | | | X | X | X | X | X | X | X | X | | | | | | | | | |
| PBSPLINE | X | X | X | X | X | X | | | X | X | X | X | X | X | X | X | | | | | | | | | |
| ELLIPSE * | X | X | X | X | X | X | | | X | X | X | X | X | X | X | X | | | | | | | | | |
| **Distribution Plots** | | | | | | | | | | | | | | | | | | | | | | | | | |
| HISTOGRAM | | | | | | | | | | | X | | | | | | X | X | | | | | | | |
| DENSITY | | | | | | | | | | | X | | | | | | X | X | | | | | | | |
| VBOX | X | X | X | X | X | X | X | X | X | X | X | | | | | | | | X | | | | | | |
| HBOX | X | X | X | X | X | X | X | X | X | X | X | | | | | | | | | X | | | | | |
| **Categorization Plots** | | | | | | | | | | | | | | | | | | | | | | | | | |
| VBAR | | | | | | | | | | | X | | | | | | | | | | X | X | | | |
| VLINE | | | | | | | | | | | X | | | | | | | | | | X | X | | | |
| HBAR | | | | | | | | | | | X | | | | | | | | | | | | X | X | X |
| HLINE | | | | | | | | | | | X | | | | | | | | | | | | X | X | X |
| DOT | | | | | | | | | | | X | | | | | | | | | | | | X | X | X |

## 2.9  Annotation

SAS 9.3 and SAS 9.4 support many new plot statements and new features that make it possible to create all types of clinical graphs. However, there are situations where we need more customizations for which we can use the SG annotation feature. The annotation feature is available starting with SAS 9.3 and it works in a manner similar to the SAS/GRAPH annotation feature, but is modified to suit the SG and GTL architecture.

The idea is to provide basic drawing function commands from an SG annotate data set that can be executed after the plot has been created. The data set contains a list of columns with predetermined names that specify the function and the data or information needed for the function. Each observation in the data set defines a single action such as drawing text as shown in Figure 2.9.1. This data set can be provided on the SGANNO option on the procedure statement.

The required column is "Function", which defines the type of drawing action to be executed. Various functions are available such as Text, Rectangle, Line, Oval, and more. The data set in Figure 2.9.1 defines three "Text" functions. Each function needs more information to complete the function. For text, we need the "Label" to be drawn. Additional information can be provided such as the (x, y) location of the text, text attributes, and the DrawSpace. Default values are used for most of these options.

**Figure 2.9.1 – SG Annotate Data Set**

| Obs | Function | X1Space | Y1Space | X1 | Y1 | TextSize | TextWeight | TextColor | Label |
|---|---|---|---|---|---|---|---|---|---|
| 1 | Text | DataValue | WallPercent | 1 | 7 | 5 | Bold | GraphData1:ContrastColor | 275 |
| 2 | Text | DataValue | WallPercent | 1 | 3 | 5 | Bold | GraphData2:ContrastColor | 406 |
| 3 | Text | DataValue | WallPercent | 2 | 7 | 5 | Bold | GraphData1:ContrastColor | 271 |

Annotate items can be drawn in any one of four graph contexts and in one of three units. The contexts are Graph, Layout, Wall, and Data as shown in Figure 2.9.2 below. The origin for each is at the lower left corner of the context. The units are Percent, Pixel, and Value. The "DrawSpace" is a combination of these two, such as "GraphPercent" or "DataValue" and so on.

The units of "Value" can only be used with context of "Data". Both X and Y can have different DrawSpace, and items can be referenced outside the DrawSpace and still be drawn. For example, X DrawSpace can be set to WallPercent, and the x value can be -10, which means 10% to the left of the left edge of the wall. The default DrawSpace is "GraphPercent".

**Figure 2.9.2 – DrawSpace for Annotation**

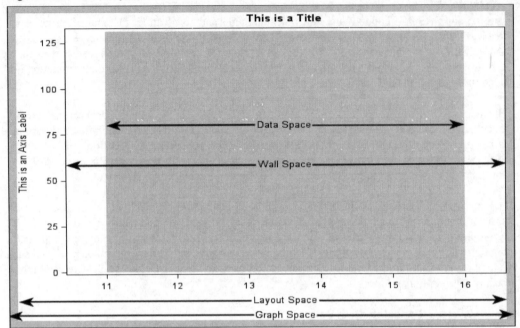

Functions that are supported include ARROW, IMAGE, LINE, OVAL, RECTANGLE, and TEXT. POLYGON and POLYLINE are also supported with the POLYGONCONT function. Additional options can be provided for each function as needed. See product documentation for more details.

## 2.10 Styles and Their Usage

The visual attributes for various elements of the graph created by the SG procedures are derived from the active style for the ODS destination. Each ODS destination has a default active style that is predefined. This active style can be changed using the appropriate options. See the ODS documentation for this information. The various elements of the style are carefully designed to create aesthetically pleasing and effective graphs by default.

A style is a collection of named elements. Each element is a bundle of named visual attributes such as color, font, marker symbol, and so on. Any output to an ODS destination derives the necessary visual information from the active style. For example, output tables derive visual attributes such as fonts and background colors for the headers, size and color of titles, and so on, from the style.

Graphs derive the visual attributes for plot colors, marker symbols, line thickness, axis label fonts, and so on, from specific named elements of the style. The association between the element of the graph and the style element is well defined and described in detail in the ODS product documentation.

You can control the visual appearance of the graphs in different ways:

1. On the ODS destination statement, use a style that is supplied by SAS.
2. Use a custom style on the ODS destination statement
3. Use the STYLEATTRS statement in the procedure syntax.
4. Use attribute maps to control group attributes.
5. Use explicit appearance options in procedure syntax.

1. **Use a style that is supplied by SAS:** Every ODS output destination has a default style. All output that is written to this destination uses this style by default. You can change the active style for an ODS output destination by setting the STYLE= option for the destination. All output that is written to that destination will then use that style.

2. **Use a custom style:** If you like one of the pre-defined SAS styles, but would prefer to change a few of the appearance settings, you can derive a new style from one of the SAS styles by using the TEMPLATE procedure. Or, you can define a style from scratch. You can also use the %MODSTYLE() macro to create a custom style. For more information about this topic, see the ODS product documentation for PROC TEMPLATE.

3. **Use the STYLEATTRS statement:** When a plot statement uses group or classification levels, the appearance attributes for each group or classification level are derived from the GRAPHDATA1 – GRAPHDATA12 style elements. Starting with SAS 9.4, these attributes can be modified on the fly using procedure syntax. You can use the STYLEATTRS statement to change the colors, marker symbols, and line patterns for the group.

4. **Use attribute maps:** Attribute maps can be used to assign specific attributes to groups by value. This is useful to ensure that a specific data value is always represented in the graph with a specific color or marker symbol, regardless of its location in the data set.

5. **Use appearance options:** You can customize the appearance of specific features of a plot statement by setting the appropriate appearance options in the procedure syntax. This overrides the settings derived from any previous global setting like styles or the STYLEATTRS statement.

## 2.11 Summary

The SGPLOT, SGPANEL, and SGSCATTER procedures give you rich, but concise, syntax to create many clinical graphs. In this chapter, our purpose was to introduce you to the methodology these procedures use to create graphs.

Describing the features or syntax of the procedures in detail is beyond the scope of this book. Chapters 3 and 4 describe in great detail how specific clinical graphs can be created using the SGPLOT procedure. Chapter 5 describes how many classification panels can be created using the SGPANEL procedure. The features of the plot statements and options will become evident through the examples.

# Chapter 3: Clinical Graphs Using the SAS 9.3 SGPLOT Procedure

When the SG procedures were first released with SAS 9.2, the underlying GTL functionality was focused on providing the features necessary to create automatic graphs from the SAS analytical procedures. Many features necessary to make clinical graphs easier were not available. So, although many simpler graphs can be built using SAS 9.2, it is not the best platform for clinical graphs.

With SAS 9.3, the SGPLOT procedure supports many useful features that enable the creation of clinical graphs. These include the following statements and features:

- Highlow plots, bubble plots, and parametric lines.
- Cluster groups for many plots like bar, box, scatter, series, highlow, and more.
- Box plot with cluster groups and interval axes.
- Discrete attribute maps.
- SG annotation for SG procedures.

With the availability of the features listed above, it became a lot easier to build most clinical graphs using the SAS 9.3 SGPLOT procedure, as shown in this chapter. This chapter will show you how to build such commonly used clinical graphs and will provide you the code that you can use directly for such graphs. Through the use of these examples, you will gain valuable insight on how to combine the plot statements to create your graph, and how to use the SG Annotate facility to fully customize the graph.

My effort is always to find ways to create the graph by layering multiple plot types to get the job done. This process is scalable and translates easily to other graphs. However, often there are cases where we have to use annotation to get just the right customization of the graph. In such cases, we will use the new SG Annotate facility.

## 3.1  Box Plot of QTc Change from Baseline

This graph displays the distribution of QTc change from baseline by week and treatment for all
subjects in a study.  The x-axis has a linear scale and is not discrete.  The "Subjects At-Risk" values
are displayed by treatment at the right location along the time axis.

### 3.1.1  Box Plot of QTc Change from Baseline with Outer Risk Table

For the graph in Figure 3.1.1.1, we will use a box plot to display the distribution of QTc change
from baseline by week and treatment on a linear x-axis.  The "Subjects At-Risk" table at the bottom
has been added by using the annotation functions as defined in the "AnnoOut" data set.

**Figure 3.1.1.1 – Box Plot of QTc Change from Baseline**

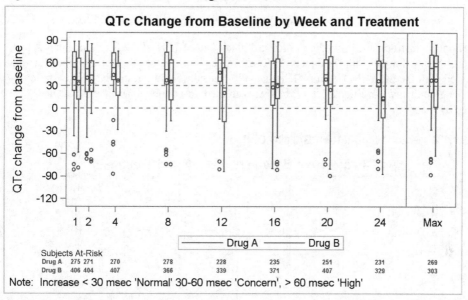

```
title 'QTc Change from Baseline by Week and Treatment';
proc sgplot data=QTcData  sganno=AnnoOut pad=(bottom=15pct);
  format week qtcweek.;
  vbox qtc / category=week group=drug groupdisplay=cluster nofill;
  refline 26 / axis=x;
  refline 0 30 60 / axis=y lineattrs=(pattern=shortdash);
  xaxis type=linear values=(1 2 4 8 12 16 20 24 28) max=29
        valueshint display=(nolabel);
  yaxis label='QTc change from baseline' values=(-120 to 90 by 30);
  keylegend / title='';
run;
```

The main body of the graph including the boxes by treatment, axes, title, and legend are created by
the statements in the procedure above.  Normally, a box plot treats the category variable as discrete,
which would have placed all the tick values on the x-axis at equally spaced intervals.  However, in

this case the values on the x-axis represent days from start of study, and we want to place the data at the correctly scaled distance along the x-axis. This can be done be explicitly setting TYPE=LINEAR on the x-axis. Now, each box is placed at the scaled location along the x-axis.

The box plot is classified by treatment, which has two values "Drug A" and "Drug B". The boxes are sized by the smallest interval along the x-axis. In this case it is 1 day at the start of the study. The effective midpoint spacing is set by that interval, and all boxes are drawn to fit in this space.

The box plot uses GROUPDISPLAY=CLUSTER to place the treatment groups side by side. We can use the NOFILL option to draw empty boxes.

Note the use of SGANNO and PAD options on the procedure statement.

```
proc sgplot data=QTcData  sganno=AnnoOut pad=(bottom=15pct);
```

The PAD option instructs the procedure to leave a blank pad of 15% of the height of the graph at the bottom. We will display the "Subjects At-Risk" values in this space using the "AnnoOut" data set provided with the SGANNO option. If we run the procedure without the SGANNO option, we will get the graph shown in Figure 3.1.1.2 below, with the extra empty space at the bottom (indicated by the arrow).

**Figure 3.1.1.2 – Graph without the SGANNO Option**

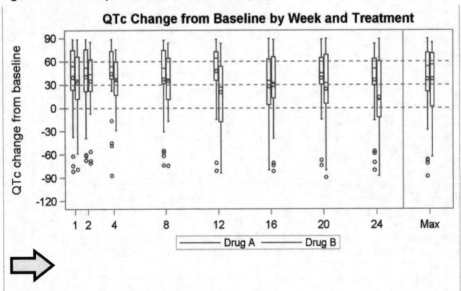

The risk table values, labels, and the header will be drawn using annotation statements defined in the annotation data set "AnnoOut". This data set is provided to the procedure using the SGANNO option. The data set contains a number of observations, each of which defines one item to be drawn. The data set contains predefined column names that determine what is to be drawn, where, and how as shown in Figure 3.1.1.3. Please see Section 2.9 for an introduction to SG annotation.

The data set "AnnoOut" has 22 observations, the first five of which are shown below. Every SGAnno data set must have a column called "Function". This column determines what is to be drawn. Multiple types of items can be drawn, including LINE, OVAL, and TEXT. In this case the risk values are displayed using the TEXT function.

**Figure 3.1.1.3 – Annotation Instructions in the Data Set**

| Obs | Function | X1Space | Y1Space | X1 | Y1 | TextSize | TextWeight | TextColor | Label |
|-----|----------|---------|---------|----|----|----------|------------|-----------|-------|
| 1 | Text | DataValue | GraphPercent | 1 | 11 | 5 | Bold | GraphData1:ContrastColor | 275 |
| 2 | Text | DataValue | GraphPercent | 1 | 8 | 5 | Bold | GraphData2:ContrastColor | 406 |
| 3 | Text | DataValue | GraphPercent | 2 | 11 | 5 | Bold | GraphData1:ContrastColor | 271 |
| 4 | Text | DataValue | GraphPercent | 2 | 8 | 5 | Bold | GraphData2:ContrastColor | 404 |
| 5 | Text | DataValue | GraphPercent | 4 | 11 | 5 | Bold | GraphData1:ContrastColor | 270 |

Additional information might be required to draw the annotation function that is provided in other columns with predefined names as needed by each function. Many of these have default values, so if they are not provided, a system default is used. For drawing text, we need at least the text string in the column named "Label". The X and Y location and the DrawSpace setting may also be required. These are explained below.

The "Function" column contains the name of the element to be drawn; in this case, it is "Text". The text function requires that we provide the text string to be displayed in the column called "Label". Other optional information such as the position of the string and its visual attributes can also be provided.

1. X1 and Y1 provide the coordinates of the location where the text is drawn.
2. The DrawSpace determines how to interpret the X1 and Y1 values provided. DrawSpace applies to all coordinates and provides the "Context" and the "Units". In this case, we want different ways to interpret X1 and Y1, so DrawSpace is not used.
3. X1Space determines the interpretation of the x1 coordinate. In this case, X1Space="DataValue". This means, the x location is in reference to the lower left corner of the "Data" space, and the units are "Value", the actual data values. So, the first text will be drawn at value of "1" along the x-axis.
4. Y1Space determines the interpretation of the y1 coordinate. Here, Y1Space="GraphPercent". This means, the y location is with reference to the lower left corner of the whole graph, and the units are "Percent". So, the first text will be drawn at 11% above the bottom of the graph.
5. All the text attributes are determined by default, but some have been set using TextSize, TextWeight, and TextColor columns.

For the first observation, Function="Text", with X1=1 and Y1=11 and Label="275". Because X1Space is "DataValue", the x location of the label "275" is aligned with "1" on the x-axis. Because Y1Space is "GraphPercent", the y location of the label is at 11% from the bottom of the graph. The label is drawn with size=5, bold weight, and color of "GraphData1:ContrastColor" to match the color for "Drug A" in the data. The risk value for "Drug B" is drawn by the second observation, using the second group color at 8% from the bottom. This process repeats for all observations in the "AnnoOut" data set.

In addition to the risk values, we need to draw additional items to complete the table. These items are defined in rows 19-22 of the "AnnoOut" data set as shown in Figure 3.1.1.4 below.

**Figure 3.1.1.4 – Annotation Data Set**

| Obs | Function | X1Space | Y1Space | X1 | Y1 | TextSize | TextWeight | TextColor | Label | Anchor |
|-----|----------|---------|---------|-----|-----|----------|------------|-----------|-------|--------|
| 19 | Text | WallPercent | GraphPercent | -1.0 | 11 | 5 | Bold | GraphData1:ContrastColor | Drug A | Right |
| 20 | Text | WallPercent | GraphPercent | -1.0 | 8 | 5 | Bold | GraphData2:ContrastColor | Drug B | Right |
| 21 | Text | WallPercent | GraphPercent | -6.5 | 14 | 7 | Normal | Black | Subjects At-Risk | Left |
| 22 | Text | GraphPercent | GraphPercent | 1.0 | 4 | 9 | Normal | Black | Note: Increase < 30 msec 'Normal' 30-60 msec 'Concern', > 60 msec 'High' | Left |

The first row of risk values is for "Drug A", so we want to place the string "Drug A" to the left of the Y-axis in line with this row. We do that using the observation # 19 in the table. The Label is "Drug A", placed at X1= -1 (WallPercent), Y1=11% (GraphPercent). The string is anchored on the right, so the string is displayed to the left of the left edge of the wall. Note, the value for x1 is negative.

Even though the x-axis coordinate is to the left of the wall area, the string is still drawn. The DrawSpace determines only the interpretation of the data, but does not clip the graphics to this area. This allows the string to be positioned by the data value in one dimension and still be drawn outside the data area in the other dimension.

Similarly, we can display the "Subjects At-Risk" header above the risk values. Finally, we can display the footnote at the bottom of the graph. For full details, see Program 3_1, available from the author's page at http://support.sas.com/matange.

## 3.1.2  Box Plot of QTc Change from Baseline with Inner Risk Table

Graphs are easier to decode when relevant information is placed as close as possible, thus reducing the amount of eye movement needed to decode the graph. Following this principle, it would be more effective to place the risk information inside the graph area, closer to the graphical information.

**Figure 3.1.2.1 – Box Plot of QTc Change from Baseline with Inner Risk Table**

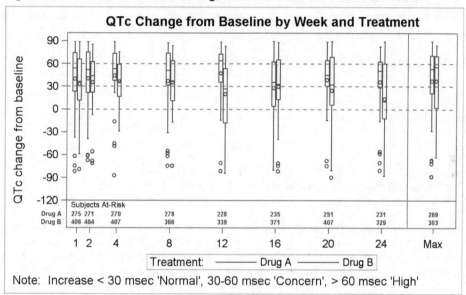

```
title 'QTc Change from Baseline by Week and Treatment';
footnote j=1 "Note:  Increase < 30 msec 'Normal', ..";
proc sgplot data=QTcData sganno=annoIn;
  format week qtcweek.;
  vbox qtc / category=week group=drug groupdisplay=cluster
       nofill name='a';
  refline 26 / axis=x;
  refline -120 / axis=y;
  xaxis type=linear values=(1 2 4 8 12 16 20 24 28) valueshint
       min=1 max=29 display=(nolabel);
  yaxis label='QTc change from baseline' values=(-120 to 90 by 30)
       offsetmin=0.14;
  keylegend 'a' / title='Treatment:';
run;
```

This graph shows an alternate layout of the table. Traditionally, the "At-Risk" table is displayed at the bottom of the graph, just above the footnote with other items in between. Such a layout places the risk data relatively far away from the plot. Even though the values are aligned with the data along the x-axis, the distance and intervening items like the legend and the axis items create a distraction.

The code for creating the box plots of QTc change by treatment and week is the same as before. We can use the VBOX statement to draw the QTc values by drug and week. The XAXIS TYPE=Linear statement is used to display the x values scaled along the x-axis. REFLINE statements are used to draw the reference lines. Options are set on the XAXIS and YAXIS statements to get the desired results.

Now, we want to place the At-Risk table above the x-axis, along with the table header as shown below, marked by the arrow. Note, this brings the table of Subjects At-Risk closer to the data, and above the x-axis and the other items such as the legend.

**Figure 3.1.2.2 – Subjects At-Risk Table Placed above the X-Axis**

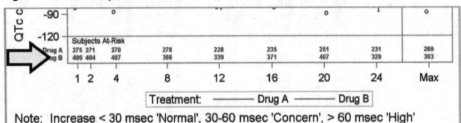

First we need to create some empty space above the x-axis line to draw the risk table. To do this, we will add an offset to the lower end of the Y-axis using the OFFSETMIN=0.14. In this case, there is no need to specify a padding at the bottom of the graph. Also, a regular footnote can be used to display the "Note" as we are not disturbing that part of the graph.

To correctly position the values along the x-axis in the right location, we will still use the X1SPACE of "DataValue". To place the values above the x-axis, we will use Y1Space of "WallPercent".

The first few observations in the data set are used for drawing the risk values as shown in Figure 3.1.2.3 below:

**Figure 3.1.2.3 – Annotation Data Set for the Values**

| Obs | Function | X1Space | Y1Space | X1 | Y1 | TextSize | TextWeight | TextColor | Label |
|---|---|---|---|---|---|---|---|---|---|
| 1 | Text | DataValue | WallPercent | 1 | 7 | 5 | Bold | GraphData1:ContrastColor | 275 |
| 2 | Text | DataValue | WallPercent | 1 | 3 | 5 | Bold | GraphData2:ContrastColor | 406 |
| 3 | Text | DataValue | WallPercent | 2 | 7 | 5 | Bold | GraphData1:ContrastColor | 271 |

The last few observations in the data set are shown in Figure 3.1.2.4 below. These draw the labels for each drug and for the table title. Note the usage of the "Anchor" value for drawing the text strings. The default anchor value is "Center". See Program 3_1 for the full code.

**Figure 3.1.2.4 – Annotation Data Set for the Labels**

| Obs | Function | X1Space | Y1Space | X1 | Y1 | TextSize | TextWeight | TextColor | Anchor | Label |
|-----|----------|---------|---------|----|----|----------|------------|-----------|--------|-------|
| 19 | Text | WallPercent | WallPercent | 1 | 12 | 6 | Normal | Black | Left | Subjects At-Risk |
| 20 | Text | WallPercent | WallPercent | -1 | 7 | 5 | Bold | GraphData1:ContrastColor | Right | Drug A |
| 21 | Text | WallPercent | WallPercent | -1 | 3 | 5 | Bold | GraphData2:ContrastColor | Right | Drug B |

## 3.1.3  Box Plot of QTc Change from Baseline in Grayscale

The graph shown in Figure 3.1.3.1 below is customized for grayscale medium.  We start with a graph that uses the Journal style, using line patterns for the two groups.  Then, we customize the graph using annotate for a different look.

**Figure 3.1.3.1 – Box Plot of QTc Change from Baseline in Grayscale**

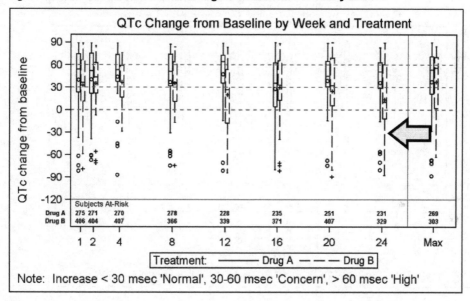

```
ods listing style=journal;
title 'QTc Change from Baseline by Week and Treatment';
footnote j=l "Note:  Increase < 30 msec 'Normal', ..";
proc sgplot data=QTcData sganno=annoIn;
   format week qtcweek.;
   vbox qtc / category=week group=drug groupdisplay=cluster
        nofill name='a';
   refline 26 / axis=x;
   refline -120 / axis=y;
   xaxis type=linear values=(1 2 4 8 12 16 20 24 28) valueshint
        min=1 max=29 display=(nolabel);
   yaxis label='QTc change from baseline' values=(-120 to 90 by 30)
        offsetmin=0.14;
   keylegend 'a' / title='Treatment:';
run;
```

The code above is identical to the code in Section 3.1.2, except we have used STYLE=Journal in the ODS LISTING statement. The Journal style is a non-color, black and white style. Since we are using unfilled boxes, the boxes for Drug A and B are both shown using black lines, one solid for Drug A and one dashed for Drug B.

Now, often dashed lines do not result in a clean representation of a box, so it might be desirable to make the lines solid for all treatments. In that case, the legend will show solid lines for both Drug A and Drug B, which is not a desirable result either.

In this case, we will suppress the automatic legend, and draw our own legend as shown in Figure 3.1.3.3 using annotation.

**Figure 3.1.3.3 – QTc Change from Baseline Graph in Grayscale**

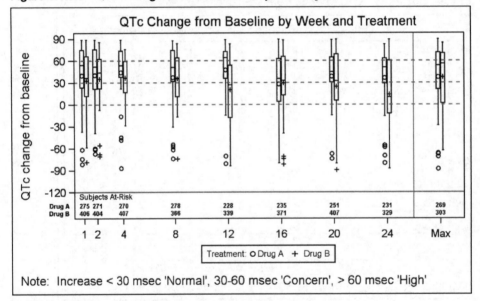

The process for creating the legend is shown below. The data set follows.

1. Create empty space above the footnote using an extra empty Footnote2 statement.
2. Add annotation functions to draw the box in the center of the wall below the axis.
3. Draw the Legend title "Treatment" on the left side.
4. To the right of this, draw the "oval", with the text "Drug A" beside it.
5. To the right of this, draw the "plus", with the text "Drug B" beside it.

**Figure 3.1.3.4 – Annotation Data Set**

| Obs | Function | X1Space | Y1Space | X1 | Y1 | TextSize | TextWeight | TextColor | Anchor | Label |
|---|---|---|---|---|---|---|---|---|---|---|
| 22 | Rectangle | WallPercent | GraphPercent | 50.00 | 14 | | | | center | |
| 23 | Text | WallPercent | GraphPercent | 34.00 | 14 | 7 | Normal | Black | left | Treatment: |
| 24 | Oval | WallPercent | GraphPercent | 46.00 | 14 | | | | center | |
| 25 | Text | WallPercent | GraphPercent | 47.00 | 14 | 7 | Normal | Black | left | Drug A |
| 26 | Line | WallPercent | GraphPercent | 56.00 | 14 | | | | | |
| 27 | Line | WallPercent | GraphPercent | 56.75 | 15 | | | | | |
| 28 | Text | WallPercent | GraphPercent | 58.75 | 14 | 7 | Normal | Black | left | Drug B |

As you can see, creating such annotated details is possible, but requires custom coding that is not scalable to other data. This is not really a solution I would suggest but I provide it mainly to provide an example of things that can be done using annotation. See the full code in Program 3_1.

## 3.2  Mean Change in QTc by Week and Treatment

This graph displays the mean and confidence of change in QTc from baseline by week and treatment for subjects in a study.  The x-axis displays weeks on a linear scale with clustered groups.

### 3.2.1  Mean Change of QTc by Week and Treatment with Outer Table

The mean values are displayed by week and treatment.  The table of subjects at visit is displayed at the bottom of the graph, below the axis in the traditional arrangement.

Figure 3.2.1.1 – Mean Change of QTc by Week and Treatment with Outer Table

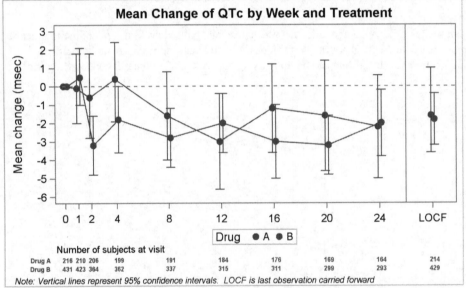

```
title 'Mean Change of QTc by Week and Treatment';
proc sgplot data=QTc_Mean_Group sganno=annoOuter pad=(bottom=14%);
   format week qtcmean.;
   scatter x=week y=mean / yerrorupper=high yerrorlower=low group=drug
           groupdisplay=cluster clusterwidth=0.5
           markerattrs=(size=7 symbol=circlefilled);
   series x=week y=mean2 / group=drug groupdisplay=cluster
           clusterwidth=0.5 lineattrs=(pattern=solid);
   refline 26 / axis=x;
   refline 0  / axis=y lineattrs=(pattern=shortdash);
   xaxis type=linear values=(0 1 2 4 8 12 16 20 24 28) max=29
         valueshint display=(nolabel);
   yaxis label='Mean change (msec)' values=(-6 to 3 by 1);
run;
```

The graph uses a SERIES plot statement of "Mean" by "Week" classified by "Drug" to display the curves.  It is possible to display the markers as part of the SERIES plot statement, but not the error bars. Hence, we have used an overlay of the SCATTER plot statement to display filled markers and also the error bars for upper and lower confidence limits.

The group values are displayed side-by-side for both the scatter and series plots, using cluster groups with CLUSTERWIDTH=0.5. This ensures tight clustering, and also ensures that the markers for each drug are connected to the line. A reference line is drawn at X=26 to separate the LOCF value and another at Y=0 to display the baseline. The x-axis is set to linear, and specific tick values are requested as shown in the code. A user-defined format is used to display the value '28' as "LOCF".

The values for LOCF are not connected to the other values, so we have used the "Mean2" variable for the series plot, where these values are missing. The HTMLBlue style is used for the graph that has an attribute priority of "color". So, we get color changes only for the two group values. Both groups use filled circle markers and solid line patterns.

The graph includes the display of the "Number of Subjects at Visit" by week and treatment at the bottom of the display. This information is added to the graph using annotation. The procedure statement includes the options SGANNO and PAD.

Using the PAD option, we have reserved 14% of the height of the graph at the bottom as blank space. We will draw the At-Risk table in this space using annotation commands from the "annoOuter" data set. This will include the table header and the footnote using annotation.

```
proc sgplot data=QTc_Mean_Group sganno=annoOuter pad=(bottom=14%);
```

The "annoOuter" data set contains all the annotation commands needed to draw the header for the table, the values for the number of subjects in the study by treatment and week, and the footnote at the bottom. The first 20 observations in the data set draw the number of subjects in the study by treatment and week. The next 4 observations draw the table header, the treatment labels, and the footnote. See Section 2.9 for an introduction to annotation functions and data set.

**Figure 3.2.1.2 – Annotation Data Set for Values**

| Obs | Function | X1Space | Y1Space | X1 | Y1 | Label | Anchor | TextSize | TextWeight | TextColor |
|---|---|---|---|---|---|---|---|---|---|---|
| 1 | text | datavalue | graphpercent | 0 | 9 | 216 | center | 5 | bold | Graphdata1:contrastcolor |
| 2 | text | datavalue | graphpercent | 0 | 6 | 431 | center | 5 | bold | GraphData2:contrastcolor |
| 3 | text | datavalue | graphpercent | 1 | 9 | 210 | center | 5 | bold | Graphdata1:contrastcolor |
| 4 | text | datavalue | graphpercent | 1 | 6 | 423 | center | 5 | bold | GraphData2:contrastcolor |
| 5 | text | datavalue | graphpercent | 2 | 9 | 206 | center | 5 | bold | Graphdata1:contrastcolor |

The values are drawn using X1Space='DataValue' to ensure that the values are correctly positioned along the x-axis with Anchor='Center' and Y1Space='GraphPercent'. The Drug A values are drawn at 9% from bottom using Graphdata1:contrastcolor, and Drug B at 6%, using Graphdata2:contrastcolor to match the colors used for the same groups in the graph.

When all the subject count values are displayed correctly, we now need to draw the labels for Drug A and Drug B to the left of the data along each row. We also need to display the table header "Number of subjects at visit" and the footnote. These annotation commands are in the last four observations in the data set, as shown below.

**Figure 3.2.1.3 – Annotation Data Set for Labels**

| Obs | Function | X1Space | Y1Space | Label | Anchor | X1 | Y1 |
|---|---|---|---|---|---|---|---|
| 21 | text | wallpercent | graphpercent | Drug B | right | -1 | 6 |
| 22 | text | wallpercent | graphpercent | Drug A | right | -1 | 9 |
| 23 | text | wallpercent | graphpercent | Number of subjects at visit | left | 0 | 13 |
| 24 | text | graphpercent | graphpercent | Note: Vertical lines represent 95% confidence intervals. LOCF is last observation carried forward | left | 2 | 2 |

The annotations from the "annoOuter" data set are drawn into the graph as shown below. See Program 3_2 for the full code.

**Figure 3.2.1.4 – Subjects at Visit Table Added Using Annotation**

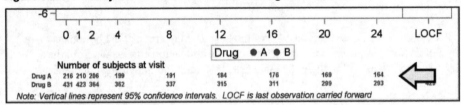

## 3.2.2  Mean Change of QTc by Week and Treatment with Inner Table

The mean values are displayed by week and treatment. The table of subjects at visit is displayed above the x-axis by using a SCATTER plot statement with MARKERCHAR on the Y2-axis. We did not use annotation for this graph. This makes it easier to understand the numbers as they are closer to the rest of the graph.

**Figure 3.2.2.1 – Mean Change of QTc by Week and Treatment with Inner Table**

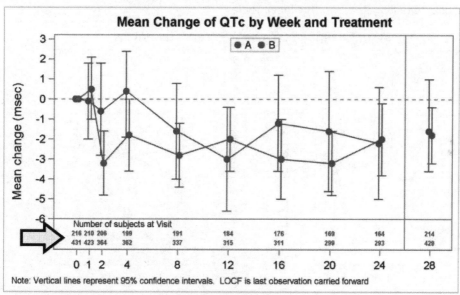

This graph shows the mean change of QTc by week and treatment, similar to the graph shown in Section 3.2.1. The main difference here is that we have positioned the "Number of subjects" table above the x-axis, closer to the graphical data. This has the benefit of proximity to the data and reduction of clutter in the graph. The other important benefit is that we do not need any annotation to create this graph.

```
title 'Mean Change of QTc by Week and Treatment';
footnote j=l h=0.8 'Note: Vertical lines represent 95% confidence
intervals.  LOCF is last observation carried forward';
proc sgplot data=QTc_Mean_Group_Header;
  format week qtcmean. N 3.0;
  scatter x=week y=mean / yerrorupper=high yerrorlower=low
          group=drug name='a' nomissinggroup groupdisplay=cluster
            clusterwidth=0.5 markerattrs=(size=7 symbol=circlefilled);
  series x=week y=mean2 / group=drug groupdisplay=cluster
          clusterwidth=0.5;
  refline 26 / axis=x;
  refline 0  / axis=y lineattrs=(pattern=shortdash);
  xaxis type=linear values=(0 1 2 4 8 12 16 20 24 28)
        max=29 valueshint display=(nolabel);
  yaxis label='Mean change (msec)' values=(-6 to 3 by 1)
```

```
          offsetmin=0.14 offsetmax=0.02;
  keylegend 'a' / location=inside position=top;
run;
```

The code shown above draws the graph shown in Figure 3.2.2.2 shown below without the "Number of Subjects" table just above the x-axis. Note, the extra blank space above the x-axis. This space is created by the YAXIS option OFFSETMIN=0.14, which leaves some blank space at the bottom.

**Figure 3.2.2.2 – Creating Space for the Inner Table**

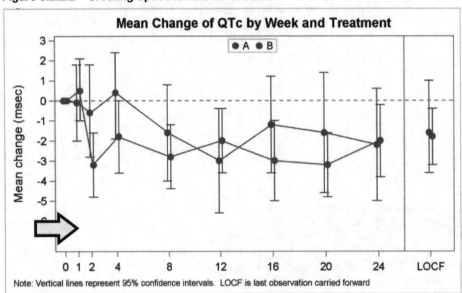

Now, we added the HIGHLOW, SCATTER with MARKERCHAR and theY2AXIS statements shown below to populate this space with the "Number of Subjects" data. Some of the options on the other statements are "thinned" to fit the code in the box.

```
proc sgplot data=QTc_Mean_Group_Header;
  format week qtcmean. N 3.0;
  scatter x=week y=mean / yerrorupper=high yerrorlower=low
          group=drug <opts>;
  series x=week y=mean2 / group=drug groupdisplay=cluster <opts>;
  highlow y=ylbl low=xlbl high=xlbl / highlabel=label y2axis
          lineattrs=(thickness=0);
  scatter x=week y=drug / markerchar=n group=drug
          markercharattrs=(size=5 weight=bold) y2axis nomissinggroup;
  refline -6  / axis=y;
  refline 26 / axis=x;
  refline 0  / axis=y lineattrs=(pattern=shortdash);
  xaxis type=linear values=(0 1 2 4 8 12 16 20 24 28) max=29 <opts>;
  yaxis label='Mean change (msec)' values=(-6 to 3 by 1)
        offsetmin=0.14 offsetmax=0.02;
  y2axis offsetmin=0.88 offsetmax=0.03 display=none reverse;
```

```
      keylegend 'a' / location=inside position=top;
run;
```

First, we have three new variables in the data: "xlbl", "ylbl", and "label". These are all missing except for three observations. This is used with the highlow plot HIGHLABEL option to display the table header in the location set by "xlbl" and "ylbl".

Next, we use the second SCATTER plot statement to display the "N" values by week and treatment using the Y2AXIS. We set the extents of the y-axis so that all the other plots are drawn in the upper part of the graph. We set the extents of the Y2-axis so that the related data is drawn in the lower part of the graph.

We draw a reference line at Y= -6 as a separator. See Program 3_2 for the full code.

### 3.2.3  Mean Change in QTc by Visit in Grayscale

Figure 3.2.3.1 shows the Mean Change in QTc graph in a grayscale format. Here we have derived a custom style from the Journal style using the %MODSTYLE macro.

**Figure 3.2.3.1 – Mean Change in QTc by Visit in Grayscale**

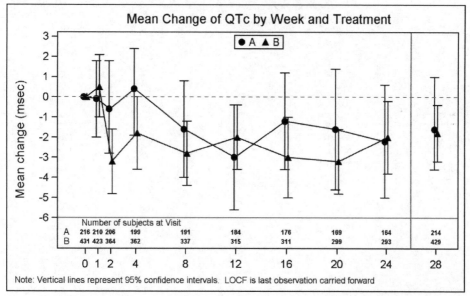

The new style is derived from the Journal with filled markers. The graph above is created using the same code except we now have lost the color hint for the classifiers for the values in the table. To fix that, we have added the display "A" and "B" labels on the left of the rows of the subjects table using the highlow plot option LOWLABEL. See Program 3_2 for the full code.

```
%modstyle(name=markers, parent=journal, type=CLM,
          markers=circlefilled trianglefilled);
```

```
ods listing style=markers;
proc sgplot data=QTc_Mean_Group_Header;
   format week qtcmean. N 3.0;
   scatter x=week y=mean / yerrorupper=high yerrorlower=low group=drug
           name='a' nomissinggroup groupdisplay=cluster
   series x=week y=mean2 / group=drug groupdisplay=cluster;
   highlow y=ylbl low=xlbl high=xlbl / highlabel=highlabel
           lowlabel=lowlabel y2axis lineattrs=(thickness=0);
   scatter x=week y=drug / markerchar=n group=drug
           markercharattrs=(size=5 weight=bold) y2axis;
   refline 26 / axis=x;
   refline -6  / axis=y;
   refline 0  / axis=y lineattrs=(pattern=shortdash);
   xaxis type=linear values=(0 1 2 4 8 12 16 20 24 28) max=29
        valueshint display=(nolabel);
   yaxis label='Mean change (msec)' values=(-6 to 3 by 1)
        offsetmin=0.14 offsetmax=0.02;
   y2axis offsetmin=0.88 offsetmax=0.03 display=none reverse;
   keylegend 'a' / location=inside position=top;
run;
```

## 3.3 Distribution of ASAT by Time and Treatment

This graph consists of three sections. The main body of the graph contains the box plot of ASAT by Week and Treatment in the middle. A table of subjects in the study by treatment is at the bottom, and the number of subjects with value > 2 by treatment is at the top of the graph.

**Figure 3.3.1 – Distribution of ASAT by Time and Treatment**

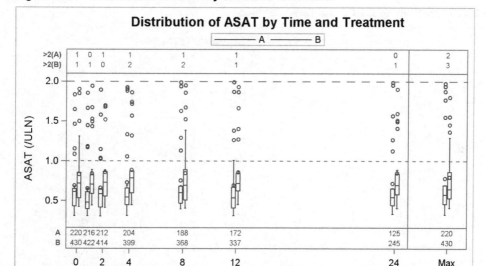

```
title 'Distribution of ASAT by Time and Treatment';
proc sgplot data=asat sganno=annoSort;
  vbox asat / category=week group=drug name='box' nofill;
  refline 1 / lineattrs=(pattern=shortdash);
  refline 2 / lineattrs=(pattern=dash);
  refline 2.1 0.16;
  refline 25 / axis=x;
  xaxis type=linear values=(0 2 4 8 12 24 28) offsetmax=0.05
  yaxis offsetmax=0.16 offsetmin=0.16;
  keylegend 'box' / position=top;
run;
```

This graph is created using a VBOX of ASAT by Week and Drug. The XAXIS TYPE is set to Linear so that the week data is plotted to scale by value. A group display of Cluster is used to place the boxes and the outliers side by side.

Reference lines on the y-axis are placed at 1.0 and 2.0. Additional reference lines are placed to act as separators between the plot and the tabular data. The legend is placed at the top, under the title to reduce the clutter with the x-axis.

The tabular data at the bottom and top of the graph are inserted using annotation and included using SGANNO=annoSort proc option. The y-axis OFFSETMIN and OFFSETMAX are set to 0.16 or 16% of the height of the graph. This creates the blank space at the top and bottom of the wall.

Without annotation, the graph looks like the one shown in Figure 3.3.2 below. Note the blank space at the top and bottom of the wall as indicated by the arrows.

**Figure 3.3.2 – Creating Space for the Table of Values**

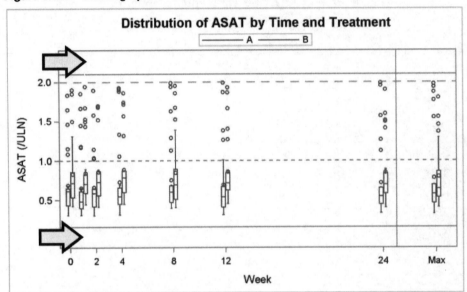

The SG Annotation data set is built from the "Asat" data set. The data set contains all the commands necessary to draw the values in the bottom and top regions of the graph and the labels for each row. Snippets of the data set are shown below. The block of observations with "Id" of "Count" is for display of the subject counts. This includes two observations to draw the labels shown in the second block below. Another similar block of observations with "Id" of "GT2" is for the values > 2 at the top of the graph.

**Figure 3.3.3 – Annotation Data Set**

| Obs | id | Function | label | x1Space | x1 | y1Space | y1 | Anchor | TextColor | TextSize | TextWeight |
|---|---|---|---|---|---|---|---|---|---|---|---|
| 1 | Count | Text | 220 | DataValue | 0 | WallPercent | 8 | Center | GraphData1:contrastcolor | 6 | |
| 2 | Count | Text | 430 | DataValue | 0 | WallPercent | 3 | Center | GraphData2:contrastcolor | 6 | |
| 3 | Count | Text | 216 | DataValue | 1 | WallPercent | 8 | Center | GraphData1:contrastcolor | 6 | |
| 4 | Count | Text | 422 | DataValue | 1 | WallPercent | 3 | Center | GraphData2:contrastcolor | 6 | |

**Figure 3.3.4 – Annotation Data Set**

| Obs | id | Function | label | x1Space | x1 | y1Space | y1 | Anchor | TextColor | TextSize | TextWeight |
|---|---|---|---|---|---|---|---|---|---|---|---|
| 17 | Count | Text | A | WallPercent | -1 | WallPercent | 8 | Right | GraphData1:contrastcolor | 6 | Bold |
| 18 | Count | Text | B | WallPercent | -1 | WallPercent | 3 | Right | GraphData2:contrastcolor | 6 | Bold |

The ID column with values of "Count" and "GT2" is added only for convenience of describing which observations are used for which part of the graph. These values play no part in the actual display of the annotations. See Program 3_3 for the full code.

## 3.4 Median of Lipid Profile by Visit and Treatment

This graph displays the median of the lipid values by visit and treatment. The visits are at regular intervals and represented as discrete data.

### 3.4.1 Median of Lipid Profile by Visit and Treatment on Discrete Axis

The values for each treatment are displayed along with the 95% confidence limits as adjacent groups using GROUPDISPLAY of "Cluster" and CLUSTERWIDTH=0.5. The HTMLBlue style is used.

**Figure 3.4.1 – Median of Lipid Profile by Visit and Treatment**

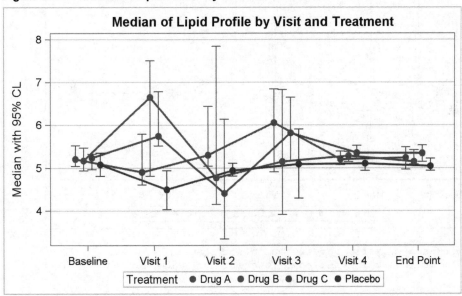

```
ods listing style=htmlblue;
title 'Median of Lipid Profile by Visit and Treatment';
proc sgplot data=lipid_grp;
  series  x=day y=median / group=trt groupdisplay=cluster
          clusterwidth=0.5 lineattrs=(thickness=2);
  scatter x=day y=median / yerrorlower=lcl yerrorupper=ucl
```

```
            group=trt  name='s' groupdisplay=cluster clusterwidth=0.5
            errorbarattrs=(thickness=1)markerattrs=(symbol=circlefilled);
  keylegend 's' / title='Treatment';
  yaxis label='Median with 95% CL' grid;
  xaxis display=(nolabel);
run;
```

A SCATTER statement is used with filled markers and error bars to display the data using cluster groups. The values across visits are joined using a series plot. Note, the series plot also uses cluster groups with the same cluster width. For full details, see Program 3_4.

### 3.4.2 Median of Lipid Profile by Visit and Treatment on Linear Axis in Grayscale

This graph displays the graph of the median of the lipid data by treatment in grayscale on a linear x-axis.

**Figure 3.4.2 – Median of Lipid Profile by Visit and Treatment on Linear Axis**

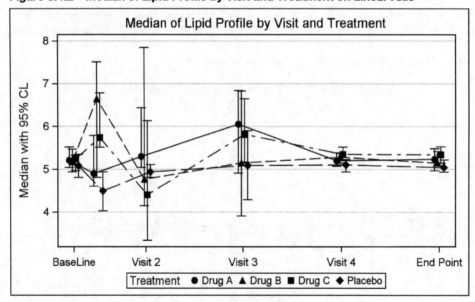

```
%modstyle(name=markers, parent=journal, type=CLM,
          markers=circlefilled trianglefilled squarefilled
                  diamondfilled);
options debug=none;
ods listing style=markers;
title 'Median of Lipid Profile by Visit and Treatment';
proc sgplot data=lipid_Liner_grp;
  series  x=n y=median /  group=trt
          groupdisplay=cluster clusterwidth=0.5;
  scatter x=n y=median / yerrorlower=lcl yerrorupper=ucl group=trt
          groupdisplay=cluster clusterwidth=0.5
```

```
        errorbarattrs=(thickness=1)markerattrs=(size=7) name='s';
  keylegend 's' / title='Treatment';
  yaxis label='Median with 95% CL' grid;
  xaxis display=(nolabel) values=(1 4 8 12 16);
run;
```

The visits are not at regular intervals and are displayed at the correct scaled location along the x-axis. The visits are at week 1, 2, 4, 8, 12, and 16. These values are formatted to the strings shown on the axis. "Visit 1" collides with "Baseline", causing alternate tick values to be dropped, so I removed "1" from the tick value list.

As you can see, the group values are displayed as clusters, and the "effective midpoint spacing" is the shortest distance between the values. The markers are reduced in size to show the clustering. This can be adjusted by setting marker SIZE=7. The %MODSTYLE macro is used to derive a new style from Journal with filled markers. For full details, see Program 3_4.

## 3.5 Survival Plot

The survival plot is one of the most popular graphs that users want to customize to their own needs. Here I have run the LIFETEST procedure to generate the data for this graph. The output is saved into the "SurvivalPlotData" data set.

### 3.5.1 Survival Plot with External "Subjects At-Risk" Table

The survival plot shown below in Figure 3.5.1.1 has the traditional arrangement where the table of Subjects At-Risk is displayed at the bottom of the graph, below the x-axis.

**Figure 3.5.1.1 – Survival Plot with External "Subjects At-Risk" Table**

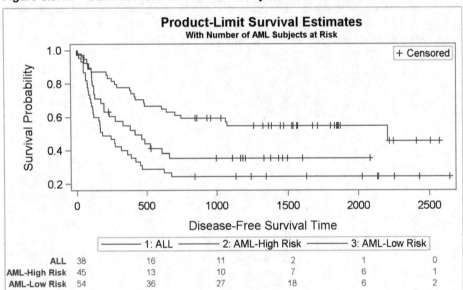

```
ods output Survivalplot=SurvivalPlotData;
proc lifetest data=sashelp.BMT
     plots=survival(atrisk=0 to 2500 by 500);
  time T * Status(0);
  strata Group / test=logrank adjust=sidak;
run;
```

For more information about the LIFETEST procedure, see the SAS/STAT documentation.

A step plot of survival by time by strata is used to display the survival curves. A scatter overlay is used to draw the censored values. A legend is drawn in the top right corner to show the censored observations, and a legend is drawn at the bottom to indicate the stratum.

```
title 'Product-Limit Survival Estimates';
title2  h=0.8 'With Number of AML Subjects at Risk';
proc sgplot data=SurvivalPlotData sganno=anno
```

```
       pad=(bottom=15pct left=6pct);
   step x=time y=survival / group=stratum
       lineattrs=(pattern=solid) name='s';
   scatter x=time y=censored / markerattrs=(symbol=plus) name='c';
   scatter x=time y=censored / markerattrs=(symbol=plus) GROUP=stratum;
   keylegend 'c' / location=inside position=topright;
   keylegend 's';
run;
```

We have set the bottom pad=15%. This reserves space of 15% of the graph height at the bottom of the graph as indicated by the arrow below. We will use annotation to draw the "Subjects At-Risk" table in this space using SGANNO=anno procedure option.

**Figure 3.5.1.2 – Survival Plot with Space for the Table of "Subjects At-Risk"**

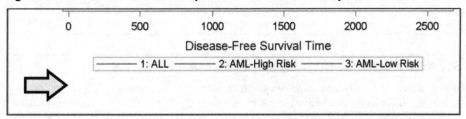

To write the table values at the bottom of the graph, we have to create an SGAnno data set. This data set contains all the commands needed to draw the values along the axis and the labels on the left. Each observation in the data set provides the information needed to draw each value using the predefined column names. The first 18 observations provide the data for the values in the table as shown below.

A row of values is drawn for each stratum level, at a fixed Y distance from the bottom of the graph. Each row also uses the text color to match the values in the graph. The values are positioned along the x-axis using X1Space=DataValue and Y1Space=GraphPercent.

**Figure 3.5.1.3 – Annotate Data Set Observations for Drawing the Table of Subjects At-Risk**

| Obs | Function | X1Space | Y1Space | X1 | Y1 | Label | TextColor | TextSize | TextWeight | Anchor |
|---|---|---|---|---|---|---|---|---|---|---|
| 1 | text | datavalue | graphpercent | 0 | 12 | 38 | GraphData1:contrastcolor | 7 | Normal | center |
| 2 | text | datavalue | graphpercent | 500 | 12 | 16 | GraphData1:contrastcolor | 7 | Normal | center |
| 3 | text | datavalue | graphpercent | 1000 | 12 | 11 | GraphData1:contrastcolor | 7 | Normal | center |

The last three observations in the data set provide the information to draw the stratum labels for each row of values. The labels are drawn using X1Space=WallPercent and X1= -1 with labels anchored on the right. The annotated part of the graph is shown below. For full details, see Program 3_5.

**Figure 3.5.1.4 – Annotate Data Set Observations for Labels**

| Obs | Function | X1Space | Y1Space | X1 | Y1 | Label | TextColor | TextSize | TextWeight | Anchor |
|-----|----------|---------|---------|-----|-----|-------|-----------|----------|------------|--------|
| 19 | text | wallpercent | graphpercent | -1 | 12 | ALL | GraphData1:contrastcolor | 7 | Bold | Right |
| 20 | text | wallpercent | graphpercent | -1 | 8 | AML-High Risk | GraphData2:contrastcolor | 7 | Bold | Right |
| 21 | text | wallpercent | graphpercent | -1 | 4 | AML-Low Risk | GraphData3:contrastcolor | 7 | Bold | Right |

**Figure 3.5.1.5 – Table of Subjects At-Risk at Bottom of Graph**

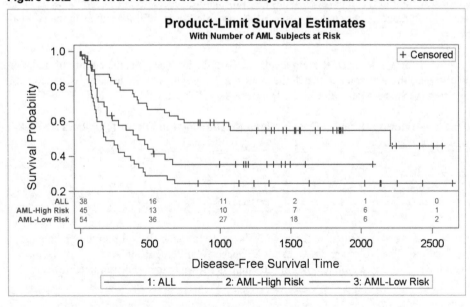

## 3.5.2  Survival Plot with Internal "Subjects At-Risk" Table

The graph shown here is mostly similar to the graph in Section 3.5.1, with the difference that the "Subjects At-Risk" table in moved above the x-axis, close to the rest of the data. Bringing all the data closer makes it easy to align the values with the data, and that improves the effectiveness of the graph.

**Figure 3.5.2 – Survival Plot with the Table of Subjects At-Risk above the X-Axis**

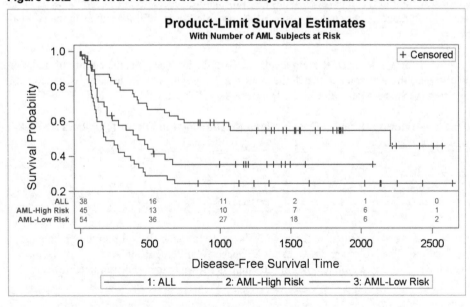

```
title 'Product-Limit Survival Estimates';
title2  h=0.8 'With Number of AML Subjects at Risk';
proc sgplot data=SurvivalPlotData sganno=anno_in pad=(left=6pct);
```

```
   step x=time y=survival / group=stratum
        lineattrs=(pattern=solid) name='s';
   scatter x=time y=censored / markerattrs=(symbol=plus) name='c';
   scatter x=time y=censored / markerattrs=(symbol=plus) GROUP=stratum;
   refline 0.2;
   yaxis offsetmin=0.2;
   keylegend 'c' / location=inside position=topright;
   keylegend 's';
run;
```

Here we use YAXIS OffsetMin=0.2 to create some space at the bottom of the y-axis. Then, we change the Y1Space from GraphPercent to WallPercent to draw the values above the wall. A reference line at y=0.2 acts as a separator.

Relevant details are shown in the code snippet above. For full details, see Program 3_5.

### 3.5.3 Survival Plot with Internal "Subjects At-Risk" Table in Grayscale

This graph shows the same survival plot using a grayscale medium.

**Figure 3.5.3 – Survival Plot in Grayscale**

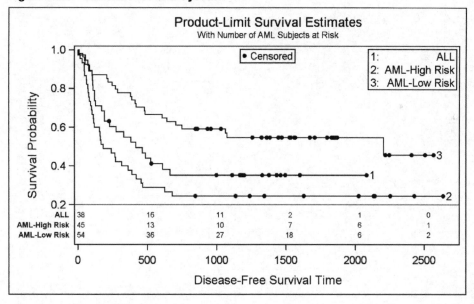

```
ods listing style=journal;
title 'Product-Limit Survival Estimates';
title2 h=0.8 'With Number of AML Subjects at Risk';
proc sgplot data=SurvivalPlotData sganno=anno_in pad=(left=6pct);
   step x=time y=survival / group=stratumnum lineattrs=(pattern=solid)
        curvelabel name='s';
   scatter x=time y=censored / name='c'
        markerattrs=(symbol=circlefilled size=4);
```

```
    keylegend 'c' / location=inside position=top;
    inset ("1:"="ALL" "2:"="AML-High Risk" "3:"="AML-Low Risk") / border;
    refline 0.2;
    yaxis offsetmin=0.2;
run;
```

Displaying the survival plot in a grayscale medium presents some challenges. Here we cannot use colors to identify the strata. Normally, the Journal style uses line patterns to identify the groups. Although line patterns work well for curves, they are not so effective with step plots because of the frequent breaks. So, it is preferable to use solid lines for all the levels of the step plot and use labels to identify the strata.

We would like to use curve labels to identify curves by stratum. However, curve labels can get long. So, we plot the curves by "stratumnum" to identify each curve, and add an inset to identify each ID. The same annotation table as in 3.5.3 is used to add the table above the x-axis.

Relevant details are shown in the code snippet above. For full details, see Program 3_5.

## 3.6  Simple Forest Plot

A forest plot is a graphical representation of a meta-analysis of the results of randomized controlled trials.

### 3.6.1  Simple Forest Plot

The graph in Figure 3.6.1 shows a simple forest plot, with the odds ratio plot in the middle by study names on the y-axis along with the tabular display of the statistics on the right.

**Figure 3.6.1.1 – Simple Forest Plot**

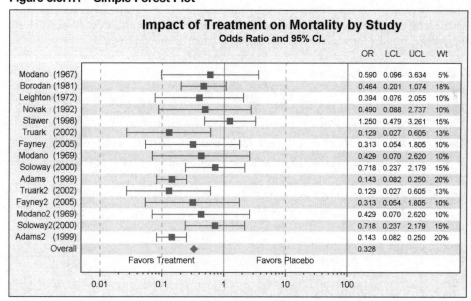

```
title "Impact of Treatment on Mortality by Study";
title2 h=8pt 'Odds Ratio and 95% CL';
proc sgplot data=forest noautolegend;
  refline study_lbl / transparency=0.95
        lineattrs=(thickness=13px color=darkgreen);
  scatter y=study x=or / xerrorupper=ucl xerrorlower=lcl group=grp;
  refline 1 100  / axis=x noclip;
  refline 0.01 0.1 10 / axis=x lineattrs=(pattern=shortdash)
        transparency=0.5 noclip;
  scatter y=study x=xlbl / markerchar=lbl ;
  scatter y=study x=or_lbl  / markerchar=or  x2axis
        markercharattrs=(size=6);
  scatter y=study x=lcl_lbl / markerchar=lcl x2axis
        markercharattrs=(size=6);
  scatter y=study x=ucl_lbl / markerchar=ucl x2axis
        markercharattrs=(size=6);
  scatter y=study x=wt_lbl  / markerchar=wt  x2axis
        markercharattrs=(size=6);
```

```
  xaxis type=log  max=100 minor display=(nolabel) valueattrs=(size=7)
        offsetmin=0.05 offsetmax=0.3;
  yaxis display=(noticks nolabel) valueattrs=(size=7) reverse;
  x2axis display=(noticks nolabel) valueattrs=(size=7)
         offsetmin=0.75 offsetmax=0.05;
run;
```

The data for this graph contains the odds ratio, the confidence limits, and the weight for each study. The studies are classified with '1' for individual study names and '2' for "Overall". We use this information to plot the graph by study using a scatter plot with error bars to plot the odds ratio on a log axis.

The %MODSTYLE macro is used to derive a new style named 'Forest' with parent='Analysis', and using two markers for group classification, "SquareFilled" and "DiamondFilled".

Let us see how we have built this graph.

1. The data contains observations for each study including "Overall".
2. Two additional observations are added for the labels at the bottom.
3. Each observation has "Grp" of 1 if it is a study, and 2 otherwise.
4. A SCATTER statement is used to draw the odds ratio and error bars in the left side of the graph.
5. This is done by setting the OFFSETMAX for the x-axis to 0.3.
6. Reference lines are drawn at 1, 100, 0.01, 0.1, and 1 on a log axis.

```
title "Impact of Treatment on Mortality by Study";
title2 h=8pt 'Odds Ratio and 95% CL';
proc sgplot data=forest noautolegend;
  scatter y=study x=or / xerrorupper=ucl xerrorlower=lcl group=grp;
  refline 1 100  / axis=x noclip;
  refline 0.01 0.1 10 / axis=x lineattrs=(pattern=shortdash) noclip;
  scatter y=study x=xlbl / markerchar=lbl;
  xaxis type=log  max=100 minor display=(nolabel)
        offsetmin=0.05 offsetmax=0.3;
  yaxis display=(noticks nolabel) reverse;
run;
```

**Figure 3.6.1.2 – Creating Space for the Statistics**

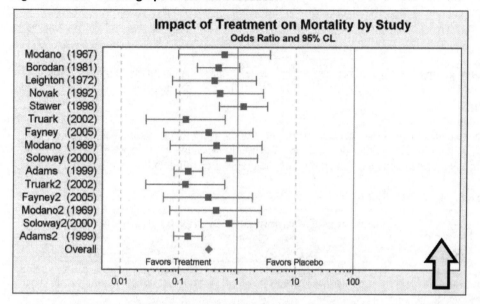

The code and the graph are shown above. The right 30% of the graph is empty, and we will use additional statements to populate this space (marked by an arrow) with the data columns.

To populate the data columns on the right of the graph as shown at the top of this section, we will use the SCATTER statement with the MARKERCHAR option as follows:

```
scatter y=study x=or_lbl / markerchar=or;
```

To make this work, we have added four columns to the data set as shown below.

**Figure 3.6.1.3 – Data for the Graph**

| Obs | Study | grp | OR | LCL | UCL | Wt | or_lbl | lcl_lbl | ucl_lbl | wt_lbl | study_lbl |
|-----|-------|-----|-----|-----|-----|-----|--------|---------|---------|--------|-----------|
| 1 | Modano (1967) | 1 | 0.590 | 0.096 | 3.634 | 5% | OR | LCL | UCL | Wt | |
| 2 | Borodan (1981) | 1 | 0.464 | 0.201 | 1.074 | 18% | OR | LCL | UCL | Wt | Borodan (1981) |
| 3 | Leighton (1972) | 1 | 0.394 | 0.076 | 2.055 | 10% | OR | LCL | UCL | Wt | |
| 4 | Novak (1992) | 1 | 0.490 | 0.088 | 2.737 | 10% | OR | LCL | UCL | Wt | Novak (1992) |

Note the columns "or_lbl", "lcl_lbl", "ucl_lbl", and "wt_lbl". Each of these columns has the same value for all the observations, and it is the text string for the description of the value. We use these columns as the X role for the scatter plot, and the corresponding value for the MARKERCHAR role.

This places the value in the "or_lbl" column as the x-axis tick value "OR", and place the value of the "OR" column as the value in each row of this column. We use four such SCATTER plot statements, one for each of OR, LCL, UCL, and Wt to place all four columns of data on the right side.

The values go on the right side because we associate all these statements with the X2AXIS, and we set the OFFSETMIN of the X2AXIS to 0.75. So, all these values are placed in the right 25% of the graph.

Note in the data shown above, we have a column "Study_Lbl". This column has a copy of the "Study" column for every other observation. We use this variable with the REFLINE statement to draw the alternating bands for ease of reading the graph. For full details, see Program 3_6.

**Figure 3.6.1.4 – Forest Plot**

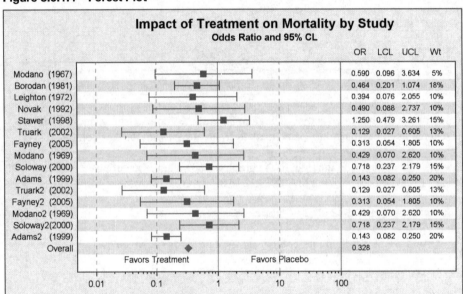

## 3.6.2 Simple Forest Plot with Study Weights

The graph below shows a simple forest plot with Study Weights, where the markers in the odds ratio plot are sized by the weight of the study.

**Figure 3.6.2 – Simple Forest Plot with Study Weights**

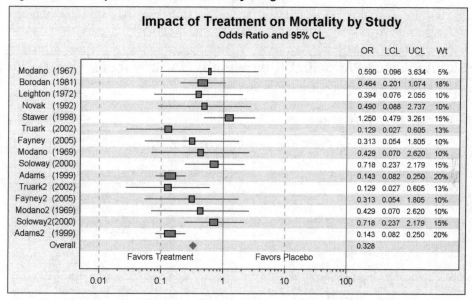

```
title "Impact of Treatment on Mortality by Study";
title2 h=8pt 'Odds Ratio and 95% CL';
proc sgplot data=forest noautolegend nocycleattrs;
  refline study_lbl / transparency=0.95 lineattrs=(color=darkgreen);
  scatter y=study x=or2 / markerattrs=graphdata2(symbol=diamondfilled);
  highlow y=study low=lcl high=ucl / type=line lineattrs=(pattern=solid);
  highlow y=study low=q1 high=q3 / type=bar barwidth=0.6
          fillattrs=graphdata1;
  refline 1 100  / axis=x noclip;
  refline 0.01 0.1 10 / axis=x transparency=0.5 noclip;
  scatter y=study x=xlbl / markerchar=lbl ;
  scatter y=study x=or_lbl  / markerchar=or  x2axis
          markercharattrs=(size=6);
  scatter y=study x=lcl_lbl / markerchar=lcl x2axis
          markercharattrs=(size=6);
  scatter y=study x=ucl_lbl / markerchar=ucl x2axis
          markercharattrs=(size=6);
  scatter y=study x=wt_lbl  / markerchar=wt  x2axis
          markercharattrs=(size=6);
  xaxis type=log  max=100 minor display=(nolabel)
        offsetmin=0.05 offsetmax=0.3;
  yaxis display=(noticks nolabel) reverse;
  x2axis display=(noticks nolabel) offsetmin=0.75 offsetmax=0.05;
run;
```

This graph uses a highlow plot to display the relative weights for each study and the confidence interval. The scatter plot uses the "OR2" variable, which is non-missing only for the "Overall" study. So, only the diamond marker is drawn by the scatter plot.

Each box is weighted by the "Wt" column. Low and high values are computed for the box and displayed using the highlow plot. This allows for a qualitative comparison between the weights, which might not be displayed as exactly proportional because of the use of the log x-axis. Some options are trimmed in the code above to fit the space. For full details, see Program 3_6.

### 3.6.3 Simple Forest Plot with Study Weights in Grayscale

Figure 3.6.3 shows the same forest plot in grayscale medium.

**Figure 3.6.3 – Forest Plot in Grayscale**

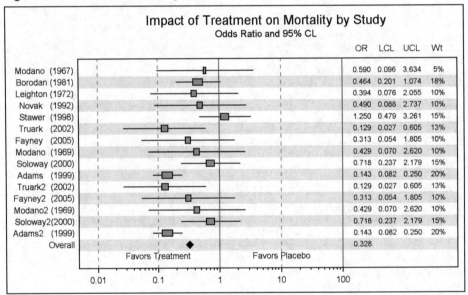

```
ods listing style=journal;
title "Impact of Treatment on Mortality by Study";
title2 h=8pt 'Odds Ratio and 95% CL';
proc sgplot data=forest noautolegend nocycleattrs;
   refline study_lbl / transparency=0.95 lineattrs=(thickness=13px);
   scatter y=study x=or2 /
           markerattrs=graphdata2(symbol=diamondfilled);
   highlow y=study low=lcl high=ucl / type=line
           lineattrs=(pattern=solid);
   highlow y=study low=q1 high=q3 / type=bar barwidth=0.6;
   refline 1 100  / axis=x noclip;
   refline 0.01 0.1 10 / axis=x transparency=0.5 noclip;
   scatter y=study x=xlbl / markerchar=lbl ;
   scatter y=study x=or_lbl  / markerchar=or   x2axis;
   scatter y=study x=lcl_lbl / markerchar=lcl x2axis;
```

```
   scatter y=study x=ucl_lbl / markerchar=ucl x2axis;
   scatter y=study x=wt_lbl  / markerchar=wt  x2axis;
   xaxis type=log  max=100 minor display=(nolabel)
         offsetmin=0.05 offsetmax=0.3;
   yaxis display=(noticks nolabel) reverse;
   x2axis display=(noticks nolabel) offsetmin=0.75 offsetmax=0.05;
run;
```

Rendering this graph in a grayscale medium does not pose a lot of challenges. Basically, we have set the ODS style to JOURNAL to produce the graph above. This is structurally similar to the graph shown in Section 3.6.2.

Some options are trimmed in the code above to fit the space. For full details, see Program 3_6.

## 3.7 Subgrouped Forest Plot

More recently, many of you have been asking for building a forest plot, where each study value has multiple subgroups. The example in Figure 3.7.1 shows two subgroups per observation.

For the graph shown below, only the hazard ratio plot in the middle is displayed using a plot statement. The rest of the tabular data is displayed using annotation.

**Figure 3.7.1 – Subgrouped Forest Plot**

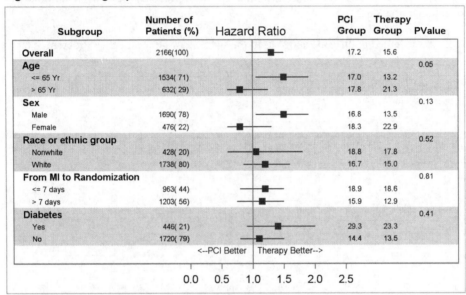

```
proc sgplot data=Forest2 nocycleattrs noautolegend
            sganno=anno pad=(top=6pct);
  refline ref / lineattrs=(thickness=15 color=cxf0f0f0);
  highlow y=obsid low=low high=high;
  scatter y=obsid x=mean / markerattrs=(symbol=squarefilled);
  scatter y=obsid x=mean / markerattrs=(size=0) x2axis;
  refline 1 / axis=x;
  refline &Rows / noclip;
  scatter y=yl x=xl / markerchar=text;
  yaxis   reverse offsetmax=0 offsetmin=0 display=none;
  xaxis   display=(noline nolabel) values=(0.0 0.5 1.0 1.5 2.0 2.5)
          offsetmin=0.4 offsetmax=0.25;
  x2axis display=(noline noticks novalues) offsetmin=0.4 offsetmax=0.25
         label='          Hazard Ratio' ;
run;
```

This graph displays the hazard ratio and confidence limits by subgroup, along with the number of patients in the study and other statistics. The key difference here is the display of the sub groups and values in the first column. The subgroup titles are displayed in a bold font, and the values are displayed in the normal font, indented to the right.

The hazard ratio plot in the middle is displayed using HIGHLOW and SCATTER plot statements. "PCI Better" and "Therapy Better" insets are displayed using SCATTER with MARKERCHAR. All the rest of the information in the graph is populated using annotation. Let us see how that was done.

The annotation data set is derived from the original forest data as shown below. In this data set, I have added two columns just for explanation of the items. These are the "Anno" and the "AnnoType" columns. The actual data has 95 observations, made up of the "Text" functions to draw each of the column values and the headers. I have used the "Anno" column to identify the column and what is in the column – "AnnoType". Then I sorted on "Anno" and kept only three observations, each to derive a reduced data set shown below.

**Figure 3.7.2 – Annotation Data Set**

| Obs | Anno | AnnoType | Function | x1space | y1Space | label | x1 | y1 | Anchor | TextWeight | textsize | width |
|---|---|---|---|---|---|---|---|---|---|---|---|---|
| 1 | 1 | Subgroups | Text | WallPercent | datavalue | Overall | 2 | 1.0 | Left | Bold | 8 | 50 |
| 2 | 1 | Subgroups | Text | WallPercent | datavalue | Age | 2 | 2.0 | Left | Bold | 8 | 50 |
| 3 | 1 | Subgroups | Text | WallPercent | datavalue | <= 65 Yr | 4 | 3.0 | Left | Normal | 6 | 50 |
| 4 | 2 | CountPct | Text | WallPercent | datavalue | 2166(100) | 40 | 1.0 | Right | Normal | 6 | 50 |
| 5 | 2 | CountPct | Text | WallPercent | datavalue | | 40 | 2.0 | Right | Normal | 6 | 50 |
| 6 | 2 | CountPct | Text | WallPercent | datavalue | 1534( 71) | 40 | 3.0 | Right | Normal | 6 | 50 |
| 7 | 3 | PCIGroup | Text | WallPercent | datavalue | 17.2 | 75 | 1.0 | Left | Normal | 6 | 50 |
| 8 | 3 | PCIGroup | Text | WallPercent | datavalue | | 75 | 2.0 | Left | Normal | 6 | 50 |
| 9 | 3 | PCIGroup | Text | WallPercent | datavalue | 17.0 | 75 | 3.0 | Left | Normal | 6 | 50 |
| 10 | 4 | Group | Text | WallPercent | datavalue | 15.6 | 83 | 1.0 | Left | Normal | 6 | 50 |
| 11 | 4 | Group | Text | WallPercent | datavalue | | 83 | 2.0 | Left | Normal | 6 | 50 |
| 12 | 4 | Group | Text | WallPercent | datavalue | 13.2 | 83 | 3.0 | Left | Normal | 6 | 50 |
| 13 | 5 | PValue | Text | WallPercent | datavalue | | 91 | 1.0 | Left | Normal | 6 | 50 |
| 14 | 5 | PValue | Text | WallPercent | datavalue | 0.05 | 91 | 2.0 | Left | Normal | 6 | 50 |
| 15 | 5 | PValue | Text | WallPercent | datavalue | | 91 | 3.0 | Left | Normal | 6 | 50 |
| 16 | 6 | Headers | Text | WallPercent | WallPercent | Subgroup | 10 | 100.8 | BottomLeft | Bold | 8 | 14 |
| 17 | 6 | Headers | Text | WallPercent | WallPercent | Number of Patients (%) | 30 | 100.8 | BottomLeft | Bold | 8 | 14 |
| 18 | 6 | Headers | Text | WallPercent | WallPercent | PCI Group | 73 | 100.8 | BottomLeft | Bold | 8 | 10 |

The first set of annotations is for the "Subgroup" and contains labels like "Overall", "Age", and "<= 65 yr". Remember, there are actually more observations for subgroups. All text annotations for the first column use x1Space="WallPercent" and y1Space='DataValue' and anchor='Left'. Recall that we have reserved the lower 40% of axis space for the left columns and 25% of upper axis space for the upper columns on the right using axis offsets. Annotated values are aligned along Y with "ObsId" values.

Subgroup headers like "Age" (id=1) are positioned at x=2%, and have bold weight with size=8pt. Values that are not header values (id=2) are indented to start at x=4%, with normal weight and with

font size=6pt.  We have similarly plotted the values for the CountPct values and the three columns
on the right.

The last few observations are for the column headers.  Here x1Space and y1Space are both
'WallPercent' as we want to draw these labels above the wall at known percent coordinates.  Text is
anchored at bottom or BottomLeft as necessary, and lined up with the X2-axis label "Hazard
Ratio".  See Program 3_7 for all the details.

## 3.8  Adverse Event Timeline by Severity

An Adverse Event Timeline graph by AEDECOD and Severity is useful to view the history of a
specific subject in a study.

**Figure 3.8.1 – Adverse Event Timeline by AEDECOD and Severity**

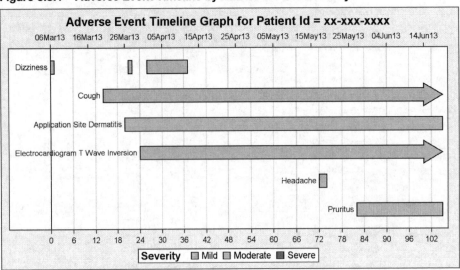

```
title "Adverse Event Timeline Graph for Patient Id = &pid";
proc sgplot data=ae2_stday dattrmap=attrmap;
  format stdate date7.;
  refline 0 / axis=x lineattrs=(color=black);
  highlow y=aedecod low=stday high=enday / type=bar group=aesev
          lineattrs=(color=black pattern=solid) barwidth=0.8
          lowlabel=aedecod highcap=highcap attrid=Severity
          nomissinggroup labelattrs=(color=black size=7);
  scatter y=aedecod x=stdate / x2axis markerattrs=(size=0);
  xaxis grid display=(nolabel) valueattrs=(size=7)
        values=(&minday to &maxday by 2) offsetmax=0.02 ;
  x2axis display=(nolabel) type=time valueattrs=(size=7)
         values=(&mindate to &maxdate) offsetmax=0.02;
  yaxis  reverse  display=(noticks novalues nolabel);
run;
```

The graph above displays each adverse event as a bar segment over its duration. The color of the event is set by the severity. The source data is in CDISC, SDTM tabulation model format, as shown below.

**Figure 3.8.2 – Data Set**

| Obs | aeseq | aedecod | aesev | aestdtc | aeendtc |
|-----|-------|---------|-------|---------|---------|
| 1 | 1 | Dizziness | Moderate | 2013-03-06 | 2013-03-06 |
| 2 | 2 | Cough | Mild | 2013-03-20 | |
| 3 | 4 | Dizziness | Mild | 2013-03-27 | 2013-03-27 |
| 4 | 5 | Electrocardiogram T Wave Inversion | Mild | 2013-03-30 | |

The data has many columns, but the ones that we are using are aeseq, aedecod, aesev, aestdtc, and aeendtc. In the example above, all aestdtc values are present and assumed to be valid. If not, some data cleaning might be needed. In the DATA step, stdate is extracted from aestdtc and endate from aeendtc. If aeendtc is missing, the largest value of endate is used, and highcap is set to "FilledArrow" to indicate the event does not have an end date. A valid end date is required to draw the event in the graph. The data set required for plotting the graph is shown below.

**Figure 3.8.3 – Data Set with Added Columns**

| Obs | aeseq | aedecod | aesev | sev | stdate | endate | stday | enday | highcap |
|-----|-------|---------|-------|-----|--------|--------|-------|-------|---------|
| 1 | 1 | Dizziness | Moderate | 2 | 06MAR2013 | 06MAR2013 | 0 | 1 | |
| 2 | 2 | Cough | Mild | 1 | 20MAR2013 | 18JUN2013 | 14 | 105 | FilledArrow |
| 3 | 6 | Application Site Dermatitis | Moderate | 2 | 26MAR2013 | 18JUN2013 | 20 | 105 | |
| 4 | 3 | Dizziness | Mild | 1 | 27MAR2013 | 27MAR2013 | 21 | 22 | |

The data set above is computed for creating the graph. Note in this data set, we do not have any observations with Severity="Severe". However, the legend in the graph does have an entry for "Severe". These dummy observations do not have valid start and end values, so they are not actually drawn in the graph. The top x-axis is enabled by using a scatter plot assigned to the x2-axis. Macro variables are used to align the x- and x2-axes.

Normally, observations with specific group values are assigned the color and other attributes from the GraphData1-12 style elements. These are assigned in the order in which they are encountered in the data. In this case, we are using specific colors for "Mild", "Moderate", and "Severe". If we just change the colors of the style elements, we will get one of the three colors, but the color assignments can shift based on the order of the data.

To ensure consistent and reliable color assignment, we will use the Discrete Attribute Map data set. Colors and the specific values of the group values are explicitly assigned. Now, the group values will get the colors by value, and not based on the order of the values in the data. In this case, LineColor is used both for lines and text.

**Figure 3.8.4 – Data Set for Attribute Map**

| Obs | Id | Show | Value | Fillcolor | Linecolor |
|-----|----|------|-------|-----------|-----------|
| 1 | Severity | Attrmap | Mild | lightgreen | darkgreen |
| 2 | Severity | Attrmap | Moderate | gold | cx9f7f00 |
| 3 | Severity | Attrmap | Severe | lightred | darkred |

Only the severity values that are present in the data are displayed in the legend. The color representing each severity is obtained from the attribute map. However, often we might want to display all the classification levels of severity that could occur, even if they might not be present in the current data set. To do this, we have to insert three observations at the start of the data, each having one of the three severity values, with missing values for other columns to prevent their inclusion in the graph.

The highlow plot is ideally suited for such a use case, and provides support to draw labels and arrowhead caps at each end. In this case, the LOWLABEL option is used to draw the event names. We have displayed the aedecod label only the first time. The HIGHCAP option is used to draw the arrowhead as shown for "Cough" at the right end. This indicates an event that does not have an end date in the data.

For the grayscale use case, we can change the high-low bar type to the default "Line". This will allow use of the line pattern as the visual element for the different severity values. Here is the graph, along with the appropriate attribute map.

**Figure 3.8.5 – Adverse Event Timeline Graph in Grayscale**

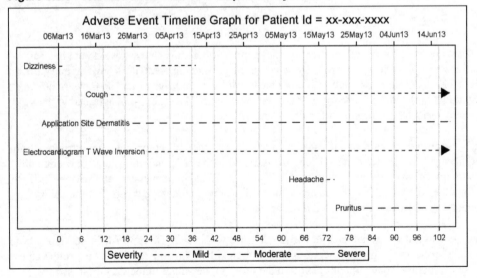

**Figure 3.8.6 – Attribute Map for Grayscale Graph**

| Obs | Id | Show | Value | Fillcolor | LinePattern | LineThickness |
|---|---|---|---|---|---|---|
| 1 | Severity | Attrmap | Mild | lightgreen | shortdash | 2 |
| 2 | Severity | Attrmap | Moderate | gold | dash | 2 |
| 3 | Severity | Attrmap | Severe | lightred | solid | 2 |

Relevant details are shown in the code snippet above. For full details, see Program 3_8.

## 3.9  Change in Tumor Size

The graph shown below is commonly known at a waterfall chart in the oncology domain. The graph displays the change in tumor size by treatment.

**Figure 3.9.1 – Change in Tumor Size by Treatment**

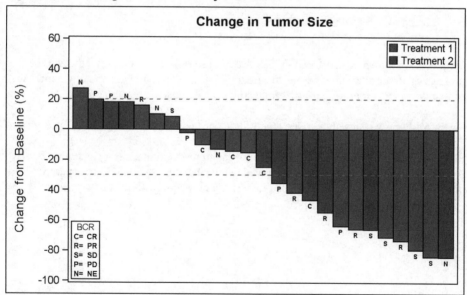

```
title 'Change in Tumor Size';
title2 'ITT Population';
proc sgplot data=TumorSizeSorted;
  vbar cid / response=change group=group datalabel=label
            groupdisplay=cluster clusterwidth=1;
  refline 20 -30 / lineattrs=(pattern=shortdash);
  xaxis display=none discreteorder=data;
  yaxis values=(60 to -100 by -20);
  inset ("C="="CR" "R="="PR" "S="="SD" "P="="PD" "N="="NE") / title='BCR'
```

```
        position=bottomleft border textattrs=(size=6 weight=bold);
  keylegend / title='' location=inside position=topright across=1 border;
run;
```

The graph displays percent change in tumor size in descending order of size increase for the population by treatment. Each bar represents one subject in the study. Values above zero indicate increase in tumor size, but values below zero indicate decrease in tumor size. The response type is shown at the end of the bar. The data is shown below in Figure 3.9.2.

**Figure 3.9.2 – Data Set for Waterfall Chart**

| Obs | Cid | Change | Id | Group | Label |
|-----|-----|--------|-----|-------------|-------|
| 1 | 1 | -14.3910 | 1 | Treatment 1 | C |
| 2 | 2 | -65.9578 | 2 | Treatment 1 | R |
| 3 | 3 | -71.1846 | 3 | Treatment 1 | S |
| 4 | 4 | 19.6850 | 4 | Treatment 2 | P |
| 5 | 5 | 18.0494 | 5 | Treatment 2 | N |

Confidence limits are shown at +20% and -30%. A partial response is generally indicated for tumor shrinkage of 30% or more. However, the author does not claim domain-specific expertise. See domain-centric papers for more information about such details.

The %MODSTYLE macro is used to create a new style derived from "Listing" for the two groups.

The graph in Figure 3.9.3 uses a different set of colors and presentation aspects, including bars with a textured look. The confidence region is displayed using a band plot with 50% transparency. For both graphs, the %MODSTYLE macro is used to derive a new style with the custom colors.

**Figure 3.9.3 – Waterfall Chart with Alternative Appearance**

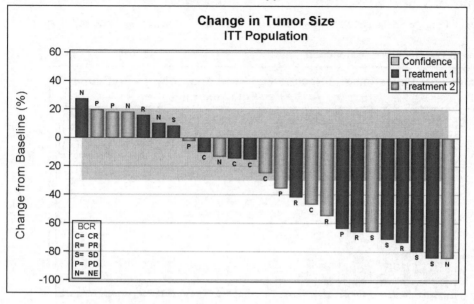

```
%modstyle(name=waterfall_2, parent=listing, type=CLM,
          numberofgroups=2,
          colors=black black, fillcolors=cxbf0000 gold);

ods listing style=waterfall_2;
title 'Change in Tumor Size';
title2 'ITT Population';
proc sgplot data=TumorSizeSorted ;
  band x=cid upper=20 lower=-30 / transparency=0.5 fill nooutline
       legendlabel='Confidence';
  vbarparm category=cid  response=change / group=group datalabel=label
           datalabelattrs=(size=5 weight=bold) dataskin=pressed;
  xaxis display=none;
  yaxis values=(60 to -100 by -20) grid;
  inset ("C="="CR" "R="="PR" "S="="SD" "P="="PD" "N="="NE") /
       title='BCR' position=bottomleft border
       textattrs=(size=6 weight=bold);
  keylegend / title='' location=inside position=topright
       across=1 border;
run;
```

A VBARPARM statement is used instead of a VBAR statement as we want to layer a band plot in the graph. Grid lines are enabled. Group display of "Cluster" is used so that we can display the bar data labels.

Relevant details are shown in the code snippet above, and some options are trimmed to fit the space. For full details, see Program 3_9.

## 3.10 Injection Site Reaction

The graph in Figure 3.10.1 shows the incidence of injection site reaction by Time and Cohort.

**Figure 3.10.1 – Injection Site Reaction**

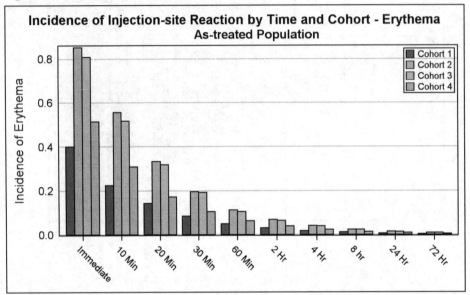

The (simulated) data is shown in Figure 3.10.2, with incidence by group over time.

```
%modstyle(name=Injection, parent=listing, type=CLM, numberofgroups=4,
          colors=black black black black,
          fillcolors=gray pink lightgreen lightblue);

ods listing style=styles.Injection;
proc sgplot data=Incidence;
  vbar time / response=incidence group=group groupdisplay=cluster;
  xaxis discreteorder=data valueattrs=(size=8) display=(nolabel);
  yaxis grid display=(noticks);
  keylegend / title='' location=inside position=topright across=1 border;
run;
```

We have used a VBAR statement with Time as the category and Group (Cohort) as the group.  The time values are treated as discrete, and each cluster of incidence bars is positioned at equidistant midpoints along the axis.

The %MODSTYLE macro is used to derive a new style from "Listing" having four groups with fill colors as specified.  The outline colors for all groups are set to black.

**Figure 3.10.2 – Data Set for Injection Site Reaction Graph**

| Obs | Time | Group | Incidence |
|---|---|---|---|
| 1 | Immediate | Cohort 1 | 0.40112 |
| 2 | Immediate | Cohort 2 | 0.85194 |
| 3 | Immediate | Cohort 3 | 0.80790 |
| 4 | Immediate | Cohort 4 | 0.51452 |

**Figure 3.10.3 – Injection Site Reaction in Grayscale**

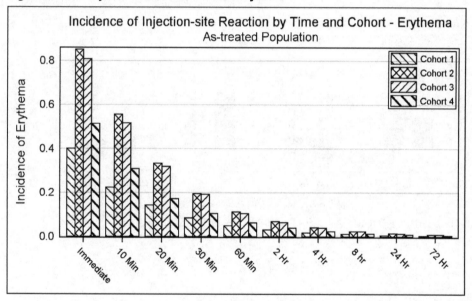

```
title 'Incidence of Injection-site Reaction by Time and Cohort -
Erythema';
title2 'As-treated Population';
ods listing style=Journal2;
proc sgplot data=Incidence;
  vbar time / response=incidence group=group groupdisplay=cluster;
  xaxis discreteorder=data valueattrs=(size=8) display=(nolabel);
  yaxis grid display=(noticks);
  keylegend / title='' location=inside position=topright across=1 border;
run;
```

The graph above uses the JOURNAL2 style suitable for submissions to journals that are published in grayscale medium. The group classifications are displayed using fill patterns.

Relevant details are shown in the code snippet above. For full details, see Program 3_10.

## 3.11  Distribution of Maximum LFT by Treatment

The graph below shows the distribution of LFT values by Test and Treatment.

### 3.11.1  Distribution of Maximum LFT by Treatment with Multi-Column Data

**Figure 3.11.1.1 – Distribution of Maximum LFT by Treatment with Multi-Column Data**

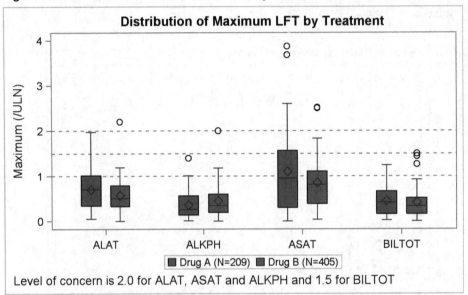

```
title 'Distribution of Maximum LFT by Treatment';
footnote j=l 'Level of concern is 2.0 for ALAT, ASAT and ALKPH and 1.5
for BILTOT';
proc sgplot data=LFT;
  refline 1 1.5 2 / lineattrs=(pattern=shortdash);
  vbox a / category=test discreteoffset=-0.15 boxwidth=0.2 name='a'
          legendlabel='Drug A (N=209)';
  vbox b / category=test discreteoffset= 0.15 boxwidth=0.2 name='b'
          legendlabel='Drug B (N=405)';
  xaxis display=(nolabel);
run;
```

The graph above shows the distribution of LFT values by Test and Treatment using the VBOX statement.  For the graph above, the data is in a multi-column format as shown in Figure 3.11.1.2.  Lab test values for each case are shown for two treatments.

**Figure 3.11.1.2 – Multi-Column Data for Graph**

| Obs | Test | A | B |
|---|---|---|---|
| 1 | ALAT | 1.05198 | 0.97755 |
| 2 | ASAT | 0.78177 | 0.59554 |
| 3 | ALKPH | 0.20475 | 0.20589 |
| 4 | BILTOT | 0.12868 | 0.10760 |
| 5 | ALAT | 1.00211 | 1.19132 |

Specific discrete offset values are used for each treatment to create side-by-side box plots. A single REFLINE statement is used to display all the concern levels.

Data with treatment as a group is more scalable as the groups are automatically positioned by the VBOX statement as shown in the next example.

## 3.11.2 Distribution of Maximum LFT by Treatment Grayscale with Group Data

This graph displays the Distribution of Maximum LFT graph by Treatment group in grayscale.

**Figure 3.11.2.1 – Distribution of Maximum LFT by Treatment Grayscale with Group Data**

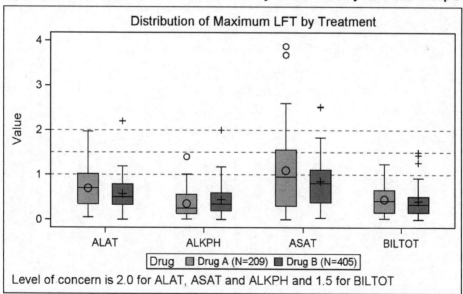

```
ods listing style=journal;
title 'Distribution of Maximum LFT by Treatment';
footnote j=l 'Level of concern is 2.0 for ALAT, ASAT and ALKPH and 1.5
for BILTOT';
```

```
proc sgplot data=lft_Grp;
   refline 1 1.5 2 / lineattrs=(pattern=shortdash);
   vbox value / category=test group=drug groupdisplay=cluster
         lineattrs=(pattern=solid) medianattrs=(pattern=solid)
         whiskerattrs=(pattern=solid);
   xaxis display=(nolabel);
run;
```

**Figure 3.11.2.2 – Grouped Data for Graph**

| Obs | Test | Drug | Value |
|-----|------|------|-------|
| 1 | ALAT | Drug A (N=209) | 1.05198 |
| 2 | ALAT | Drug B (N=405) | 0.97755 |
| 3 | ASAT | Drug A (N=209) | 0.78177 |
| 4 | ASAT | Drug B (N=405) | 0.59554 |
| 5 | ALKPH | Drug A (N=209) | 0.20475 |

In this example, the data is arranged by group, instead of multi-column as in 3.11.1. We are using the Journal style, which uses different gray shades for the fill color for each group. Line patterns for the box, median, and whiskers are set to solid.

Relevant details are shown in the code snippet above. For full details, see Program 3_11.

## 3.12 Clark Error Grid

The Clark Error Grid graph is used to quantify the clinical accuracy of blood glucose levels generated by the meters.   The sensor response and the reference value are plotted on the grid.

### 3.12.1 Clark Error Grid

The graph includes demarcated zones that indicate the divergence of the meter values from reference values.  Zone "A" demarcates the zone where the divergence is < 20%.  Zone "B" has divergence > 20%, but not leading to improper treatment.  Other zones indicate dangerous or confusing results.

**Figure 3.12.1 – Clark Error Grid for Blood Glucose Measurement Accuracy**

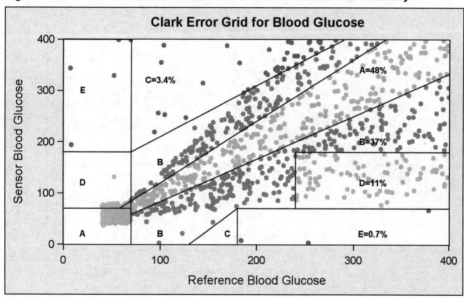

```
title 'Clark Error Grid for Blood Glucose';
proc sgplot data=plotZoneCount noautolegend dattrmap=attrmap;
  scatter x=x y=y / group=zone attrid=A
          markerattrs=(symbol=circlefilled);
  series x=rfbg y=sbg / group=id nomissinggroup
          lineattrs=graphdatadefault(color=black) ;
  scatter x=xl y=yl / markerchar=label markercharattrs=(weight=bold);
  xaxis min=0 max=400 offsetmin=0 offsetmax=0
        label='Reference Blood Glucose';
  yaxis min=0 max=400 offsetmin=0 offsetmax=0
        label='Sensor Blood Glucose';
  run;
```

The data for this graph includes the measured and reference glucose level observations, data for zone boundaries, and the zone labels and data for zone labels.

The scatter plot in the program is used to draw the metered glucose values by reference. The series plot is used to display the boundaries of each zone, and the scatter plot is used to display the zone name. A discrete attribute map is used to color the markers in each zone appropriately.

### 3.12.2 Clark Error Grid in Grayscale

Figure 3.12.2 shows the Clark Error Grid in grayscale. Different marker shapes are used for each zone. Zone labels are highlighted with a circle.

**Figure 3.12.2 – Clark Error Grid in Grayscale**

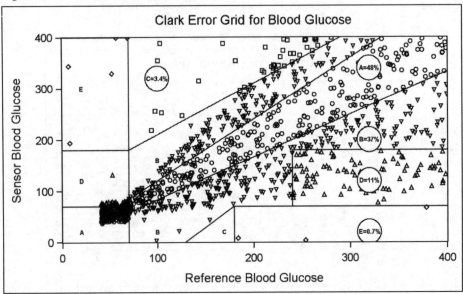

```
%modstyle(name=Clark, parent=journal, type=CLM, numberofgroups=5,
          markers=triangle circle square diamond triangledown);

ods listing style=Clark;
title 'Clark Error Grid for Blood Glucose';
proc sgplot data=plotZoneCount noautolegend;
  scatter x=x y=y / group=zone attrid=A markerattrs=(size=5);
  series x=rfbg y=sbg / group=id nomissinggroup
          lineattrs=graphdatadefault(color=black);
  bubble x=xl y=yl size=size / bradiusmin=14 bradiusmax=15
          fillattrs=(color=white);
  scatter x=xl y=yl / markerchar=label
          markercharattrs=(size=5 weight=bold);
  xaxis min=0 max=400 offsetmin=0 offsetmax=0
        label='Reference Blood Glucose';
  yaxis min=0 max=400 offsetmin=0 offsetmax=0
          label='Sensor Blood Glucose';
run;
```

The same graph as in Section 3.12.1 is rendered here for a grayscale medium. The key difference is to ensure the correct decoding of the data in the five zones. Here, I have used the %MODSTYLE macro to define five groups, each with a distinct marker shape.

The labels for each zone do not stand out against the markers of the same color--especially in the dense areas. So, I used a bubble plot to draw a filled white bubble behind the zone label. All axis offsets are set to zero to ensure that the zone boundaries touch the axes. This also removes the effect of any offset contributions by the scatter plot with MARKERCHAR.

Relevant details are shown in the code snippet above. For full details, see Program 3_12.

## 3.13 The Swimmer Plot

This "swimmer plot" displays the response of the tumor to the study drug over time in months. Each horizontal bar represents one subject in the study.

### 3.13.1 The Swimmer Plot for Tumor Response over Time

This graph shows the tumor response by subject over time.[1] Each horizontal bar in the graph represents one subject. The inset line indicates complete or partial response with start and end times.

**Figure 3.13.1.1 – Tumor Response Graph**

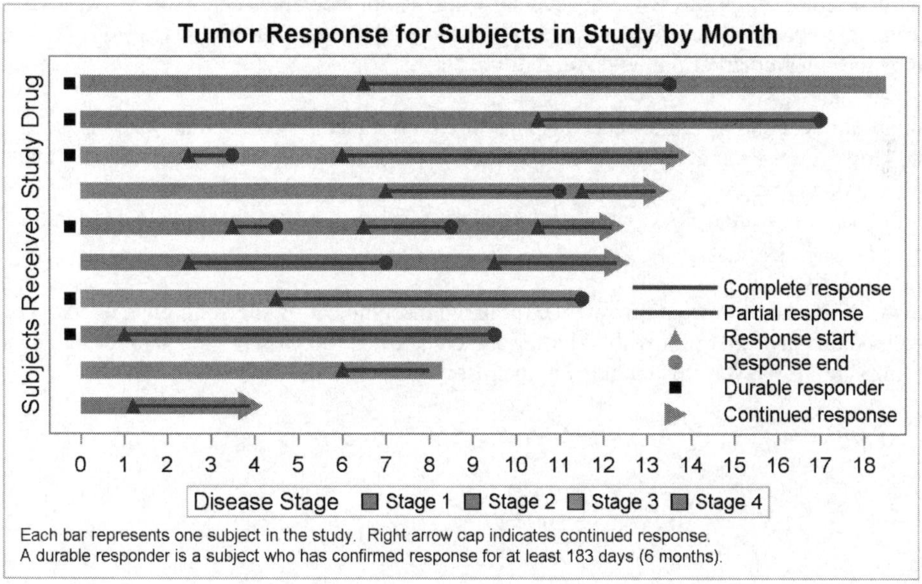

```
title 'Tumor Response for Subjects in Study by Month';
proc sgplot data= swimmer dattrmap=attrmap nocycleattrs;
   highlow y=item low=low high=high / highcap=highcap type=bar group=stage
           fill nooutline name='stage' nomissinggroup transparency=0.3;
   highlow y=item low=startline high=endline / group=status
```

```
            name='status' nomissinggroup attrid=statusC;
  scatter y=item x=start / name='s' legendlabel='Response start'
          markerattrs=(symbol=trianglefilled size=8 color=darkgray);
  scatter y=item x=end / name='e' legendlabel='Response end'
          markerattrs=(symbol=circlefilled size=8 color=darkgray);
  scatter y=item x=xmin / name='x' legendlabel='Continued response '
          markerattrs=(symbol=trianglerightfilled size=12
                       color=darkgray);
  scatter y=item x=durable / name='d' legendlabel='Durable responder'
          markerattrs=(symbol=squarefilled size=6 color=black);
  scatter y=item x=start / group=status attrid=status
          markerattrs=(symbol=trianglefilled size=8);
  scatter y=item x=end / group=status attrid=status
          markerattrs=(symbol=circlefilled size=8);
  xaxis display=(nolabel) label='Months'
        values=(0 to 20 by 1) valueshint;
  yaxis reverse display=(noticks novalues noline)
        label='Subjects Received ...';
  keylegend 'stage' / title='Disease Stage';
  keylegend 'status' 's' 'e' 'd' / location=inside
            position=bottomright across=1;
run;
```

An arrowhead on the right indicates continuing response. The bar contains durations over which the "Complete" or "Partial" response is indicated, with a start and end time. The disease stage is indicated by the color of the bar, with a legend showing the unique values below the x-axis. An inset is included to decode the different markers in the event bar. A "Durable" response is indicated by the square marker on the left end of the bar.

Note that the start and end points for each response are represented by colored markers inside each event bar. However, the same are shown in grayscale in the inset table. This is achieved by first plotting the markers in a gray color, and overdrawing those by colored markers using GROUP=Status. The scatter plots that plot the gray markers are the ones that are included in the inset.

Also note the existence of a "right arrow" marker in the inset indicating the continuing event. This is done by including a scatter plot with a right triangle marker in the plot, but the data for this marker is missing. However, it is included in the inset.

The structure of the data set needed for the graph is shown below.

**Figure 3.13.1.2 – Data for Tumor Response Graph**

| Obs | Item | Stage | Low | High | Highcap | Status | Start | End | Durable | Startline | Endline | Xmin |
|-----|------|-------|-----|------|---------|--------|-------|-----|---------|-----------|---------|------|
| 1 | 1 | Stage 1 | 0 | 18.5 | | Complete response | 6.5 | 13.5 | -0.25 | 6.5 | 13.5 | . |
| 2 | 2 | Stage 2 | 0 | 17.0 | | Complete response | 10.5 | 17.0 | -0.25 | 10.5 | 17.0 | . |
| 3 | 3 | Stage 3 | 0 | 14.0 | FilledArrow | Partial response | 2.5 | 3.5 | -0.25 | 2.5 | 3.5 | . |
| 4 | 3 | | 0 | 14.0 | FilledArrow | Partial response | 6.0 | . | | 6.0 | 13.7 | . |
| 5 | 4 | Stage 4 | 0 | 13.5 | FilledArrow | Partial response | 7.0 | 11.0 | | 7.0 | 11.0 | . |
| 6 | 4 | | 0 | 13.5 | FilledArrow | Partial response | 11.5 | . | | 11.5 | 13.2 | . |
| 7 | 5 | Stage 1 | 0 | 12.5 | FilledArrow | Complete response | 3.5 | 4.5 | -0.25 | 3.5 | 4.5 | . |
| 8 | 5 | | 0 | 12.5 | FilledArrow | Complete response | 6.5 | 8.5 | | 6.5 | 8.5 | . |
| 9 | 5 | | 0 | 12.5 | FilledArrow | Partial response | 10.5 | . | | 10.5 | 12.2 | . |
| 10 | 6 | Stage 2 | 0 | 12.6 | FilledArrow | Partial response | 2.5 | 7.0 | | 2.5 | 7.0 | . |

Note, although the program for this graph is longer than some other ones, it can be built one part at a time.

- First, plot the full duration from Low to High by Item using a grouped High Low plot with a High Cap and TYPE=BAR. Include this in the outside legend.
- Layer the individual "Response" events from Startline to Endline by Status using a High Low bar with the default line type. Include this in the inset legend.
- Layer the Start and End events in gray color. Include these in the inset legend.
- Layer the Start and End events again using GROUP=Status.
- Add a scatter plot with missing data to include the "Right Arrow" in the legend.

The Discrete Attribute Map data set contains two maps, one for the colored graph called "StatusC", and one for the grayscale graph called "StatusJ". AttrId=StatusC is used in this graph. For full details, see Program 3_12.

### 3.13.2  The Swimmer Plot for Tumor Response in Grayscale

The tumor response graph appears in grayscale.  The disease stage is shown on the left as we cannot use a color indicator.

**Figure 3.13.1 – Tumor Response Graph in Grayscale**

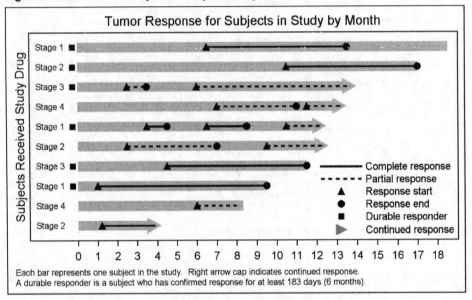

```
proc sgplot data= swimmer2 dattrmap=attrmap nocycleattrs;
  highlow y=item low=low high=high / highcap=highcap type=bar
          group=stage fill nooutline lineattrs=(color=black)
          fillattrs=(color=lightgray)
          name='stage' barwidth=1 nomissinggroup;
  highlow y=item low=startline high=endline / group=status
          lineattrs=(thickness=2)
          name='status' nomissinggroup  attrid=statusJ;
  scatter y=item x=start / markerattrs=(symbol=trianglefilled size=8)
          name='s' legendlabel='Response start';
  scatter y=item x=end / markerattrs=(symbol=circlefilled size=8)
          name='e' legendlabel='Response end';
  scatter y=item x=xmin / name='x' legendlabel='Continued response '
          markerattrs=(symbol=trianglerightfilled size=12
          color=darkgray);
  scatter y=item x=durable / name='d' legendlabel='Durable responder'
          markerattrs=(symbol=squarefilled size=6 color=black);
  scatter y=item x=start / attrid=statusJ
          markerattrs=(symbol=trianglefilled size=8) group=status;
  scatter y=item x=end / attrid=statusJ
          markerattrs=(symbol=circlefilled size=8) group=status;
  highlow y=item low=stagex high=stagex / lowlabel=stage
          lineattrs=(thickness=0);
  xaxis   display=(nolabel) label='Months'
```

```
           values=(0 to 20 by 1) valueshint;
   yaxis   reverse display=(noticks novalues noline)
           label='Subjects Received Study Drug';
   keylegend 'status' 's' 'e' 'd' 'x' / noborder location=inside
           position=bottomright across=1;
run;
```

Patterned lines are used to draw the response events and a highlow plot to draw the stage labels on the left. AttrId=StatusJ is used in this graph. For full details, see Program 3_13.

## 3.14  CDC Chart for Length and Weight Percentiles

The CDC chart for length and weight for boys and girls from birth to 36 months is widely used in pediatric practices to track vital statistics. This graph is shown in Figure 3.14.1, and the entire chart is created using the SGPLOT procedure. The purpose is primarily to evaluate the features of the procedure.

**Figure 3.14.1 – CDC Chart for Length and Weight Percentiles**

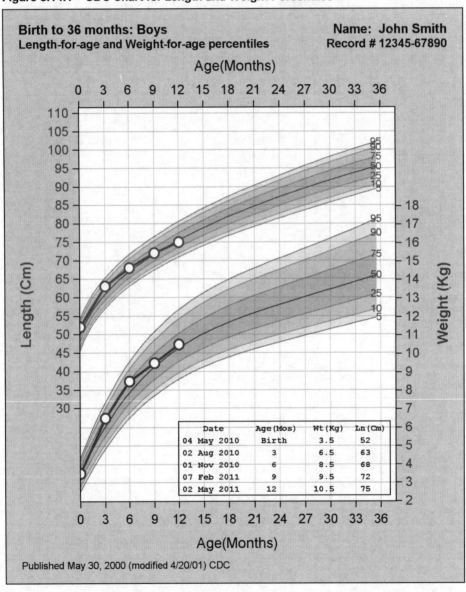

| Date | Age(Mos) | Wt(Kg) | Ln(Cm) |
|---|---|---|---|
| 04 May 2010 | Birth | 3.5 | 52 |
| 02 Aug 2010 | 3 | 6.5 | 63 |
| 01 Nov 2010 | 6 | 8.5 | 68 |
| 07 Feb 2011 | 9 | 9.5 | 72 |
| 02 May 2011 | 12 | 10.5 | 75 |

The graph above renders the full CDC chart for Length and Weight Percentiles from the data for one subject. The original graph was a bit taller, but I shrank it to fit this page. The data required is created by appending the CDC percentile data with the historical data for one subject. The CDC data is included in the file named "3_14_CDC_Cleaned.csv".

The CDC data for the percentile curves is shown below. Only a few of the observations are displayed to conserve space. Also, the data contains all the columns for 5, 10, 25, 50, 75, 90, and 95 percentiles, but only a few columns are included to fit in the space.

**Figure 3.14.2 – Data for CDC Graph**

| Sex | Agemos | W5 | W25 | W75 | W95 | H5 | H25 | H75 | H95 |
|---|---|---|---|---|---|---|---|---|---|
| 1 | 0 | 2.52690402 | 3.150611082 | 3.879076559 | 4.34029274 | 45.5684091 | 48.189373814 | 51.771257485 | 54.307211972 |
| 1 | 0.5 | 2.964655655 | 3.597395573 | 4.387422565 | 4.910130108 | 48.558092059 | 50.979188895 | 54.440543134 | 56.999077373 |
| 1 | 1.5 | 3.774848862 | 4.428872952 | 5.327327567 | 5.967101615 | 52.726106587 | 54.979104409 | 58.350594078 | 60.964653792 |

The historical data for the subject is appended at the bottom of the curve data, using the column names Sex, Age, Height, and Length, as shown below.

**Figure 3.14.3 – Data for CDC Graph**

| Obs | Sex | Agemos | W5 | W50 | W95 | H5 | H50 | H95 | Age | Height | Weight |
|---|---|---|---|---|---|---|---|---|---|---|---|
| 36 | Male | 34.5 | 11.86229971 | 14.1150324 | 17.10619066 | 88.703007448 | 94.808229231 | 101.43177049 | . | . | . |
| 37 | Male | 35.5 | 11.98045644 | 14.25779618 | 17.30646132 | 89.332418366 | 95.446369813 | 102.11744722 | . | . | . |
| 38 | Male | . | . | . | . | . | . | . | 0 | 52 | 3.5 |
| 39 | Male | . | . | . | . | . | . | . | 3 | 63 | 6.5 |

```
title j=l h=9pt 'Birth to 36 months: Boys' j=r "Name:  John Smith";
title2 j=l h=8pt "Length-for-age and Weight-for-age percentiles" j=r
"Record # 12345-67890";
footnote j=l h=7pt "Published May 30, 2000 (modified 4/20/01) CDC";
proc sgplot data=Chart_Patient noautolegend;
  where sex=1;
   refline 3 4 5 6 / axis=y2 lineattrs=graphgridlines;

   /*--Curve bands--*/
   band x=agemos lower=w5  upper=w95 / y2axis fillattrs=graphdata1
         transparency=0.9;
   band x=agemos lower=w10 upper=w90 / y2axis fillattrs=graphdata1
         transparency=0.8;
   band x=agemos lower=w25 upper=w75 / y2axis fillattrs=graphdata1
         transparency=0.8;

   /*--Curves--*/
   series x=agemos y=w5 / y2axis lineattrs=graphdata1 transparency=0.5;
 series x=agemos y=w10 / y2axis lineattrs=graphdata1 transparency=0.7;
 series x=agemos y=w25 / y2axis lineattrs=graphdata1 transparency=0.7;
 series x=agemos y=w50 / y2axis x2axis lineattrs=graphdata1;
```

```
   series x=agemos y=w75 / y2axis lineattrs=graphdata1 transparency=0.7;
   series x=agemos y=w90 / y2axis lineattrs=graphdata1 transparency=0.7;
   series x=agemos y=w95 / y2axis lineattrs=graphdata1 transparency=0.5;
```

The program that is required to draw all the elements of this graph is long, but easy to understand. So, I have shown it in parts across the following pages. The first part of the program is shown above, with titles, footnotes, and percentile curves for Weight. The bands are drawn with three transparent overlays to create the appearance of color gradation. The curves are overlaid on the bands.

```
/*--Curve labels--*/
scatter x=agemos y=w5  / markerchar= l5 y2axis textattrs=graphdata1;
scatter x=agemos y=w10 / markerchar=l10 y2axis textattrs=graphdata1;
scatter x=agemos y=w25 / markerchar=l25 y2axis textattrs=graphdata1;
scatter x=agemos y=w50 / markerchar=l50 y2axis textattrs=graphdata1;
scatter x=agemos y=w75 / markerchar=l75 y2axis textattrs=graphdata1;
scatter x=agemos y=w90 / markerchar=l90 y2axis textattrs=graphdata1;
scatter x=agemos y=w95 / markerchar=l95 y2axis textattrs=graphdata1;

/*--Patient datas--*/
series x=age y=weight / y2axis lineattrs=graphdata1(thickness=2)
      markers markerattrs=(symbol=circlefilled size=11);
series x=age y=weight / y2axis lineattrs=graphdata1(thickness=2)
      markers markerattrs=(symbol=circlefilled size=7, color=white);
```

The code section above draws the curve labels for the percentile curves on the right. This is overlaid by the historical subject weight data as a series plot. The code for Height is shown below.

```
/*--Curve bands--*/
band x=agemos lower=h5  upper=h95 / fillattrs=graphdata3
        transparency=0.9;
band x=agemos lower=h10 upper=h90 / fillattrs=graphdata3
        transparency=0.8;
band x=agemos lower=h25 upper=h75 / fillattrs=graphdata3
        transparency=0.8;

/*--Curves--*/
series x=agemos y=h5 / lineattrs=graphdata3(pattern=solid)
        transparency=0.5;
series x=agemos y=h10 /lineattrs=graphdata3(pattern=solid)
        transparency=0.7;
series x=agemos y=h25 /lineattrs=graphdata3(pattern=solid)
        transparency=0.7;
series x=agemos y=h50 /lineattrs=graphdata3(pattern=solid) x2axis;
series x=agemos y=h75 /lineattrs=graphdata3(pattern=solid)
        transparency=0.7;
series x=agemos y=h90
/lineattrs=graphdata3(pattern=solid)transparency=0.7;
series x=agemos y=h95 /lineattrs=graphdata3(pattern=solid)
transparency=0.5;
```

```
/*--Curve labels--*/
scatter x=agemos y=h5   / markerchar = 15 textattrs=graphdata3;
scatter x=agemos y=h10  / markerchar =l10 textattrs=graphdata3;
scatter x=agemos y=h25  / markerchar =l25 textattrs=graphdata3;
scatter x=agemos y=h50  / markerchar =l50 textattrs=graphdata3;
scatter x=agemos y=h75  / markerchar =l75 textattrs=graphdata3;
scatter x=agemos y=h90  / markerchar =l90 textattrs=graphdata3;
scatter x=agemos y=h95  / markerchar =l95 textattrs=graphdata3;

/*--Patient datas--*/
series x=age y=height / lineattrs=graphdata3(pattern=solid thickness=2)
       markers markerattrs=(symbol=circlefilled size=11);
series x=age y=height / lineattrs=graphdata3(pattern=solid thickness=2)
       markers markerattrs=(symbol=circlefilled size=7, color=white);
```

The Height (Length) and Weight data ranges are different, and these need to be plotted with different vertical scales and axis details. We can do that by using two separate Y axes for each column. Here we used the Y2AXIS for Weight and YAXIS for Height. This breaks the link between the two variables scales thus allowing us to draw the Height and Weight curves and data independently.

```
/*--Table--*/
inset "    Date        Age(Mos)   Wt(Kg)   Ln(Cm)"
         "04 May 2010    Birth       3.5       52"
         "02 Aug 2010      3         6.5       63"
         "01 Nov 2010      6         8.5       68"
         "07 Feb 2011      9         9.5       72"
         "02 May 2011     12        10.5       75" / border
         textattrs=(family='Courier' size=6 weight=bold)
                   position=bottomright;

xaxis grid offsetmin=0  integer values=(0 to 36 by 3);
x2axis grid offsetmin=0 integer values=(0 to 36 by 3);
yaxis  grid offsetmin=0.25 offsetmax=0.0 label="Length (Cm)"
       integer values=(30 to 110 by 5)
       labelattrs=graphdata3(weight=bold) valueattrs=graphdata3;
y2axis offsetmin=0.0 offsetmax=0.25 label="Weight (Kg)" integer
       values=(2 to 18 by 1) labelattrs=graphdata1(weight=bold)
       valueattrs=graphdata1;
run;
```

Note the options on the YAXIS and the Y2AXIS statements. The Y2AXIS has OFFSETMAX=0.25, which means that all items that are associated with it are displayed only in the lower 75% of the graph height. This causes all the "Weight" related items and the axis (drawn in blue) to be drawn in the lower part.

Similarly, the YAXIS has OFFSETMIN =0.25, so all the "Height or Length" related items are drawn in the upper part of the graph. More importantly, the scaling for each axis is independent, allowing us to draw different tick values on the axes. To make the graph easier to read, we have taken care to position the Y grid lines so that they line up with the values on each side.

The program snippet above also shows how we can include the historical data as a tabular display in the chart for easy reference. I have used the INSET statement to create a tabular display. Although the values here are hardcoded, we can use macro variables assigned from the DATA step.

Relevant details are shown in the code snippet above. For full details, see Program 3_14.

## 3.15 Summary

The graphs discussed in this chapter represent a large fraction of the graphs commonly used in the clinical trials industry and in Health and Life Sciences in general. Most of these are "single-cell" graphs where the main data is displayed in one cell in the middle, along with other information.

As we have seen in the examples, the SAS 9.3 SGPLOT procedure provides you with a large selection of plot statements and features that can be used to create many graphs. Many of these plot statements can be combined in creative ways to create almost any graph that might be needed.

The SG Annotate facility further enhances your ability to create custom graphs using the SGPLOT procedure. As seen in many examples, statistics tables or tables of subjects in the study can be displayed correctly positioned along the x- or y-axis, either outside the data area, or inside the data area.

Group attributes such as colors or marker symbol shapes can be assigned by specific group values using the Attribute Map feature. This ensures that attributes are correctly mapped regardless of the data order, or whether some groups are present or not.

---

[1] My graph is based on ideas presented in a paper. See Phillips, Stacey D. 2014. "Swimmer Plot: Tell a Graphical Story of Your Time to Response Data Using PROC SGPLOT." *Proceedings of the Pharmaceutical Industry SAS Users Group* (PharmaSug) 2014 Conference. San Diego, CA: SAS Institute Inc. Available at http://www.pharmasug.org/2014-proceedings.html.

# Chapter 4: Clinical Graphs Using the SAS 9.4 SGPLOT Procedure

Clinical graphs often display the data in one cell along with derived statistics and other details that aid in the decoding of the information in the graph. Most of these single-cell graphs can be created using the SGPLOT procedure.

With SAS 9.4, the SGPLOT procedure supports some new and useful features that simplify the creation of such graphs. These include the following new statements and features:

- **XAXISTABLE and YAXISTABLE.** These two statements support axis tables along the x- and y-axes. These statements can be used to draw "At-Risk" tables along the X-axis, or study names and statistic values along the Y-axis. Rows and columns of textual data can be displayed inside the data area or outside.

- **TEXT plot.** This statement displays a text string from a column at the specified location. It replaces the need for using a SCATTER plot statement with the MARKERCHAR option. Because a text plot draws only text strings, other features are available for this function, including control of offsets that might be driven by the text values.

- **POLYGON plot.** This statement displays polygons in the graph based on the columns in the data set. This is useful in drawing ranges in the graph for various levels, including complex regions in graphs for device evaluation like the Clark Error Grid.

The goal in this chapter is to cover in detail the creation of some commonly used clinical graphs using SAS 9.4. The chapter will provide not only code that you can use directly for such graphs, but will also provide ideas on how you can use or combine plot statements to create your own custom graph.

The SG Annotate facility features are also available for you to use in cases where the result cannot be achieved using plot layers. SG Annotate was used extensively in Chapter 3 to create the clinical graphs. See Section 2.9 for an introduction to this feature.

## 4.1 Box Plot of QTc Change from Baseline

This graph displays the distribution of QTc change from baseline by week and treatment for all subjects in a study. The x-axis has a linear scale. The "Subjects At-Risk" values are displayed by treatment at the right location along the time axis.

### 4.1.1 Box Plot of QTc Change from Baseline

For the graph in Figure 4.1.1, we will use a box plot to display the distribution of QTc change from baseline by week and treatment on a linear x-axis. The "Subjects At-Risk" table is shown in the traditional arrangement at the bottom of the graph using the XAXISTABLE statement.

**Figure 4.1.1 – Graph of QTc Change from Baseline with the Subjects Table at the Bottom**

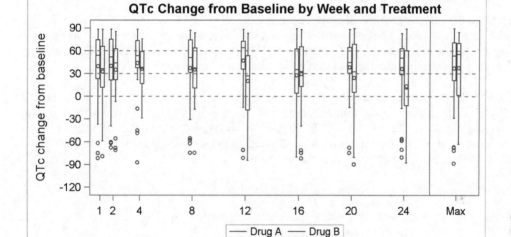

```
title 'QTc Change from Baseline by Week and Treatment';
footnote j=l "Note:  Increase < 30 msec 'Normal', "
             "30-60 msec 'Concern', > 60 msec 'High' ";
proc sgplot data=QTcData;
  format week qtcweek.;
  vbox qtc / category=week group=drug groupdisplay=cluster nofill;
  xaxistable risk / class=drug colorgroup=drug;
  refline 26 / axis=x;
  refline 0 30 60 / axis=y lineattrs=(pattern=shortdash);
  xaxis type=linear values=(1 2 4 8 12 16 20 24 28) max=29
        display=(nolabel);
  yaxis label='QTc change from baseline' values=(-120 to 90 by 30);
  keylegend / title='' linelength=20;
run;
```

Normally, a box plot treats the category variable as discrete, which would have placed all the tick values on the x-axis at equally spaced intervals. However, in this case the values on the x-axis represent days from start of study, and we want to place the data at the correctly scaled distance along the x-axis. This can be done be explicitly setting TYPE=LINEAR on the x-axis. Now, each box is placed at the scaled location along the x-axis.

The box plot is classified by treatment, which has two values "Drug A" and "Drug B". The boxes are sized by the smallest interval along the x-axis. In this case, it is one day at the start of the study. Hence, the effective midpoint spacing is set by that interval, and all boxes are drawn to fit in this space.

The box plot uses the GROUPDISPLAY=CLUSTER option to place the groups side by side. We have used the NOFILL option to draw empty boxes.

The table of the subjects at risk is displayed using the XAXISTABLE statement, showing risk values by week and drug. The optional X role is not specified, so the table uses the X role that is active; in this case, it is from the VBOX statement. The option LOCATION=OUTSIDE is used to display the risk values outside the data area at the default bottom position.

The XAXISTABLE is classified by treatment by setting CLASS=DRUG. Now, the values for risk are displayed in separate rows by drug. The value of the classifier DRUG is shown in the row label on the left of the data. The option COLORGROUP=DRUG is used to color the risk values by drug for easier association. Display attributes such as font size and font weight are set for both the risk values and labels using the appropriate options:

```
xaxistable risk / class=drug colorgroup=drug
                  valueattrs=(size=6 weight=bold)
                  labelattrs=(size=6 weight=bold);
```

Reference lines are placed on the y-axis at y= 0, 30, and 60 to represent the levels of concern. A reference line is also placed on the x-axis at x=26 to separate MAX value.

The axis tick value "Max" has a value of x=28, and a format is used to display the tick value. The tick values displayed on the x-axis are determined by the VALUES option on the XAXIS statement, and the option MAX is set to 29 to allow an even display of the tick values.

The y-axis places the tick values from -120 to 90 by 30, and also sets the displayed axis range.

A legend is automatically added by the procedure because the box plot has a GROUP role. We have used the KEYLEGEND statement to customize some aspects of the legend. The legend title is removed, and the lengths of the line segments representing each classification value are shortened using the LINELENGTH option.

Normally, the procedure draws longer lines for each class value in the legend in order to represent the full line pattern. In this case, however, we are using the HTMLBlue style, which uses the attribute priority of color. So, most line styles used are solid, and a long line segment is not required.

Relevant details are shown in the code snippet above. For full details, see Program 4_1, available from the author's page at http://support.sas.com/matange.

## 4.1.2 Box Plot of QTc Change from Baseline with Inner Risk Table and Bands

The traditional graph commonly in use in the industry, as shown in Figure 4.1.1, shows the "At-Risk" table at the bottom of the graph, just above the footnote with other items in between. Such a layout places the risk data relatively far away from the graph. Even though the values are aligned with the data along the x-axis, the distance and intervening items like the legend and the axis items create a distraction.

**Figure 4.1.2 – Graph of QTc Change from Baseline with Subjects Table inside**

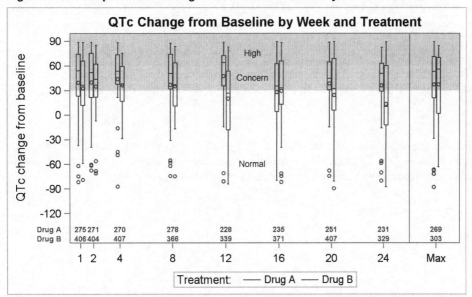

Graphs are easier to decode when relevant information is placed as close as possible, thus reducing the amount of eye movement needed to decode the graph. Following this principle, it would be more effective to place the risk information inside the graph area, closer to the graphical information. This arrangement is shown in the Figure 4.1.2. It was achieved by placing the XAXISTABLE with LOCATION=INSIDE, as shown in the code snippet below.

Another improvement would be to represent the levels of concern as colored bands with direct labels. This reduces the eye movement that is required to decode the information in the data. We can do this by using the BAND plot statements. A text plot is used to label each band with the level of concern "Normal", "Concern", and "High". The columns needed are included in the data. The code snippet for inclusion of bands, band labels, and the inner risk table is shown below.

```
title 'QTc Change from Baseline by Week and Treatment';
proc sgplot data=QTcBand;
  format week qtcweek.;
  band x=wk lower=L0  upper=L30 / fill legendlabel='Normal' name='a'
       fillattrs=(color=white transparency=0.6) ;
  band x=wk lower=L30 upper=L60 / fill legendlabel='Concern' name='b'
       fillattrs=(color=gold transparency=0.6) ;
  band x=wk lower=L60 upper=L90 / fill legendlabel='High' name='c'
       fillattrs=(color=pink transparency=0.6);
  vbox qtc / category=week group=drug groupdisplay=cluster
       nofill name='d';
  text x=wk y=ylabel text=label / contributeoffsets=none;
  xaxistable risk / class=drug colorgroup=drug location=inside;
  refline 26 / axis=x;
  xaxis type=linear values=(1 2 4 8 12 16 20 24 28) valueshint
        min=1 max=29 display=(nolabel)
        colorbands=odd colorbandsattrs=(transparency=1);
  yaxis label='QTc change from baseline' values=(-120 to 90 by 30);
  keylegend 'a' / title='Treatment:' linelength=20;
run;
```

For graphs that are consumed in a color medium, this graph provides all the information in a compact form that is free of clutter. The levels of concern are color coded with direct labels, and risk values are moved closer to the rest of the data. For full details, see Program 4_1.

### 4.1.3 Box Plot of QTc Change from Baseline in Grayscale

The graph in Figure 4.1.3 is created for a grayscale medium using the Journal style, along with a few other customizations.

**Figure 4.1.3 – Box Plot of QTc Change from Baseline in Grayscale**

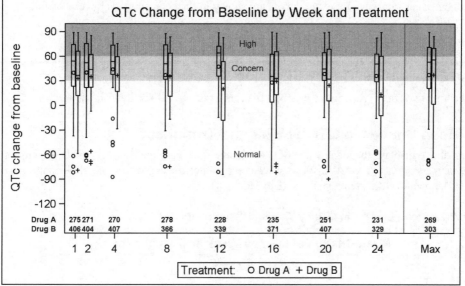

```
title 'QTc Change from Baseline by Week and Treatment';
proc sgplot data=QTcBand;
   format week qtcweek.;
   styleattrs datalinepatterns=(solid);
   band x=wk lower=L0  upper=L30 / fill legendlabel='Normal'
        fillattrs=(color=white transparency=0.6);
   band x=wk lower=L30 upper=L60 / fill  legendlabel='Concern'
        fillattrs=(color=lightgray transparency=0.6);
   band x=wk lower=L60 upper=L90 / fill legendlabel='High'
        fillattrs=(color=gray transparency=0.6) ;
   vbox qtc / category=week group=drug groupdisplay=cluster nofill;
   scatter x=wk y=QTc / group=drug name='a' nomissinggroup;
   text x=wk y=ylabel text=label / contributeoffsets=none;
   xaxistable risk / class=drug colorgroup=drug location=inside;
   refline 26 / axis=x;
   xaxis type=linear values=(1 2 4 8 12 16 20 24 28) valueshint
         min=1 max=29 display=(nolabel)
         colorbands=odd colorbandsattrs=(transparency=1);
   yaxis label='QTc change from baseline' values=(-120 to 90 by 30);
   keylegend 'a' / title='Treatment:' linelength=20;
run;
```

Box plots are represented in the legend using the display characteristics of the box. In this case, the boxes are not filled. Normally, when using grayscale, the line style for the second group is a dashed line. To avoid drawing boxes with patterned lines, we have specified only one solid pattern for all groups in the STYLEATTRS statement. So, using lines in the legend will not be effective.

To distinguish the two groups, we would like to display markers in the legend. To do this, we added a scatter plot that plots QTc by Week and Drug, except that all these QTc values are missing. So, no markers are actually drawn in the plot, but the legend that is derived from the scatter plot displays the marker symbols. Relevant details are shown in the code snippet above. For full details, see Program 4_1.

## 4.2  Mean Change in QTc by Visit and Treatment

In this section we discuss creating the graph of the mean change in QTc by visit and treatment.

### 4.2.1  Mean Change in QTc by Visit and Treatment

The graph above displays the mean value of QTc change from baseline by week and treatment for all subjects in a study. The x-axis displays weeks on a numeric scale, with week 28 formatted to "LOCF". The mean values are clustered side by side.

**Figure 4.2.1 – Mean Change in QTc by Visit and Treatment**

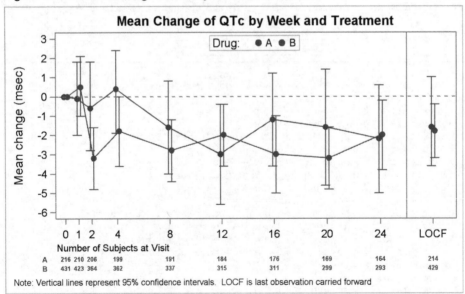

```
title 'Mean Change of QTc by Week and Treatment';
proc sgplot data=QTc_Mean_Group;
   format week qtcmean.;
   format n 3.0;
   scatter x=week y=mean / yerrorupper=high yerrorlower=low
          group=drug groupdisplay=cluster clusterwidth=0.5
          markerattrs=(size=7 symbol=circlefilled) name='a';
```

```
    series x=week y=mean2 / group=drug groupdisplay=cluster
          clusterwidth=0.5 lineattrs=(pattern=solid);
    xaxistable n / class=drug colorgroup=drug location=outside
          title='Number of Subjects at Visit' titleattrs=(size=8);
    refline 26 / axis=x;
    refline 0  / axis=y lineattrs=(pattern=shortdash);
    xaxis type=linear values=(0 1 2 4 8 12 16 20 24 28)
          max=29 valueshint;
    yaxis label='Mean change (msec)' values=(-6 to 3 by 1);
    keylegend 'a' / title='Drug: ' location=inside position=top;
run;
```

The overlaid series plot could have also used the same response variable "Mean", but then the last value on the x-axis, "LOCF", would have been joined to the previous one.

To avoid this, we have copied the values from the variable "Mean" to the variable "Mean2", with a missing value for the x=28. The series plot uses "Mean2" as the response variable, which excludes the last value to avoid connecting to the "LOCF" value.

Note, both the SCATTER and SERIES statements use GROUPDISPLAY=CLUSTER. This option spreads the position of each group value on the x-axis. CLUSTERWIDTH=0.5 is set to keep the clusters tight. This means that all the class values will be spread within 50% of the midpoint spacing. Since both statements use same setting for group display and cluster width, the lines and markers match for each group value.

An XAXISTABLE is used to display the "Number of Subjects" values at the bottom of the graph. The display variable is "N", and the x-axis variable is the same as the x variable for the primary plot – "Week". So, the optional X role does not need to be specified in the statement.

```
  xaxistable n / class=drug colorgroup=drug location=outside
          valueattrs=(size=5 weight=bold) labelattrs=(size=6 weight=bold)
          title='Number of Subjects at Visit' titleattrs=(size=8);
```

The graph is classified by "Drug". We have specified "Drug" for the CLASS role for the axis table. This causes the values for the two values of "Drug" to be displayed in separate rows. COLORGROUP is also set to "Drug", so the values are colored by "Drug".

The table of subjects is displayed at the bottom of the graph by setting LOCATION=OUTSIDE, which is also the default setting. The table has a title, which was set using the TITLE option. Text attributes for the values, labels, and title are specified using the appropriate options.

The Y reference line is drawn at y=0, and the X reference line is drawn at X=26, which acts like a separator for the "LOCF" value. A user-defined format is used to display "LOCF" for x=28.

The legend is generated by default by the procedure because group is in effect. But to prevent multiple items in the legend, we specify the KEYLEGEND statement with the name of only one statement. The legend is placed at the top center of the wall.

Relevant details are shown in the code snippet above. For full details, see Program 4_2.

## 4.2.2 Mean Change in QTc by Visit and Treatment with Inner Table of Subjects

In this graph, the table of subjects at visit is displayed above the x-axis. This makes it easier to understand the numbers because they are closer to the rest of the graph.

**Figure 4.2.2 – Mean Change in QTc by Visit and Treatment**

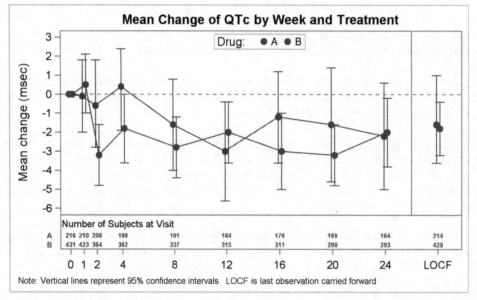

```
proc sgplot data=QTc_Mean_Group;
  format week qtcmean.;
  format n 3.0;
  scatter x=week y=mean / yerrorupper=high yerrorlower=low
          group=drug groupdisplay=cluster clusterwidth=0.5
          markerattrs=(size=7 symbol=circlefilled) name='a';
  series x=week y=mean2 / group=drug
          groupdisplay=cluster clusterwidth=0.5;
  xaxistable n / class=drug colorgroup=drug location=inside
            valueattrs=(size=5 weight=bold)
            labelattrs=(size=6 weight=bold) separator
            title='Number of Subjects at Visit' titleattrs=(size=8);
  refline 26 / axis=x;
  refline 0  / axis=y lineattrs=(pattern=shortdash);
  xaxis type=linear values=(0 1 2 4 8 12 16 20 24 28) max=29
        valueshint display=(nolabel);
  yaxis label='Mean change (msec)' values=(-6 to 3 by 1);
  keylegend 'a' / title='Drug: ' location=inside position=top;
run;
```

The graph above is mostly similar to 4.2.1, with the key difference of placing the "Subjects at Visit" inside the data area instead of at the bottom of the graph. This improves the readability of the graph.

The key difference in the code is the use of LOCATION=Inside for the XAXISTABLE. We also use the SEPARATOR option to draw the line above the table. A reference line is used to separate the "LOCF" value. Relevant details are shown in the code snippet above. For full details, see Program 4_2.

## 4.2.3  Mean Change in QTc by Visit and Treatment in Grayscale

The graph shown in Figure 4.2.3 shows the Mean Change in QTc graph in grayscale.

**Figure 4.2.3 – Mean Change in QTc by Visit and Treatment in Grayscale**

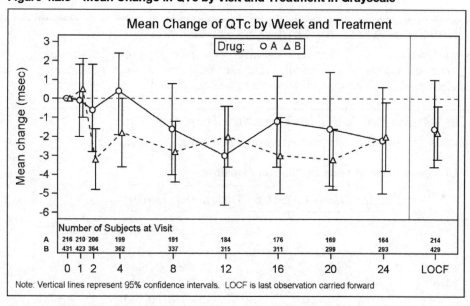

```
ods listing style=journal;
proc sgplot data=QTc_Mean_Group;
  styleattrs datasymbols=(circlefilled trianglefilled)
             datalinepatterns=(solid shortdash);
  format week qtcmean.;
  format n 3.0;
  series x=week y=mean2 / group=drug groupdisplay=cluster c
         clusterwidth=0.5;
  scatter x=week y=mean / yerrorupper=high yerrorlower=low
          group=drug name='a' groupdisplay=cluster
          clusterwidth=0.5 markerattrs=(size=7)
          filledoutlinedmarkers markerfillattrs=graphwalls;
  xaxistable n / class=drug colorgroup=drug location=inside
          title='Number of Subjects at Visit' separator;
  refline 26 / axis=x;
```

```
    refline 0  / axis=y lineattrs=(pattern=shortdash);
    xaxis type=linear values=(0 1 2 4 8 12 16 20 24 28) max=29 valueshint;
    yaxis label='Mean change (msec)' values=(-6 to 3 by 1);
    keylegend 'a' / title='Drug: ' location=inside position=top;
run;
```

To create an effective graph in grayscale, we have run the same graph as in 4.2.2 with ODS Style=JOURNAL. Also, we have used STYLEATTRS option to customize the group attributes.

Note the use of FILLEDOUTLINEDMARKERS. When we are using the filled markers that are specified here, the markers are drawn with fill and outline. MARKERFILLATTRS=GRAPHWALLS is used. Relevant details are shown in the code snippet above. For full details, see Program 4_2.

## 4.3 Distribution of ASAT by Time and Treatment

The graphs below consist of three sections. The main body of the graph contains the display of ASAT by Week and Treatment in the middle. A table of subjects in the study by treatment is at the bottom, and the number of subjects with value > 2 by treatment is at the top of the graph.

### 4.3.1 Distribution of ASAT by Time and Treatment

The values of ASAT by week and treatment are displayed using a box plot. The x-axis type is linear.

**Figure 4.3.1 – Distribution of ASAT by Time and Treatment**

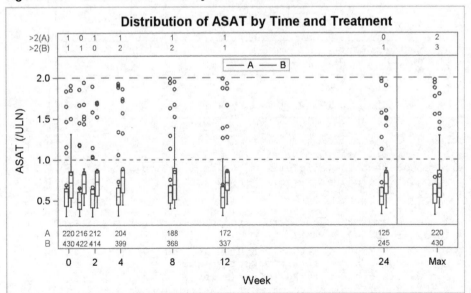

This graph is likely one of the most complex displays that can be created using the SGPLOT procedure. This graph displays the distribution of ASAT by treatment over time using a grouped box plot on a linear x-axis. The visit values are scaled correctly on the time axis. The smallest interval between the visits determines the "effective" midpoint spacing used for adjacent placement of the treatment values.

```
title 'Distribution of ASAT by Time and Treatment';
proc sgplot data=asat;
  vbox asat / category=week group=drug name='box' nofill;
  xaxistable gt2 / class=drugGT colorgroup=drugGT position=top
          location=inside separator valueattrs=(size=6)
          labelattrs=(size=7);
  xaxistable count / class=drug colorgroup=drug position=bottom
          location=inside separator valueattrs=(size=6)
          labelattrs=(size=7);
  refline 1 / lineattrs=(pattern=shortdash);
  refline 2 / lineattrs=(pattern=dash);
  refline 25 / axis=x;
  xaxis type=linear values=(0 2 4 8 12 24 28) offsetmax=0.05
        valueattrs=(size=7) labelattrs=(size=8);
  yaxis offsetmax=0.1 valueattrs=(size=7) labelattrs=(size=8);
  keylegend 'box' / location=inside position=top linelength=20;
run;
```

An XAXISTABLE statement is used to display the "Number of Subjects" values at the bottom of the graph. A second XAXISTABLE at the top is used to display the count of values above 2.0 by treatment.

### 4.3.2  Distribution of ASAT by Time and Treatment in Grayscale

The graph in Figure 4.3.2 is the same as above in grayscale.  Markers are used in the legend for treatment.

**Figure 4.3.2 – Distribution of ASAT by Time and Treatment in Grayscale**

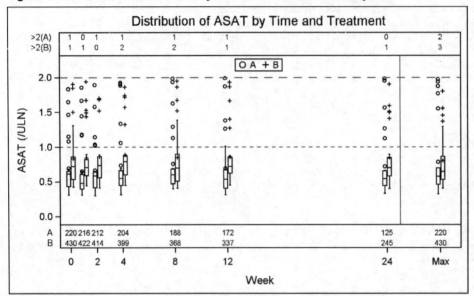

Drawing this graph using the Journal style poses a few challenges, mainly in the drawing of the boxes and their representation in the legend.  Using the Journal style, the boxes for Drug "B" will get drawn using dashed lines.  Because those look odd, I set the STYLEATTRS option to use only solid lines.

```
ods listing style=journal;
title 'Distribution of ASAT by Time and Treatment';
proc sgplot data=asat2;
  styleattrs datalinepatterns=(solid);
  vbox asat / category=week group=drug nofill;
  scatter x=week y=asat2 / group=drug name='s';
  xaxistable gt2 / class=drugGT colorgroup=drugGT position=top
        location=inside;
  xaxistable count / class=drug colorgroup=drug position=bottom
        location=inside;
  refline 1 / lineattrs=(pattern=shortdash);
  refline 2 / lineattrs=(pattern=dash);
  refline 25 / axis=x;
  xaxis type=linear values=(0 2 4 8 12 24 28) offsetmax=0.05;
  yaxis offsetmax=0.1 valueattrs=(size=8) labelattrs=(size=9);
  keylegend 's' / location=inside position=top linelength=20;
run;
```

Although this improves the rendering of the boxes, it will put two solid lines in the legend for "A" and "B". It would be better to show the mean markers in the legend instead. To do this, I have to add a scatter plot of asat2 by Week and Drug and include that in the legend. Because values in "asat2" are all missing, no markers are displayed in the graph itself, but the group markers are displayed in the legend. Relevant details are shown in the code snippet above. For full details, see Program 4_3.

## 4.4 Median of Lipid Profile by Visit and Treatment

This graph displays the median of the lipid values by visit and treatment. The visits are at regular intervals and represented as discrete data.

### 4.4.1 Median of Lipid Profile by Visit and Treatment on Discrete Axis

The values for each treatment are displayed along with the 95% confidence limits as adjacent groups using GROUPDISPLAY option of "Cluster" and the option CLUSTERWIDTH=0.5. The HTMLBlue style is used.

**Figure 4.4.1 – Median of Lipid Profile by Visit and Treatment**

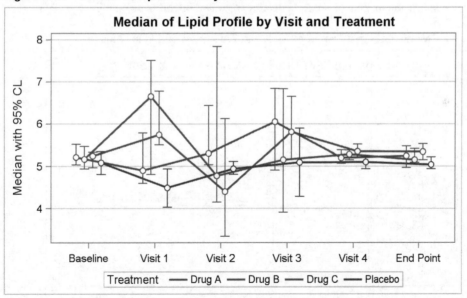

```
title 'Median of Lipid Profile by Visit and Treatment';
proc sgplot data=lipid_grp;
    series   x=day y=median / lineattrs=(pattern=solid) group=trt name='s'
             groupdisplay=cluster clusterwidth=0.5 lineattrs=(thickness=2);
    scatter x=day y=median / yerrorlower=lcl yerrorupper=ucl group=trt
             groupdisplay=cluster clusterwidth=0.5
             errorbarattrs=(thickness=1) filledoutlinedmarkers
             markerattrs=(symbol=circlefilled)
```

```
        markerfillattrs=(color=white);
  keylegend 's' / title='Treatment' linelength=20;
  yaxis label='Median with 95% CL' grid;
  xaxis display=(nolabel);
run;
```

This graph displays the median of the lipid data by visit and treatment. The visits are at regular intervals and represented as discrete data. However, they could also be on a time axis with unequal intervals. The values for each treatment are displayed along with the 95% confidence limits as adjacent groups using GROUPDISPLAY=Cluster and CLUSTERWIDTH=0.5.

The values across visits are joined using a series plot. Note, the series plot also uses cluster groups with the same cluster width. The lengths of the line segments in the legends are reduced using the LINELENGTH option. Markers with fill and outlines are used with specific fill attributes.

Relevant details are shown in the code snippet above. For full details, see Program 4_4.

## 4.4.2  Median of Lipid Profile by Visit and Treatment on Linear Axis in Grayscale

This graph displays the median of the lipid data by treatment in grayscale on a linear x-axis.

**Figure 4.4.2 – Median of Lipid Profile by Visit and Treatment on Linear Axis**

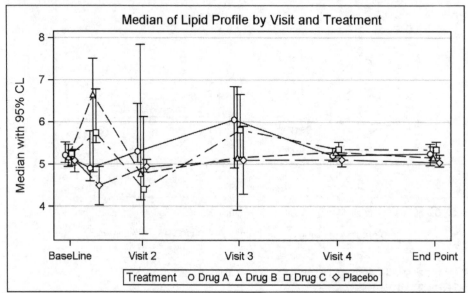

```
title 'Median of Lipid Profile by Visit and Treatment';
proc sgplot data=lipid_Liner_grp;
  styleattrs datasymbols=(circlefilled trianglefilled
            squarefilled diamondfilled);
  series  x=n y=median /  group=trt groupdisplay=cluster
```

```
              clusterwidth=0.5;
  scatter x=n y=median / yerrorlower=lcl yerrorupper=ucl group=trt
          groupdisplay=cluster clusterwidth=0.5
          errorbarattrs=(thickness=1) filledoutlinedmarkers
          markerattrs=(size=7) name='s'
          markerfillattrs=(color=white);
  keylegend 's' / title='Treatment' linelength=20;
  yaxis label='Median with 95% CL' grid;
  xaxis display=(nolabel) values=(1 4 8 12 16);
run;
```

The visits are not at regular intervals and are displayed at the correct scaled location along the x-axis. The visits are at week 1, 2, 4, 8, 12, and 16. These values are formatted to the strings shown on the axis. "Visit 1" collides with "Baseline", causing alternate tick values to be dropped, so I removed "1" from the tick value list.

As you can see, the group values are displayed as clusters, and the "effective midpoint spacing" is the shortest distance between the values. The markers are reduced in size to show the clustering. This can be adjusted by setting marker SIZE=7. Four filled markers are assigned to the list of markers.

Relevant details are shown in the code snippet above. For full details, see Program 4_4.

## 4.5  Survival Plot

The survival plot is one of the most popular graphs that users want to customize to their own needs. Here I have run the LIFETEST procedure to generate the data for this graph. The output is saved into the "SurvivalPlotData" data set. For more information about the LIFETEST procedure, see the SAS/STAT documentation.

### 4.5.1  Survival Plot with External "Subjects At-Risk" Table

The survival plot shown below in Figure 4.5.1 has the traditional arrangement where the table of Subjects At-Risk is displayed at the bottom of the graph, below the x-axis.

**Figure 4.5.1 – Survival Plot with External "Subjects At-Risk" Table**

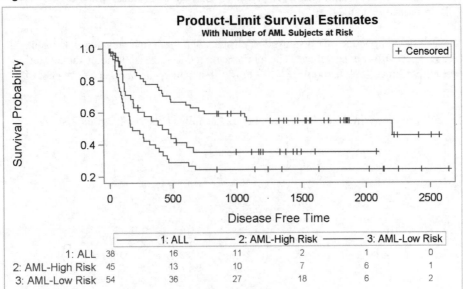

```
ods output Survivalplot=SurvivalPlotData;
proc lifetest data=sashelp.BMT plots=survival(atrisk=0 to 2500 by 500);
   time T * Status(0);
   strata Group / test=logrank adjust=sidak;
   run;
```

A step plot of survival by time by strata displays the curves. A scatter overlay is used to draw the censored values, and an XAXISTABLE statement is used to display the at-risk values at the bottom of the graph. Relevant details are shown in the code snippet above. For full details, see Program 4_5.

```
title 'Product-Limit Survival Estimates';
title2  h=0.8 'With Number of AML Subjects at Risk';
proc sgplot data=SurvivalPlotData;
  step x=time y=survival / group=stratum
```

```
              lineattrs=(pattern=solid) name='s';
    scatter x=time y=censored / markerattrs=(symbol=plus) name='c';
    scatter x=time y=censored / markerattrs=(symbol=plus) GROUP=stratum;
    xaxistable atrisk/x=tatrisk location=outside class=stratum
            colorgroup=stratum;
    keylegend 'c' / location=inside position=topright;
    keylegend 's';
run;
```

## 4.5.2  Survival Plot with Internal "Subjects At-Risk" Table

The graph shown here is mostly similar to the graph in Section 4.5.1, with the difference that the "Subjects At-Risk" table is moved above the x-axis, close to the rest of the data.  Bringing all the data closer makes it easy to align the values with the data, and that improves the effectiveness of the graph.

**Figure 4.5.2 – Survival Plot with Internal "Subjects At-Risk" Table**

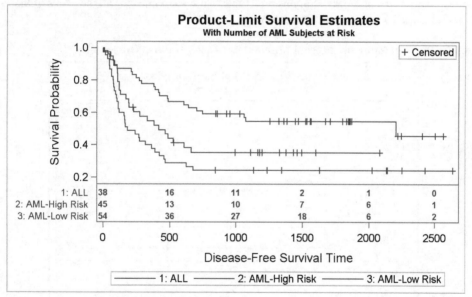

```
title 'Product-Limit Survival Estimates';
title2  h=0.8 'With Number of AML Subjects at Risk';
proc sgplot data=SurvivalPlotData;
    step x=time y=survival / group=stratum lineattrs=(pattern=solid)
        name='s';
    scatter x=time y=censored / markerattrs=(symbol=plus) name='c';
    scatter x=time y=censored / markerattrs=(symbol=plus) GROUP=stratum;
    xaxistable atrisk / x=tatrisk location=inside class=stratum
        colorgroup=stratum separator valueattrs=(size=7 weight=bold)
        labelattrs=(size=8);
```

```
      keylegend 'c' / location=inside position=topright;
      keylegend 's';
run;
```

All this graph needs is to simply specify LOCATION=Inside for the XAXISTABLE statement. In addition to that, we have switched on the separator that draws the horizontal line between the table and the curves.

Relevant details are shown in the code snippet above. For full details, see Program 4_5.

### 4.5.3 Survival Plot with Internal "Subjects At-Risk" Table in Grayscale

Displaying the survival plot in a grayscale medium presents some challenges.

Here we cannot use colors to identify the strata. Normally, the Journal style uses line patterns to identify the groups. Although line patterns work well for curves, they are not so effective with step plots because of the frequent breaks. So, it is preferable to use solid lines for all the levels of the step plot and to use markers to identify the strata.

**Figure 4.5.3 – Survival Plot with Internal "Subjects At-Risk" Table in Grayscale**

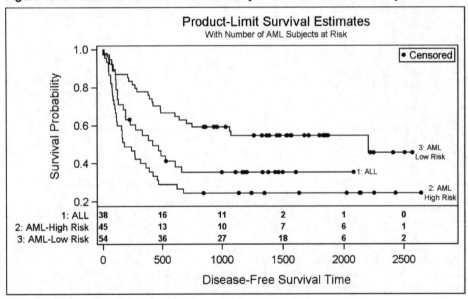

```
      title 'Product-Limit Survival Estimates';
      title2  h=0.8 'With Number of AML Subjects at Risk';
      proc sgplot data=SurvivalPlotData;
        step x=time y=survival / group=stratum lineattrs=(pattern=solid)
              name='s' curvelabel curvelabelattrs=(size=6) splitchar='-';
        scatter x=time y=censored / name='c'
              markerattrs=(symbol=circlefilled size=4);
        xaxistable atrisk / x=tatrisk location=inside class=stratum
```

```
        colorgroup=stratum separator valueattrs=(size=7 weight=bold)
        labelattrs=(size=8);
    keylegend 'c' / location=inside position=topright;
run;
```

In this case, markers are also used to identify the censored observations. So, I have chosen to use the CURVELABEL option with the SPLITCHAR option to identify the curves. This results in a clean and effective graph, without the need for a legend for the strata.

Relevant details are shown in the code snippet above. For full details, see Program 4_5.

## 4.6 Simple Forest Plot

This forest plot is a graphical representation of a meta-analysis of the results of randomized controlled trials.

### 4.6.1 Simple Forest Plot

The graph in Figure 4.6.1 shows a simple forest plot, with the odds ratio plot in the middle by study, along with the tabular display of the statistics on the right.

**Figure 4.6.1 – Simple Forest Plot**

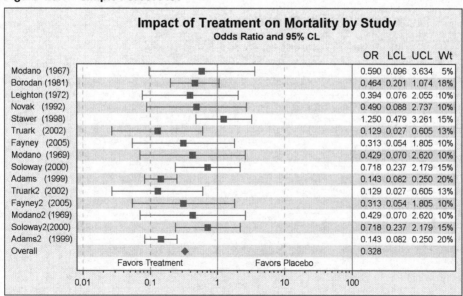

```
title "Impact of Treatment on Mortality by Study";
title2 h=8pt 'Odds Ratio and 95% CL';
proc sgplot data=forest noautolegend nocycleattrs;
  styleattrs datasymbols=(squarefilled diamondfilled);
  scatter y=study x=or / xerrorupper=ucl xerrorlower=lcl group=grp;
```

```
      yaxistable or lcl ucl wt / y=study location=inside position=right;
      refline 1 100  / axis=x noclip;
      refline 0.01 0.1 10 / axis=x lineattrs=(pattern=shortdash) noclip;
      text y=study x=xlbl text=lbl  / position=center contributeoffsets=none;
      xaxis type=log  max=100 minor display=(nolabel)  valueattrs=(size=7);
      yaxis display=(noticks nolabel)  fitpolicy=none reverse
            valueshalign=left colorbands=even )  valueattrs=(size=7);
run;
```

The data for this graph contains the odds ratio, the confidence limits, and the weight for each study. The studies are reclassified with "1" for individual study names and "2" for "Overall". We use this information to plot the graph by study using SCATTERPLOT and YAXISTABLE statements. Note that this graph uses the Analysis style that has an attribute priority of "None", and producing the display of varying markers by group.

We have used the TEXT statement to place the "Favors" strings at the bottom, using a study value of NBSP. Y-axis tick values are left-aligned, and the fit policy is set to "none" so that all tick values are displayed regardless of congestion. For full details, see Program 4_6.

## 4.6.2  Simple Forest Plot with Study Weights
The graph below shows a simple forest plot with Study Weights, where the markers in the odds ratio plot are sized by the weight of the study.

**Figure 4.6.2 – Simple Forest Plot with Study Weights**

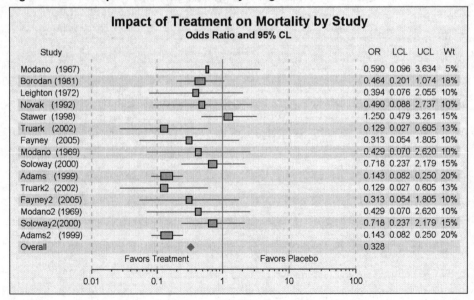

```
title "Impact of Treatment on Mortality by Study";
title2 h=8pt 'Odds Ratio and 95% CL';
proc sgplot data=forest noautolegend nocycleattrs nowall noborder;
```

```
styleattrs axisextent=data;
scatter y=study x=or2 / markerattrs=graphdata2(symbol=diamondfilled);
highlow y=study low=lcl high=ucl / type=line;
highlow y=study low=q1 high=q3 / type=bar barwidth=0.6;
yaxistable study / y=study location=inside position=left
        labelattrs=(size=7);
yaxistable or lcl ucl wt / y=study location=inside position=right;
refline 1  / axis=x noclip;
refline 0.01 0.1 10 100 / axis=x lineattrs=(pattern=shortdash noclip;
text y=study x=xlbl text=lbl  / position=center contributeoffsets=none;
xaxis type=log  max=100 minor display=(nolabel)  valueattrs=(size=7);
yaxis display=none fitpolicy=none reverse valueshalign=left
   colorbands=even colorbandsattrs=Graphdatadefault(transparency=0.75);
run;
```

This graph uses a highlow plot to display the relative weights for each study and the confidence interval. The scatter plot uses the "OR2" variable, which is non-missing only for the "Overall" study. So, only the diamond marker is drawn by the scatter plot.

The width of each marker is proportional to the weight in linear scale. However, because we have used a log x-axis, the widths might not be represented accurately in log scale. So, this can provide a qualitative representation of the weight.

The graph has no wall or wall borders and the x-axis line is displayed only to the extent of the data by using the AXISEXTENT=DATA option on the STYLEATTRS statement. The y-axis is replaced by a YAXISTABLE on the left side so that the bands extend across the full graph.

Relevant details are shown in the code snippet above. For full details, see Program 4_6.

### 4.6.3 Simple Forest Plot with Study Weights in Grayscale

Figure 4.6.3 shows the same forest plot in grayscale medium.

**Figure 4.6.3 – Simple Forest Plot with Study Weights in Grayscale**

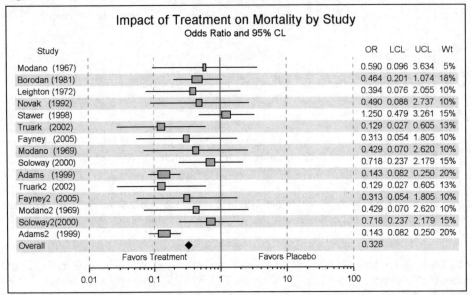

```
ods listing style=journal;
title "Impact of Treatment on Mortality by Study";
title2 h=8pt 'Odds Ratio and 95% CL';
proc sgplot data=forest noautolegend nocycleattrs nowall noborder;
  styleattrs axisextent=data;
  scatter y=study x=or2 / markerattrs=graphdata2(symbol=diamondfilled);
  highlow y=study low=lcl high=ucl / type=line;
  highlow y=study low=q1 high=q3 / type=bar barwidth=0.6;
  yaxistable study / y=study location=inside position=left
          labelattrs=(size=7);
  yaxistable or lcl ucl wt / y=study location=inside position=right
          labelattrs=(size=7);
  refline 1  / axis=x noclip;
  refline 0.01 0.1 10 100 / axis=x lineattrs=(pattern=shortdash)noclip;
  text y=study x=xlbl text=lbl  / position=center contributeoffsets=none;
  xaxis type=log  max=100 minor display=(nolabel)  valueattrs=(size=7);
  yaxis display=none fitpolicy=none reverse valueshalign=left
        colorbands=even valueattrs=(size=7)
        colorbandsattrs=Graphdatadefault(transparency=0.8);
run;
```

Rendering this graph in a grayscale medium does not pose a lot of challenges. Basically, we have set the ODS style to JOURNAL to produce the graph above. This is structurally similar to the graph shown in Section 4.6.2.

Relevant details are shown in the code snippet above. For full details, see Program 4_6.

## 4.7  Subgrouped Forest Plot

More recently, many of you have been asking for building a forest plot, where each study value has multiple subgroups. The example in Figure 4.7.1 shows two subgroups per observation.

For the graph shown below, only the hazard ratio plot in the middle is displayed using a plot statement. The tabular data is displayed in axis tables.

**Figure 4.7.1 – Subgrouped Forest Plot**

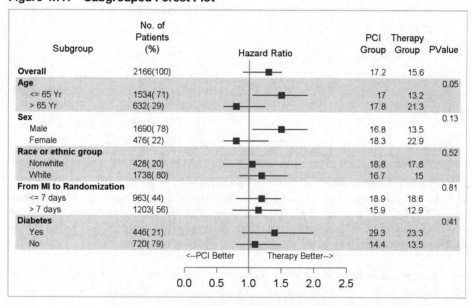

```
proc sgplot data=forest_subgroup_2 nowall noborder nocycleattrs
dattrmap=attrmap;
  styleattrs axisextent=data;
  refline ref / lineattrs=(thickness=13 color=cxf0f0f0);
  highlow y=obsid low=low high=high;
  scatter y=obsid x=mean / markerattrs=(symbol=squarefilled);
  scatter y=obsid x=mean / markerattrs=(size=0) x2axis;
  refline 1 / axis=x;
  text x=xl y=obsid text=text / position=center contributeoffsets=none;
  yaxistable subgroup  / location=inside position=left textgroup=id
        labelattrs=(size=8) textgroupid=text indentweight=indentWt;
  yaxistable countpct / location=inside position=left;
  yaxistable PCIGroup group pvalue / location=inside position=right;
  yaxis reverse display=none colorbands=odd
        colorbandsattrs=(transparency=1);
```

```
   xaxis display=(nolabel) values=(0.0 0.5 1.0 1.5 2.0 2.5);
   x2axis label='Hazard Ratio' display=(noline noticks novalues);
run;
```

The graph above displays the hazard ratio and confidence limits by subgroup, along with the number of patients in the study and other statistics. The key difference here is the display of the subgroups and values in the first column. The subgroup titles are displayed in a bold font, and the values are displayed in a normal font and indented to the right.

**Table 4.7.2 - Data for Subgrouped Forest Plot**

| Obs | ObsId | Id | Subgroup | indentWt | Count | Percent | Mean | Low | High | PCIGroup | Group | PValue | ref |
|-----|-------|-----|----------|----------|-------|---------|------|------|------|----------|-------|--------|-----|
| 1 | 1 | 1 | Overall | 0 | 2166 | 100 | 1.3 | 0.90 | 1.50 | 17.2 | 15.6 | . | . |
| 2 | 2 | 1 | Age | 0 | . | . | . | . | . | . | . | 0.05 | 2 |
| 3 | 3 | 2 | <= 65 Yr | 1 | 1534 | 71 | 1.5 | 1.05 | 1.90 | 17.0 | 13.2 | . | 3 |
| 4 | 4 | 2 | > 65 Yr | 1 | 632 | 29 | 0.8 | 0.60 | 1.25 | 17.8 | 21.3 | . | 4 |
| 5 | 5 | 1 | Sex | 0 | . | . | . | . | . | . | . | 0.13 | . |
| 6 | 6 | 2 | Male | 1 | 1690 | 78 | 1.5 | 1.05 | 1.90 | 16.8 | 13.5 | . | . |
| 7 | 7 | 2 | Female | 1 | 476 | 22 | 0.8 | 0.60 | 1.30 | 18.3 | 22.9 | . | . |

The data for the graph is shown above. The study values come from the "Subgroup" column and are displayed by "ObsId" order. For subgroup labels like "Overall", the Id value is "1", and for the values in the subgroup, the ID is "2". This ID is used to control the attributes of the values that are displayed in the first column of the graph using the attribute map as defined below. Text attributes are defined by the value. Id=1 values are displayed with a bigger, bold font.

In addition, the indention of some of the values in column 1 are controlled by "IndentWt" column. The default indention value is 1/8 inch, and can be changed using the INDENT option. Actual indention amount is based on the INDENTWEIGHT * INDENT.

**Figure 4.7.3 – Attribute Map for Font Attributes**

| Obs | id | value | textcolor | textsize | textweight |
|-----|------|-------|-----------|----------|------------|
| 1 | text | 1 | Black | 7 | bold |
| 2 | text | 2 | Black | 5 | normal |

The second column contains a combination of patient count and percentage and is displayed by another YAXISTABLE statement. The hazard ratio graph in the middle is displayed using a highlow plot and a scatter plot. Then, the three columns on the right are displayed using another YAXISTABLE, with three columns.

The insets at the bottom, "<- PCI Better" and "Therapy Better ->", are displayed in a text plot using the "text", "xl", and "ObsId" columns. The text is center justified. See the full code for this information in the data set, available from the author's page at http://support.sas.com/matange.

Finally, the wide horizontal bands across the graph are drawn using the REFLINE statement with the "Ref" column. This column is a copy of the ObsId column where alternate 3 observations are set to missing. Reference lines are not drawn when the value is missing. Also note, the x-axis line is drawn only to the extent of the actual data, and not all the way using the AXISEXTENT option on the STYLEATTRS statement.

Relevant details are shown in the code snippet above. For full details, see Program 4_7.

## 4.8  Adverse Event Timeline by Severity

An Adverse Event Timeline graph by AEDECOD and Severity is useful to view the history of a specific subject in a study.

**Figure 4.8.1 – Adverse Event Timeline by Severity**

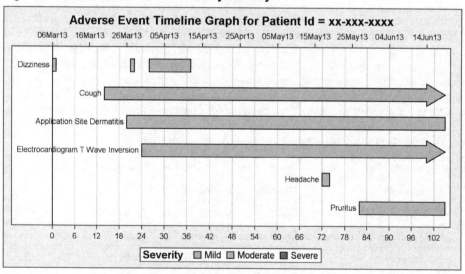

```
title "Adverse Event Timeline Graph for Patient Id = &pid";
proc sgplot data=ae3s dattrmap=attrmap;
   format stdate date7.;
   refline 0 / axis=x lineattrs=(color=black);
   highlow y=aedecod low=stday high=enday / type=bar group=aesev
           lineattrs=(color=black pattern=solid) barwidth=0.8
           lowlabel=aedecod highcap=highcap attrid=Severity
           nomissinggroup labelattrs=(color=black size=7);
   scatter y=aedecod x=stdate / x2axis markerattrs=(size=0);
   xaxis grid display=(nolabel) valueattrs=(size=7)
```

```
        values=(&minday to &maxday by 2) offsetmax=0.02 ;
  x2axis display=(nolabel) type=time valueattrs=(size=7) v
        alues=(&mindate to &maxdate) offsetmax=0.02;
  yaxis  reverse  display=(noticks novalues nolabel);
  run;
```

The graph above displays each adverse event as a bar segment over its duration. The color of the event is set by the severity. The source data is in CDISC, using the SDTM tabulation model format, as shown below.

**Figure 4.8.2 – Data Set for Adverse Event Timeline Graph**

| Obs | aeseq | aedecod | aesev | aestdtc | aeendtc |
|---|---|---|---|---|---|
| 1 | 1 | Dizziness | Moderate | 2013-03-06 | 2013-03-06 |
| 2 | 2 | Cough | Mild | 2013-03-20 | |
| 3 | 4 | Dizziness | Mild | 2013-03-27 | 2013-03-27 |
| 4 | 5 | Electrocardiogram T Wave Inversion | Mild | 2013-03-30 | |

The data has many columns, but the ones that we are using are aeseq, aedecod, aesev, aestdtc, and aeendtc. In the example above, all aestdtc values are present and assumed to be valid. If not, some data cleaning might be needed. In the DATA step, stdate is extracted from aestdtc and endate from aeendtc. If aeendtc is missing, the largest value of endate is used, and highcap is set to "FilledArrow" to indicate that the event does not have an end date. A valid end date is required to draw the event in the graph. The data set that is required for plotting the graph is shown below.

**Figure 4.8.3 – Data Set for Adverse Event Timeline Graph with Caps**

| Obs | aeseq | aedecod | aesev | sev | stdate | endate | stday | enday | highcap |
|---|---|---|---|---|---|---|---|---|---|
| 1 | 1 | Dizziness | Moderate | 2 | 06MAR2013 | 06MAR2013 | 0 | 1 | |
| 2 | 2 | Cough | Mild | 1 | 20MAR2013 | 18JUN2013 | 14 | 105 | FilledArrow |
| 3 | 6 | Application Site Dermatitis | Moderate | 2 | 26MAR2013 | 18JUN2013 | 20 | 105 | |
| 4 | 3 | Dizziness | Mild | 1 | 27MAR2013 | 27MAR2013 | 21 | 22 | |

The data set below is computed for creating the graph. Note that in this data set, we do not have any observations with Severity="Severe". However, the legend in the graph does have an entry for "Severe". These dummy observations do not have valid start and end values, so they are not actually drawn in the graph. The top x-axis is enabled by using a scatter plot assigned to the x2-axis. Macro variables are used to align the x- and x2-axes.

Observations with specific group values are assigned the color and other attributes from the GraphData1-12 style elements. These are assigned in the order in which they are encountered in the data. In this case, we are using specific colors for "Mild", "Moderate", and "Severe". If we just change the colors of the style elements, we will get one of the three colors, but the color assignments can shift based on the order of the data.

To ensure consistent and reliable color assignment, we will use the Discrete Attribute Map data set. Colors and the specific values of the group values are explicitly assigned. Now, the group values will get the colors by value, and not those based on the order of the values in the data. In this case, LineColor is used both for lines and text.

**Figure 4.8.4 – Discrete Attribute Map Data Set**

| Obs | Id | Show | Value | Fillcolor | Linecolor |
|---|---|---|---|---|---|
| 1 | Severity | Attrmap | Mild | lightgreen | darkgreen |
| 2 | Severity | Attrmap | Moderate | gold | cx9f7f00 |
| 3 | Severity | Attrmap | Severe | lightred | darkred |

Another benefit of using the attribute map is based on the SAS 9.4 option "Show" in the map data set. This applies to every map "ID" that is defined in the data set. In this case, there is only one "Severity". By default, only the values that occur in the data are included in the legend. But, if Show is set to "AttrMap", then all the values from the attribute map ID are shown in the legend. In this case, even though the aesev value of "Severe" never occurs in the data, it is still shown in the legend. Another benefit of this feature is that the values that are shown in the legend are sorted in the same order in which they appear in the attribute map. So, we can get a custom sorting of the legend by using this feature.

The highlow plot is ideally suited for such a use case, and provides support for drawing labels and arrowhead caps at each end. In this case, the LOWLABEL option is used to draw the event names. We have displayed the aedecod label only the first time. The HIGHCAP option is used to draw the arrowhead as shown for "Cough" at the right end. This indicates an event that does not have an end date in the data.

For the grayscale use case, we can change the highlow bar type to the default "Line". This will allow use of the line pattern as the visual element for the different severity values. Here is the graph, along with the appropriate attribute map.

**Figure 4.8.5 – Adverse Event Timeline for Grayscale**

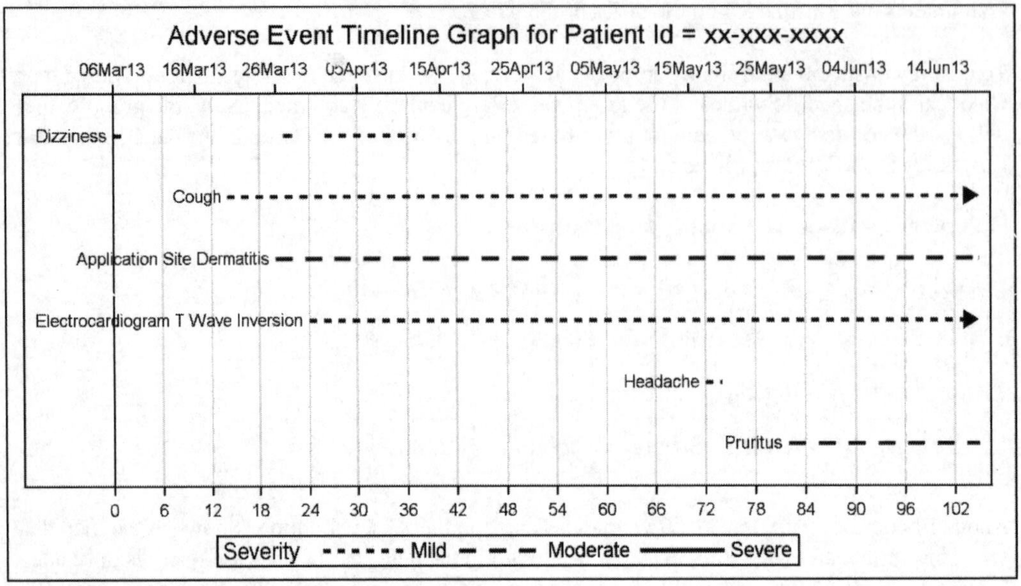

Adverse Event Timeline Graph for Patient Id = xx-xxx-xxxx

**Figure 4.8.6 – Attribute Map for Grayscale Graph**

| Obs | Id | Show | Value | Fillcolor | LinePattern | LineThickness |
|-----|----|----|----|----|----|----|
| 1 | Severity | Attrmap | Mild | lightgreen | shortdash | 2 |
| 2 | Severity | Attrmap | Moderate | gold | dash | 2 |
| 3 | Severity | Attrmap | Severe | lightred | solid | 2 |

Relevant details are shown in the code snippet above.  For full details, see Program 4_8.

## 4.9 Change in Tumor Size

The graph shown below is commonly known at a "waterfall chart" in the oncology domain. The graph displays the change in tumor size by treatment.

**Figure 4.9.1 – Graph of Change in Tumor Size**

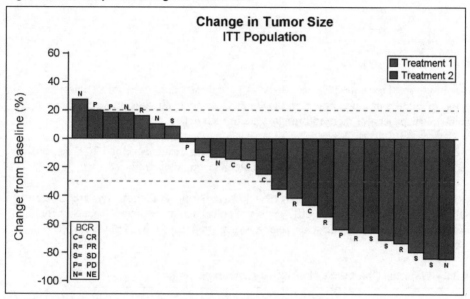

```
title 'Change in Tumor Size';
title2 'ITT Population';
proc sgplot data=TumorSize nowall noborder;
  styleattrs datacolors=(cxbf0000 cx4f4f4f) datacontrastcolors=(black);
  vbar cid / response=change group=group categoryorder=respdesc
       datalabel=label datalabelattrs=(size=5) groupdisplay=cluster
       clusterwidth=1;
  refline 20 -30 / lineattrs=(pattern=shortdash);
  xaxis display=none;
  yaxis values=(60 to -100 by -20);
  inset ("C="="CR" "R="="PR" "S="="SD" "P="="PD" "N="="NE") / title='BCR'
       position=bottomleft border textattrs=(size=6)
       titleattrs=(size=7);
  keylegend / title='' location=inside position=topright across=1 border;
run;
```

The graph displays the change in tumor size in descending order of size increase for the population by treatment. The data is shown on the right. The response type is shown at the end of the bar.

**Figure 4.9.2 – Data for Waterfall Chart**

| Obs | Cid | Change | Id | Group | Label |
|-----|-----|--------|----|-------|-------|
| 1 | 1 | -14.3910 | 1 | Treatment 1 | C |
| 2 | 2 | -65.9578 | 2 | Treatment 1 | R |
| 3 | 3 | -71.1846 | 3 | Treatment 1 | S |
| 4 | 4 | 19.6850 | 4 | Treatment 2 | P |
| 5 | 5 | 18.0494 | 5 | Treatment 2 | N |

Confidence limits are shown at +20% and -30%. A partial response is generally indicated for tumor shrinkage of 30% or more; however, the author does not claim domain-specific expertise. See domain-centric papers for more information about such details.

The STYLEATTRS statement is used to control the colors for treatments 1 and 2. For specific assignment of colors by treatment, a discrete attribute map would be preferred.

A serious clinical graph does not necessarily have to have boring aesthetics. The graph below displays the same information using a different set of colors and presentation aspects, including bars with a textured look. The confidence region is displayed using a band plot with 50% transparency.

**Figure 4.9.3 – Waterfall Chart with Alternative Appearance**

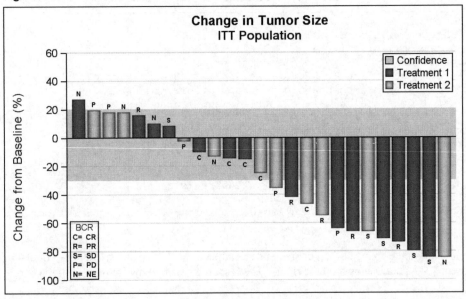

```
title 'Change in Tumor Size';
title2 'ITT Population';
proc sgplot data=TumorSizeDesc nowall noborder;
```

```
styleattrs datacolors=(cxbf0000 gold) datacontrastcolors=(black);
band x=cid upper=20 lower=-30 /transparency=0.5
     filllegendlabel='Confidence';
vbarparm category=cid  response=change / group=group datalabel=label
          datalabelattrs=(size=5 weight=bold) groupdisplay=cluster
          dataskin=pressed;
xaxis display=none;
yaxis values=(60 to -100 by -20) grid gridattrs=(color=cxf0f0f0);
inset ("C="="CR" "R="="PR" "S="="SD" "P="="PD" "N="="NE") / title='BCR'
     position=bottomleft border textattrs=(size=6)
     titleattrs=(size=7);
keylegend / title='' location=inside position=topright
     across=1 border opaque;
run;
```

A VBARPARM statement is used instead of a VBAR statement because we want to layer a band plot in the graph.  Grid lines are enabled, and the legend has an opaque background.  Group display of "Cluster" is used so that we can display the bar data labels.

Relevant details are shown in the code snippet above.  For full details, see Program 4_9.

## 4.10 Injection Site Reaction

The graph in Figure 4.10.1 shows the incidence of injection site reaction by Time and Cohort.

### 4.10.1 Injection Site Reaction

The (simulated) data is shown on the right, with incidence by group over time.

**Figure 4.10.1.1 – Graph of Injection Site Reaction**

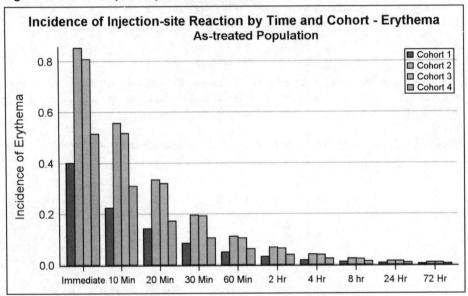

```
title 'Incidence of Injection-site Reaction by Time and Cohort -
Erythema';
title2 'As-treated Population';
ods listing style=listing;
proc sgplot data=Incidence nowall noborder;
  styleattrs datacolors=(gray pink lightgreen lightblue)
          datacontrastcolors=(black);
  vbar time / response=incidence group=group groupdisplay=cluster;
  xaxis discreteorder=data valueattrs=(size=8) fitpolicy=none
        display=(nolabel);
  yaxis grid display=(noticks);
  keylegend / title='' location=inside position=topright across=1 border
        autoitemsize valueattrs=(size=8);
run;
```

We have used a VBAR statement with Time as the category and Cohort (Group) as the group. The time values are treated as discrete, and each cluster of incidence bars is positioned at equidistant midpoints along the axis.

**Figure 4.10.1.1 – Data Set for Injection Site Reaction Graph**

| Obs | Time | Group | Incidence |
|---|---|---|---|
| 1 | Immediate | Cohort 1 | 0.40112 |
| 2 | Immediate | Cohort 2 | 0.85194 |
| 3 | Immediate | Cohort 3 | 0.80790 |
| 4 | Immediate | Cohort 4 | 0.51452 |

The STYLEATTRS statement is used to set the four colors for the group values. Y-axis grid lines are enabled, and the tick marks are removed.

## 4.10.2 Injection Site Reaction in Grayscale

The graph above uses the JOURNAL2 style that is suitable for submissions to journals that are published in grayscale medium. The group classifications are displayed using fill patterns.

**Figure 4.10.2 – Graph of Injection Site Reaction in Grayscale**

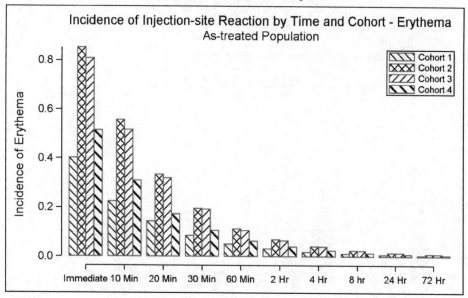

```
title 'Incidence of Injection-site Reaction by Time and Cohort - ';
title2 'As-treated Population';
ods listing style=Journal2;
proc sgplot data=Incidence nowall noborder;
  styleattrs datacolors=(gray pink lightgreen lightblue )
             datacontrastcolors=(black) axisextent=data;
  vbar time / response=incidence group=group groupdisplay=cluster
```

```
                baselineattrs=(thickness=0) outlineattrs=(color=gray);
  xaxis discreteorder=data valueattrs=(size=8) fitpolicy=none
        display=(nolabel);
  yaxis offsetmin=0.04 grid display=(noticks);
  keylegend / title='' location=inside position=topright across=1 border
             autoitemsize valueattrs=(size=8);
run;
```

We have used a new SAS 9.4 feature to display the axis only for the extent of the data using the AXISEXTENT=DATA on the STYLEATTRS statement. This produces results that are preferred by many users.

Relevant details are shown in the code snippet above. For full details, see Program 4_10.

## 4.11 Distribution of Maximum LFT by Treatment

The graph below shows the distribution of LFT values by Test and Treatment.

### 4.11.1 Distribution of Maximum LFT by Treatment with Multi-Column Data

The graph shows the distribution of LFT values by Test and Treatment using multi-column data.

**Figure 4.11.1.1 – Distribution of Maximum LFT by Treatment**

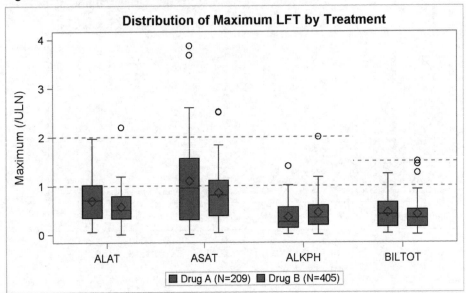

```
title 'Distribution of Maximum LFT by Treatment';
footnote j=l 'Level of concern is 2.0 for ALAT, ASAT, ALKPH and 1.5
for BILTOT';
```

```
proc sgplot data=LFT;
   refline 1 / lineattrs=(pattern=shortdash);
   dropline x='BILTOT' y=2.0 / dropto=y discreteoffset=-0.5;
   dropline x='BILTOT' y=1.5 / y2axis dropto=y discreteoffset=-0.5;
   vbox a / category=test discreteoffset=-0.15 boxwidth=0.2 name='a'
            legendlabel='Drug A (N=209)';
   vbox b / category=test discreteoffset= 0.15 boxwidth=0.2 name='b'
            legendlabel='Drug B (N=405)';
   vbox a / category=test y2axis transparency=1;
   vbox b / category=test y2axis transparency=1;
   keylegend 'a' 'b';
   xaxis display=(nolabel);
   y2axis display=none;
run;
```

The graph above uses two VBOX statements, one each for the values for drugs A and B.

**Figure 4.11.1.2 – Data for Graph Using Multiple Columns**

| Obs | Test | A | B |
|-----|-------|---------|---------|
| 1 | ALAT | 1.05198 | 0.97755 |
| 2 | ASAT | 0.78177 | 0.59554 |
| 3 | ALKPH | 0.20475 | 0.20589 |
| 4 | BILTOT | 0.12868 | 0.10760 |
| 5 | ALAT | 1.00211 | 1.19132 |

The levels of concern for the lab tests are different, so we have used the DROPLINE statement to draw the levels differently for the upper and lower values. Discrete offset is used to start the drop line halfway between the lab values.

## 4.11.2  Distribution of Maximum LFT by Treatment Grayscale with Group Data

This graph displays the Distribution of Maximum LFT graph by Treatment group in grayscale.

**Figure 4.11.2.1 – Distribution of Maximum LFT by Treatment**

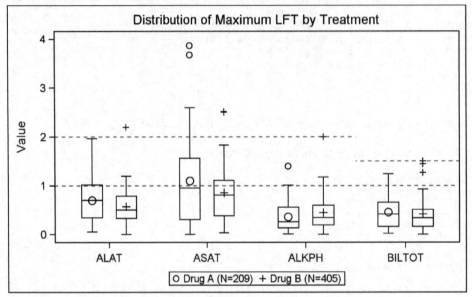

```
title 'Distribution of Maximum LFT by Treatment';
proc sgplot data=lft_Grp;
   styleattrs datalinepatterns=(solid);
   refline 1 / lineattrs=(pattern=shortdash);
   dropline x='BILTOT' y=2.0 / dropto=y discreteoffset=-0.5;
   dropline x='BILTOT' y=1.5 / y2axis dropto=y discreteoffset=-0.5;
   vbox value / category=test group=drug groupdisplay=cluster nofill;
   scatter x=test y=out / y2axis group=drug name='a';
   keylegend 'a';
   xaxis display=(nolabel);
   y2axis display=none min=0 max=4;
run;
```

In this example, the data is arranged by group, instead of by multi-column as in 4.11.1. We are using empty boxes in a black and white medium using the Journal style. We have set all lines to solid, so we need another way to indicate the treatment name.

**Figure 4.11.2.2 – Data for Graph Using Group Data**

| Obs | Test | Drug | Value | Out |
|---|---|---|---|---|
| 1 | ALAT | Drug A (N=209) | 1.05198 | 5 |
| 2 | ALAT | Drug B (N=405) | 0.97755 | 5 |
| 3 | ASAT | Drug A (N=209) | 0.78177 | 5 |
| 4 | ASAT | Drug B (N=405) | 0.59554 | 5 |
| 5 | ALKPH | Drug A (N=209) | 0.20475 | 5 |

Here we used a scatter overlay, with Y=OUT, on a column that has all values > 4. We also set the y-axis MAX=4 in order to remove these fake markers while still retaining them in the legend.

Relevant details are shown in the code snippet above. For full details, see Program 4_11.

## 4.12  Clark Error Grid

The Clark Error Grid graph is used to quantify the clinical accuracy of blood glucose levels that are generated by the meters.  The sensor response and the reference value are plotted on the grid.

### 4.12.1  Clark Error Grid

The graph includes demarcated zones that indicate the divergence of the meter values from reference values.  Zone "A" demarcates the zone where the divergence is < 20%.  Zone "B" has divergence > 20%, but not leading to improper treatment.  Other zones indicate dangerous or confusing results.

**Figure 4.12.1 – Clark Error Grid for Blood Glucose Measurement Accuracy**

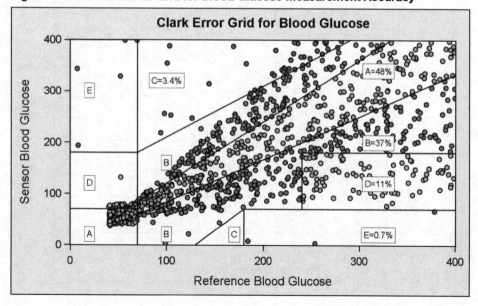

```
title 'Clark Error Grid for Blood Glucose';
proc sgplot data=plotZoneCount noautolegend dattrmap=attrmap;
   scatter x=x y=y / group=zone attrid=A filledoutlinedmarkers
          markerattrs=(symbol=circlefilled size=5);
   series x=rfbg y=sbg / group=id nomissinggroup
          lineattrs=graphdatadefault(color=black) ;
   text x=xl y=yl text=label / backfill fillattrs=(color=white) outline;
   xaxis min=0 max=400 offsetmin=0 offsetmax=0
         label='Reference Blood Glucose';
   yaxis min=0 max=400 offsetmin=0 offsetmax=0
         label='Sensor Blood Glucose';
run;
```

The data for this graph includes the measured and reference glucose level observations, data for zone boundaries and the zone labels, and data for zone labels.

The scatter plot in the program is used to draw the metered glucose values by reference. The series plot is used to display the boundaries of each zone, and the text plot is used to display the zone name. The text plot is optimized for display of textual items in a graph. A discrete attributes map is used to color the markers in each zone appropriately.

## 4.12.2 Clark Error Grid in Grayscale

The same graph as in Section 4.12.1 is rendered here for a grayscale medium. The key difference in approach is that we need to ensure the correct decoding of the data in the five zones. Here, we have used filled markers for each zone as specified in the STYLEATTRS statement. The marker fill color is set to "White".

**Figure 4.12.2 – Clark Error Grid in Grayscale**

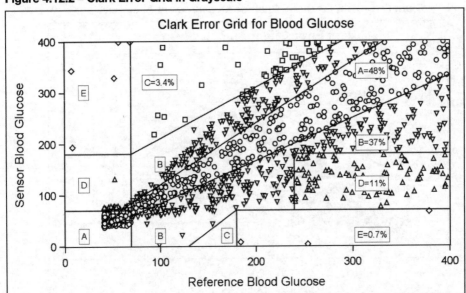

```
ods listing style=journal;
title 'Clark Error Grid for Blood Glucose';
proc sgplot data=plotZoneCount noautolegend;
  styleattrs datasymbols=(trianglefilled circlefilled
           squarefilled diamondfilled triangledownfilled);
  scatter x=x y=y / group=zone attrid=A markerattrs=(size=5)
          filledoutlinedmarkers markerfillattrs=(color=white);
  series x=rfbg y=sbg / group=id nomissinggroup;
  text x=xl y=yl text=label / backfill fillattrs=(color=white) outline;
  xaxis min=0 max=400 offsetmin=0 offsetmax=0
       label='Reference Blood Glucose';
  yaxis min=0 max=400 offsetmin=0 offsetmax=0
       label='Sensor Blood Glucose';
  run;
```

The attribute map is not used here because the zones are clearly marked in the graph itself. It is only helpful to have different markers in each zone, but not necessary. However, if it does become necessary to place the same markers across different graphs for each zone, this can be ensured by using a discrete attribute map.

All axis offsets are set to zero to ensure the zone boundaries touch the axes. This also removes the effect of any offset contributions preferred by the text plot.

Relevant details are shown in the code snippet above. For full details, see Program 4_12.

## 4.13 The Swimmer Plot

This "swimmer plot" displays the response of the tumor to the study drug over time in months. Each horizontal bar represents one subject in the study.

### 4.13.1 The Swimmer Plot for Tumor Response over Time

This graph shows the tumor response by subject over time[1]. Each horizontal bar in the graph represents one subject. The inset line indicates complete or partial response with start and end times.

**Figure 4.13.1.1 – The Swimmer Plot for Tumor Response over Time**

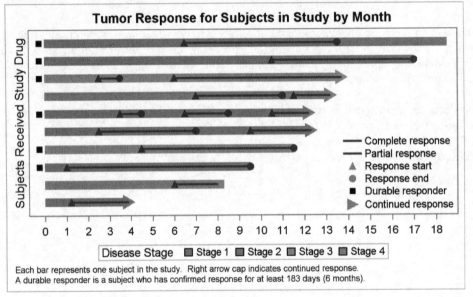

```
title 'Tumor Response for Subjects in Study by Month';
proc sgplot data= swimmer dattrmap=attrmap nocycleattrs;
  highlow y=item low=low high=high / highcap=highcap type=bar group=stage
          fill nooutline name='stage' nomissinggroup transparency=0.3;
  highlow y=item low=startline high=endline / group=status
          name='status' nomissinggroup attrid=statusC;
  scatter y=item x=start / name='s' legendlabel='Response start'
          markerattrs=(symbol=trianglefilled size=8 color=darkgray);
  scatter y=item x=end / name='e' legendlabel='Response end'
          markerattrs=(symbol=circlefilled size=8 color=darkgray);
  scatter y=item x=xmin / name='x' legendlabel='Continued response '
          markerattrs=(symbol=trianglerightfilled
          size=12 color=darkgray);
  scatter y=item x=durable / name='d' legendlabel='Durable responder'
          markerattrs=(symbol=squarefilled size=6 color=black);
  scatter y=item x=start / group=status attrid=status
          markerattrs=(symbol=trianglefilled size=8);
```

```
scatter y=item x=end / group=status attrid=status
        markerattrs=(symbol=circlefilled size=8);
xaxis display=(nolabel) label='Months'
      values=(0 to 20 by 1) valueshint;
yaxis reverse display=(noticks novalues noline)
      label='Subjects Received ...';
keylegend 'stage' / title='Disease Stage';
keylegend 'status' 's' 'e' 'd' / noborder location=inside
          position=bottomright across=1 linelength=20;
run;
```

An arrowhead on the right indicates continuing response. The bar contains durations over which the "Complete" or "Partial" response is indicated, with a start and end time. The disease stage is indicated by the color of the bar, with a legend showing the unique values below the x-axis. An inset is included to decode the different markers in the event bar. A "Durable" response is indicated by the square marker on the left end of the bar.

Note that the start and end points for each response are represented by colored markers inside each event bar. However, the same points are shown in grayscale in the inset table. This is achieved by first plotting the markers in a gray color, and overdrawing those by colored markers using GROUP=Status. The scatter plots that plot the gray markers are the ones that are included in the inset.

Also note the existence of a "right arrow" marker in the inset indicating the continuing event. This is done by including a scatter plot with a right triangle marker in the plot, but the data for this marker is missing. However, it is included in the inset.

The structure of the data set that is needed for the graph is shown below.

**Figure 4.13.1.2 – Data Set for Tumor Response Graph**

| Obs | Item | Stage | Low | High | Highcap | Status | Start | End | Durable | Startline | Endline | Xmin |
|-----|------|-------|-----|------|---------|--------|-------|-----|---------|-----------|---------|------|
| 1 | 1 | Stage 1 | 0 | 18.5 | | Complete response | 6.5 | 13.5 | -0.25 | 6.5 | 13.5 | . |
| 2 | 2 | Stage 2 | 0 | 17.0 | | Complete response | 10.5 | 17.0 | -0.25 | 10.5 | 17.0 | . |
| 3 | 3 | Stage 3 | 0 | 14.0 | FilledArrow | Partial response | 2.5 | 3.5 | -0.25 | 2.5 | 3.5 | . |
| 4 | 3 | | 0 | 14.0 | FilledArrow | Partial response | 6.0 | . | | 6.0 | 13.7 | . |
| 5 | 4 | Stage 4 | 0 | 13.5 | FilledArrow | Partial response | 7.0 | 11.0 | . | 7.0 | 11.0 | . |
| 6 | 4 | | 0 | 13.5 | FilledArrow | Partial response | 11.5 | . | . | 11.5 | 13.2 | . |
| 7 | 5 | Stage 1 | 0 | 12.5 | FilledArrow | Complete response | 3.5 | 4.5 | -0.25 | 3.5 | 4.5 | . |
| 8 | 5 | | 0 | 12.5 | FilledArrow | Complete response | 6.5 | 8.5 | | 6.5 | 8.5 | . |
| 9 | 5 | | 0 | 12.5 | FilledArrow | Partial response | 10.5 | . | . | 10.5 | 12.2 | . |
| 10 | 6 | Stage 2 | 0 | 12.6 | FilledArrow | Partial response | 2.5 | 7.0 | . | 2.5 | 7.0 | . |

Note, although the program for this graph is longer than some other ones, it can be built one part at a time.

- First, plot the full duration from Low to High by Item using a grouped highlow plot with a High Cap and TYPE=BAR. Include this in the outside legend.
- Layer the individual "Response" events from Startline to Endline by Status using a high-low bar with the default line type. Include this in the inset legend.
- Layer the Start and End events in a gray color. Include these in the inset legend.
- Layer the Start and End events again using GROUP=Status.
- Add a scatter plot with missing data to include the "Right Arrow" in the legend.

The Discrete Attribute Map data set contains two maps, one for the colored graph "StatusC", and one for the grayscale graph called "StatusJ". AttrId=StatusC is used in this graph. For full details, see Program 4_12.

## 4.13.2 The Swimmer Plot for Tumor Response over Time in Grayscale

The tumor response graph is shown in grayscale. The disease stage is shown on the left as we cannot use a color indicator.

Patterned lines are used to draw the response events, and a YAXISTABLE is used to draw the stage labels on the left. ATTRID=StatusJ is used in this graph. For full details, see Program 4_13.

**Figure 4.13.2 – The Swimmer Plot for Tumor Response over Time in Grayscale**

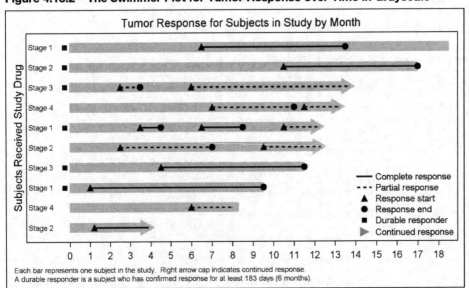

```
ods listing style=journal;
title 'Tumor Response for Subjects in Study by Month';
proc sgplot data= swimmer dattrmap=attrmap nocycleattrs;
```

```
    styleattrs datalinepatterns=(solid shortdash);
    highlow y=item low=low high=high / highcap=highcap type=bar group=stage
            nooutline lineattrs=(color=black) fillattrs=(color=lightgray)
            name='stage' barwidth=1 nomissinggroup fill;
    highlow y=item low=startline high=endline / group=status name='status'
            lineattrs=(thickness=2) nomissinggroup  attrid=statusJ;
    scatter y=item x=start / name='s' legendlabel='Response start'
            markerattrs=(symbol=trianglefilled size=8);
    scatter y=item x=end / name='e' legendlabel='Response end'
            markerattrs=(symbol=circlefilled size=8);
    scatter y=item x=xmin / name='x' legendlabel='Continued response'
            markerattrs=(symbol=trianglerightfilled size=12
            color=darkgray);
    scatter y=item x=durable / name='d' legendlabel='Durable responder'
            markerattrs=(symbol=squarefilled size=6 color=black);
    scatter y=item x=start / group=status attrid=statusJ;
    scatter y=item x=end / group=status attrid=statusJ;
    yaxistable stage / location=inside position=left nolabel
               attrid=statusJ;
    xaxis display=(nolabel) label='Months'
          values=(0 to 20 by 1) valueshint;
    yaxis reverse display=(noticks novalues noline)
          label='Subjects Received ...';
    keylegend 'status' 's' 'e' 'd' 'x' / noborder location=inside across=1
              position=bottomright linelength=20;
run;
```

## 4.14 CDC Chart for Length and Weight Percentiles

The CDC chart for length and weight for boys and girls from birth to 36 months is widely used in pediatric practices to track vital statistics. This graph is shown in Figure 4.14.1, and the entire chart is created using the SGPLOT procedure. The purpose is primarily to evaluate the features of the procedure.

**Figure 4.14.1 – CDC Chart for Length and Weight Percentiles**

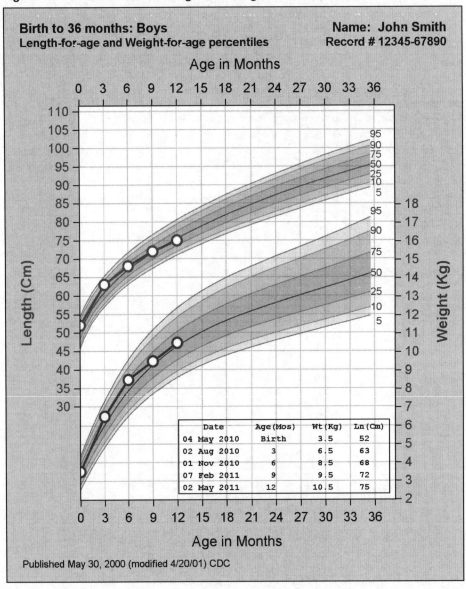

The graph above renders the full CDC chart for Length and Weight Percentiles from the data for one subject. The original graph was a bit taller, but I shrank it to fit this page. The data that is required is created by appending the CDC percentile data with the historical data for one subject. The CDC data is included in the file named "4_14_CDC_Cleaned.csv".

The CDC data for the percentile curves is shown below. Only a few of the observations are displayed to conserve space. Also, the data contains all the columns for 5, 10, 25, 50, 75, 90, and 95 percentiles, but only a few columns are included to fit in the space.

**Figure 4.14.2 – Data for CDC Chart**

| Sex | Agemos | W5 | W25 | W75 | W95 | H5 | H25 | H75 | H95 |
|---|---|---|---|---|---|---|---|---|---|
| 1 | 0 | 2.52690402 | 3.150611082 | 3.879076559 | 4.34029274 | 45.5684091 | 48.189373814 | 51.771257485 | 54.307211972 |
| 1 | 0.5 | 2.964655655 | 3.597395573 | 4.387422565 | 4.910130108 | 48.558092059 | 50.979188895 | 54.440543134 | 56.999077373 |
| 1 | 1.5 | 3.774848862 | 4.428872952 | 5.327327567 | 5.967101615 | 52.726106587 | 54.979104409 | 58.350594078 | 60.964653792 |

The historical data for the subject is appended at the bottom of the curve data, using the column names Sex, Age, Height, and Length, as shown below.

**Figure 4.14.3 – Data for CDC Chart**

| Obs | Sex | Agemos | W5 | W50 | W95 | H5 | H50 | H95 | Age | Height | Weight |
|---|---|---|---|---|---|---|---|---|---|---|---|
| 36 | Male | 34.5 | 11.86229971 | 14.1150324 | 17.10619066 | 88.703007448 | 94.808229231 | 101.43177049 | . | . | . |
| 37 | Male | 35.5 | 11.98045644 | 14.25779618 | 17.30646132 | 89.332418366 | 95.446369813 | 102.11744722 | . | . | . |
| 38 | Male | . | . | . | . | . | . | . | 0 | 52 | 3.5 |
| 39 | Male | . | . | . | . | . | . | . | 3 | 63 | 6.5 |

```
title j=l h=9pt 'Birth to 36 months: Boys' j=r "Name:  John Smith";
title2 j=l h=8pt "Length-for-age and Weight-for-age percentiles" j=r
"Record # 12345-67890";
footnote j=l h=7pt "Published May 30, 2000 (modified 4/20/01) CDC";
proc sgplot data=Chart_Patient noautolegend;
  where sex=1;
    refline 3 4 5 6 / axis=y2 lineattrs=graphgridlines;

    /*--Curve bands--*/
    band x=agemos lower=w5  upper=w95 / y2axis fillattrs=graphdata1
        transparency=0.9;
    band x=agemos lower=w10 upper=w90 / y2axis fillattrs=graphdata1
        transparency=0.8;
    band x=agemos lower=w25 upper=w75 / y2axis fillattrs=graphdata1
        transparency=0.8;

    /*--Curves--*/
    series x=agemos y=w5 / y2axis lineattrs=graphdata1 transparency=0.5;
    series x=agemos y=w10 / y2axis lineattrs=graphdata1 transparency=0.7;
    series x=agemos y=w25 / y2axis lineattrs=graphdata1 transparency=0.7;
    series x=agemos y=w50 / y2axis x2axis lineattrs=graphdata1;
    series x=agemos y=w75 / y2axis lineattrs=graphdata1 transparency=0.7;
```

```
series x=agemos y=w90 / y2axis lineattrs=graphdata1 transparency=0.7;
series x=agemos y=w95 / y2axis lineattrs=graphdata1 transparency=0.5;
```

The program that is required to draw all the elements of this graph is long, but easy to understand. So, I have shown it in parts across the following pages. The first part of the program is shown above, with titles, footnotes, and percentile curves for Weight. The bands are drawn with three transparent overlays to create the appearance of color gradation. The curves are overlaid on the bands.

```
/*--Curve labels--*/
text x=agemos y=w5  text=15  / y2axis textattrs=graphdata1
             position=right;
text x=agemos y=w10 text=110 / y2axis textattrs=graphdata1
             position=right;
text x=agemos y=w25 text=125 / y2axis textattrs=graphdata1
             position=right;
text x=agemos y=w50 text=150 / y2axis textattrs=graphdata1
             position=right;
text x=agemos y=w75 text=175 / y2axis textattrs=graphdata1
             position=right;
text x=agemos y=w90 text=190 / y2axis textattrs=graphdata1
             position=right;
text x=agemos y=w95 text=195 / y2axis textattrs=graphdata1
             position=right;


/*--Patient datas--*/
series x=age y=weight / lineattrs=graphdata1(thickness=2)
        y2axis markers markerattrs=(symbol=circlefilled size=11)
        filledoutlinedmarkers markerfillattrs=(color=white)
        markeroutlineattrs=graphdata1(thickness=2);
```

The code section above draws the curve labels for the percentile curves on the right. This is overlaid by the historical subject weight data as a series plot. The code for Height is shown below.

```
/*--Curve bands--*/
band x=agemos lower=h5  upper=h95 / fillattrs=graphdata3
transparency=0.9;
band x=agemos lower=h10 upper=h90 / fillattrs=graphdata3
transparency=0.8;
band x=agemos lower=h25 upper=h75 / fillattrs=graphdata3
transparency=0.8;


/*--Curves--*/
series x=agemos y=h5 / lineattrs=graphdata3(pattern=solid)
        transparency=0.5;
series x=agemos y=h10 /lineattrs=graphdata3(pattern=solid)
        transparency=0.7;
series x=agemos y=h25 /lineattrs=graphdata3(pattern=solid)
        transparency=0.7;
series x=agemos y=h50 /lineattrs=graphdata3(pattern=solid) x2axis;
series x=agemos y=h75 /lineattrs=graphdata3(pattern=solid)
```

```
        transparency=0.7;
series x=agemos y=h90 /lineattrs=graphdata3(pattern=solid)
        transparency=0.7;
series x=agemos y=h95 /lineattrs=graphdata3(pattern=solid)
transparency=0.5;

/*--Curve labels--*/
text x=agemos y=h5  text=l5  / textattrs=graphdata3
      position=bottomright;
text x=agemos y=h10 text=l10 / textattrs=graphdata3 position=right;
text x=agemos y=h25 text=l25 / textattrs=graphdata3 position=right;
text x=agemos y=h50 text=l50 / textattrs=graphdata3 position=right;
text x=agemos y=h75 text=l75 / textattrs=graphdata3 position=right;
text x=agemos y=h90 text=l90 / textattrs=graphdata3 position=right;
text x=agemos y=h95 text=l95 / textattrs=graphdata3 position=topright;

/*--Patient datas--*/
series x=age y=height /
       lineattrs=graphdata3(pattern=solid thickness=2)
       markers markerattrs=(symbol=circlefilled size=11)
       filledoutlinedmarkers markerfillattrs=(color=white)
       markeroutlineattrs=graphdata3(thickness=2);
```

The Height (Length) and Weight data ranges are different, and these need to be plotted with different vertical scales and axis details. We can do that by using two separate Y-axes for each column. Here we used the Y2AXIS for Weight and YAXIS for Height. This breaks the link between the two variables scales, thus allowing us to draw the Height and Weight curves and data independently.

```
/*--Table--*/
inset "    Date       Age(Mos)    Wt(Kg)   Ln(Cm)"
         "04 May 2010     Birth      3.5      52"
         "02 Aug 2010       3        6.5      63"
         "01 Nov 2010       6        8.5      68"
         "07 Feb 2011       9        9.5      72"
         "02 May 2011      12       10.5      75" / border
         textattrs=(family='Courier' size=6 weight=bold)
         position=bottomright;

xaxis grid offsetmin=0  integer values=(0 to 36 by 3);
x2axis grid offsetmin=0 integer values=(0 to 36 by 3);
yaxis  grid offsetmin=0.25 offsetmax=0.0 label="Length (Cm)" integer
       values=(30 to 110 by 5) labelattrs=graphdata3(weight=bold)
       valueattrs=graphdata3;
       y2axis offsetmin=0.0 offsetmax=0.25 label="Weight (Kg)" integer
       values=(2 to 18 by 1) labelattrs=graphdata1(weight=bold)
       valueattrs=graphdata1;
run;
```

Note the options on the YAXIS and the Y2AXIS statements. The Y2AXIS has OFFSETMAX=0.25, which means that all items that are associated with it are displayed only in the lower 75% of the graph height. This causes all the "Weight" related items and the axis (drawn in blue) to be drawn in the lower part.

Similarly, the YAXIS has OFFSETMIN =0.25, so all the "Height or Length" related items are drawn in the upper part of the graph. More importantly, the scaling for each axis is independent, allowing us to draw different tick values on the axes. To make the graph easier to read, we have taken care to position the Y grid lines so that they line up with the values on each side.

The program snippet above also shows how we can include the historical data as a tabular display in the chart for easy reference. I have used the INSET statement to create a tabular display. Although the values here are hardcoded, we can use macro variables assigned from the DATA step.

Relevant details are shown in the code snippet above. For full details, see Program 4_14.

## 4.15 Summary

The graphs discussed in this chapter represent a large fraction of the graphs commonly used in the clinical trials industry and in Health and Life Sciences in general. Most of these are "single-cell" graphs where the main data is displayed in one cell in the middle, along with other information.

In this chapter, we have used the SAS 9.4 SGPLOT procedure, which provides you with a large selection of plot statements that can be used to create many graphs on their own. Many of these plot statements can be combined in creative ways to create almost any graph that might be needed. Some new statements, such as the axis tables, and options newly added to SAS 9.4 make it much easier to create these graphs.

The SG Annotate facility further enhances your ability to create custom graphs using the SGPLOT procedure. Although we have not used it in these examples, annotation can be very useful to add some custom details that are otherwise hard to do using plot layers.

Group attributes such as colors or marker symbol shapes can be assigned by specific group values using the Attribute Map feature. This ensures that attributes are correctly mapped regardless of the data order, or whether some groups are present or not.

---

[1] My graph is based on ideas presented in a paper. See Phillips, Stacey D. 2014. "Swimmer Plot: Tell a Graphical Story of Your Time to Response Data Using PROC SGPLOT." *Proceedings of the Pharmaceutical Industry SAS Users Group (PharmaSug) 2014 Conference*. San Diego, CA: SAS Institute Inc. Available at http://www.pharmasug.org/2014-proceedings.html.

# Chapter 5: Clinical Graphs Using the SGPANEL Procedure

In Chapters 3 and 4, we discussed many types of single-cell graphs that are commonly used in the clinical domain. Most of these graphs have only one region for displaying the data. Some of the complex graphs seem to use additional cells to display important items such as the associated table of subjects in the study for a survival plot or the columns of numeric data values in a forest plot.

Graphs like the survival plot or forest plot, especially in SAS 9.4, actually have more than one cell in the generated GTL code. Such additional cells are automatically generated for us by the SGPLOT procedure, and they take care of table placement when those tables are positioned outside the main graph area. So, behind the scenes, these are multi-cell graphs, and we will see more details about them as well as about GTL in Chapters 7 and 8.

Another important type of multi-cell graph is the classification panel shown in Figure 5.0. It was created using the SGPANEL procedure. Note, this graph displays the distribution of Systolic blood pressure by Weight_Status. The procedure determines the number of unique values for the panel variable or variables and creates one cell for each unique value or crossing of the panel variable or variables as shown below. The typical PROC SGPANEL code for the graph is also included.

**Figure 5.0 – Classification Panel Graph**

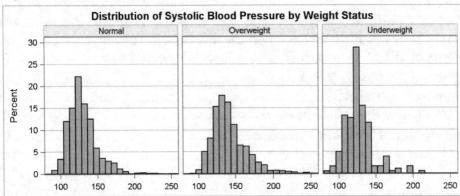

```
title "Distribution of Systolic Blood Pressure by Weight Status";
proc sgpanel data=sashelp.heart;
  panelby weight_status / <options>;
  histogram systolic;
run;
```

These graphs enable us to understand the data by different classifiers. Using the SAS 9.4 SGPANEL procedure, this chapter will review many examples of real-world panel graphs that are commonly used in the clinical domain.

## 5.1 Panel of LFT Shifts from Baseline to Maximum by Treatment

The graph below displays Maximum by Baseline values for four lab results. The classification panel is created using the SGPANEL procedure.

### 5.1.1 Panel of LFT Shifts with Common Clinical Concern Levels

Here is the classification panel with common level of concern lines. The values are grouped by treatment.

**Figure 5.1.1 – Panel of LFT Shifts with Common Clinical Concern Levels**

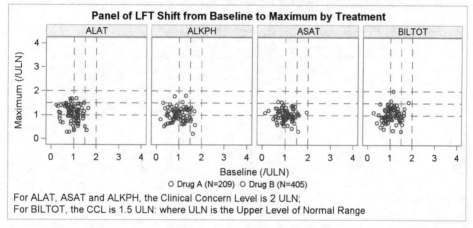

```
title "Panel of LFT Shift from Baseline to Maximum by Treatment";
footnote1 j=l "For ALAT, ASAT and ALKPH, the Clinical Concern Level is 2
ULN;";
footnote2 j=l "For BILTOT, the CCL is 1.5 ULN: where ULN is the Upper
Level of Normal Range";
proc sgpanel data=LFTShiftNorm;
  format Drug $drug.;
  panelby Test / layout=panel columns=4 spacing=10 novarname;
  scatter x=base y=max / group=drug;
  refline 1 1.5 2 / axis=Y lineattrs=(pattern=dash);
  refline 1 1.5 2 / axis=X lineattrs=(pattern=dash);
  rowaxis integer min=0 max=4;
  colaxis integer min=0 max=4;
  keylegend / title="" noborder;
run;
```

Figure 5.1.1 displays a plot of the Maximum values to Baseline by "Test" for subjects in a study. The data is simulated. The Test variable has four distinct values: ALAT, ALKPH, ASAT, and BILTOT. The procedure determines that there are four unique values for the class variable and subdivides the graph area into four cells. Each cell is then populated by the same plots that are specified in the procedure syntax. This includes the scatter plot of Maximum by Baseline by treatment as well as the reference lines. Row and column axis options are specified to customize the axes.

Note the use of two REFLINE statements, one each for the X and the Y reference lines drawn at "1", "1.5", and "2" in each cell. An automatic legend is created and has been customized to exclude the legend title and border. ROWAXIS and COLAXIS statements are used to customize the axes.

For the full code, see Program 5_1, available from the author's page at http://support.sas.com/matange.

## 5.1.2 Panel of LFT Shifts with Individual Clinical Concern Levels

Figure 5.1.2 shows the graph of Maximum by Baseline values for subjects in a study. In the panel, each cell has individual clinical concern level reference lines as indicated by the arrow.

**Figure 5.1.2 – Panel of LFT Shifts with Individual Clinical Concern Levels**

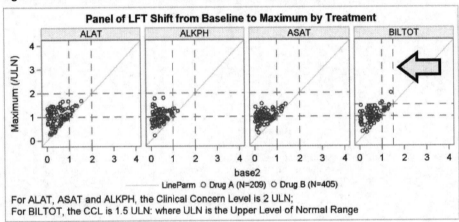

```
title "Panel of LFT Shift from Baseline to Maximum by Treatment";
footnote1 j=l "For ALAT, ASAT and ALKPH, the Clinical Concern Level is 2
ULN;";
footnote2 j=l "For BILTOT, the CCL is 1.5 ULN: where ULN is the Upper
Level of Normal Range";
proc sgpanel data=LFTShiftNormRef;
  format Drug $drug.;
  panelby Test / layout=panel columns=4 spacing=10 novarname;
  scatter x=base y=max / group=drug;
  refline ref / axis=Y lineattrs=(pattern=dash);
  refline ref / axis=X lineattrs=(pattern=dash);
  rowaxis integer min=0 max=4;
  colaxis integer min=0 max=4;
  keylegend / title="" noborder;
run;
```

This graph is very similar to the one shown in Figure 5.1.1 and displays a plot of the Maximum values to Baseline by "Test" for simulated data. The Test variable has four distinct values: ALAT, ALKPH, ASAT, and BILTOT. One cell is created for each unique value of the panel variable.

Each cell is then populated by a scatter plot of Maximum by Baseline by treatment, with a 45-degree line and reference lines. Row and column axis options are specified to customize the axes.

The main difference between Figure 5.1.1 and Figure 5.1.2 is that the reference lines shown in each cell are not all the same. The clinical concern level for ALAT, ASAT, and ALKPH is 2 ULN, and for BILTOT it is 1.5 ULN. Instead of showing reference lines at 1, 1.5, and 2 in each cell, it is preferable to draw the appropriate ULN level for each cell. To do this, the reference values are added to the data set for each cell as appropriate in the "Ref" variable. Only one observation per test value is added to avoid over-plotting.

The REFLINE statement is used to draw these specific reference lines using the "Ref" column. Now the first three cells, one each for ALAT, ALKPH, and ASAT, have reference lines at 1.0 and 2.0. By contrast, the fourth cell has reference lines at 1 and 1.5 as indicated in Figure 5.1.2 by the arrow.

For the full code, see Program 5_1.

## 5.2 Immunology Profile by Treatment

The graph in Figure 5.2.1 displays immunology values over time by drug and lab parameters for eight different subjects as indicated in the legend. Lab values for each subject are represented as a series plot.

### 5.2.1 Immunology Panel

Four cycles of 30 days each are displayed in each cell, marked by the colored zones. The values 1 to 12 on the x-axis are replaced to show four cycles of 0 to 30 using the VALUESDISPLAY option.

**Figure 5.2.1 – Immunology Panel**

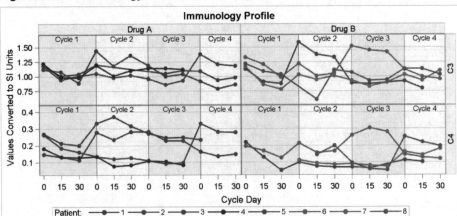

```
title "Immunology Profile";
proc sgpanel data=immune2;
   panelby trt lbparm / layout=lattice novarname uniscale=column;
   block x=xval block=cyc / transparency = .75 filltype=alternate;
   series x=xval y=sival / group=pt name='a' markers
          lineattrs=(thickness=2) markerattrs=(symbol=circlefilled);
   colaxis values=(1 to 12 by 1) integer label='Cycle Day'
        valuesdisplay=("0" "15" "30" "0" "15" "30"
                       "0" "15" "30" "0" "15" "30");
   rowaxis offsetmax=.1 label="Values Converted to SI Units " grid;
   keylegend 'a' / title="Patient:";
run;
```

This is done by plotting the data over x values of 1-12, and labeling each of the three values (in a cycle) as "0", "15", and "30" using the VALUEDISPLAY option.

A BLOCK plot statement is used to display the cycles using X=xval and BLOCK=cyc. An alternate coloring scheme is used to display the blocks for each cycle. See Program 5_2 for the full code.

## 5.2.2 Immunology Panel in Grayscale

Here is the immunology panel using the grayscale medium. Each patient is represented by a curve using different marker shapes--four filled and four unfilled.

**Figure 5.2.2 – Immunology Panel in Grayscale**

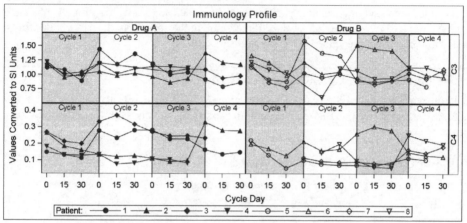

```
ods listing style=journal;
title "Immunology Profile";
proc sgpanel data=immune2;
  styleattrs datasymbols=(circlefilled trianglefilled diamondfilled
                          triangledownfilled circle triangle diamond
                          triangledown);
  panelby trt lbparm / layout=lattice novarname uniscale=column;
  block x=xval block=cyc / filltype=alternate;
  series x=xval y=sival / group=pt lineattrs=(pattern=solid)
        markers markerattrs=(color=cx2f2f2f size=8) name='a';

  colaxis values=(1 to 12 by 1) integer label='Cycle Day'
      valuesdisplay=("0" "15" "30" "0" "15" "30"
                     "0" "15" "30" "0" "15" "30");
  rowaxis offsetmax=.1 label="Values Converted to SI Units " grid;
  keylegend 'a' / title="Patient:";
run;
```

This graph displays immunology values over time by drug and lab parameter for eight different subjects. Lab values for each subject are represented by a series plot classified by treatment and lab values similar to the graph in Section 5.2.1.

The main difference is the output is in grayscale using the Journal style. By default, the Journal style uses patterned lines for drawing the line plots by patient. So, each patient would get a line of a different pattern.

However, line patterns can often get a bit confusing. So here I have set the line pattern for all curves to solid with a 1-pixel thickness. I have used the STYLEATTRS statement to assign eight different markers, one for each patient. An alternate fill color for the band plot is set to white with full opacity for clarity. See Program 5_2 for the full code.

## 5.3 LFT Safety Panel, Baseline vs Study

This graph displays the study by baseline (/ULN) values for each lab test by visit for all subjects in a study. I have reduced the number of rows to fit the graph in the space, but the same code will work for any number of unique values of labs or visits.

### 5.3.1 LFT Safety Panel, Baseline vs Study

Figure 5.3.1 displays a panel of Study by Baseline values (/ULN) by "Labtest" and "VisitNum". The results are classified by "LabTest" as the column classifier and "VisitNum" as the row classifier.

**Figure 5.3.1 – LFT Safety Panel, Baseline vs Study**

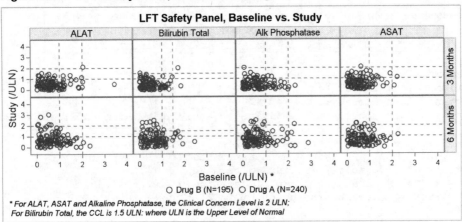

```
proc sgpanel data=labs(where=(visitnum ne 1));
panelby labtest visitnum / layout=lattice onepanel novarname;
   scatter x=baseline y=study/ group=drug markerattrs=(size=9)
           nomissinggroup;
   refline ref / axis=Y lineattrs=(pattern=shortdash);
   refline ref / axis=X lineattrs=(pattern=shortdash);
   rowaxis integer min=0 max=4 label='Study (/ULN)' valueattrs=(size=7);
   colaxis integer min=0 max=4 label='Baseline (/ULN) *'
           valueattrs=(size=7);;
   keylegend/title=" " noborder;
run;
```

Values for the different reference lines are added to the end of the data set for each visit and test. For "Billirubin Total", the clinical concern level is 1.5, and the correct reference lines are drawn in each cell.

As you can see, a relatively complex graph can be created using a few lines of code and the SGPANEL procedure. See Program 5_3 for the full code.

## 5.3.2 LFT Safety Panel, Baseline vs Study

This graph shows the LFT panel by lab test and visit in grayscale.

**Figure 5.3.2 – LFT Safety Panel, Baseline vs Study in Grayscale**

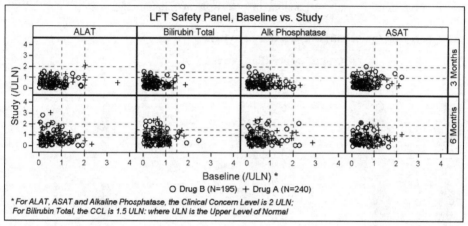

```
ods listing style=journal;
proc sgpanel data=labs(where=(visitnum ne 1));
panelby labtest visitnum / layout=lattice onepanel novarname;
  scatter x=baseline y=study/ group=drug markerattrs=(size=9)
          nomissinggroup;
  refline ref / axis=Y lineattrs=(pattern=shortdash);
  refline ref / axis=X lineattrs=(pattern=shortdash);
  rowaxis integer min=0 max=4 label='Study (/ULN)' valueattrs=(size=7);
  colaxis integer min=0 max=4 label='Baseline (/ULN) *'
          valueattrs=(size=7);;
  keylegend/title=" " noborder;
run;
```

This graph displays the study by baseline values for each lab test by visit for all subjects in a study. The graph is shown in grayscale using the Journal style. The results are classified by "LabTest" as column classifier and "Visit" as the row classifier. I have reduced the number of rows to fit the graph in the space, but the same code will work for any number of unique values of labs or visits.

Values for the different reference lines are added to the end of the data set for each visit and test. For "Billirubin Total", the clinical concern level is 1.5, and the correct reference lines are drawn in each cell.

As you can see, a relatively complex graph can be created using a few lines of code and the SGPANEL procedure. See Program 5_3 for the full code.

## 5.4 Lab Test Panel

This graph shows the lab results for WBC and Differential by visit for all subjects in the study by visit. Different lab values are shown in the panel of rows, with one row for each lab value.

### 5.4.1 Lab Test Panel with Clinical Concern Limits

This graph shows the results for only two lab tests to fit the space. This will work equally well if the line classifier has multiple values. Each lab test has its own Y data range.

**Figure 5.4.1 – Lab Test Panel with Clinical Concern Limits**

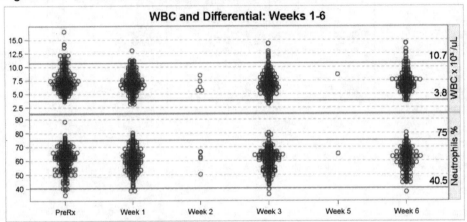

```
title 'WBC and Differential: Weeks 1-6';
proc sgpanel data=labs2;
  panelby line / onepanel uniscale=column layout=rowlattice novarname;
  refline numlow / label noclip;
  refline numhi / label noclip;
  scatter x=visitnum y=result / jitter transparency=0.5;
  rowaxis display=(nolabel) valueattrs=(size=7) grid
          gridattrs=(pattern=dash);
  colaxis display=(nolabel) offsetmax=0.1 valueattrs=(size=7)
          type=discrete;
run;
```

The name of the test is shown in the row header on the right. Note the use of Unicode characters ($10^3$) in the header of the top row. This is done by specifying Unicode values in the format for the column.

Also note, the range of data on the y-axis is not uniform. The y-axis for each row shows the data range that is appropriate for each test. Clinical concern levels are displayed as reference lines with values for the lower and upper levels on the right. Each lab test has different CCL values, so these values have to be inserted into the data for plotting. The scatter plot is "jittered", so that we can see the values spread out over the midpoint range. Discrete jittering is used by setting the COLAXIS TYPE=Discrete.

The actual lab panel can have many rows, and the panel will break up into multiple pages if needed. In this example, I have restricted the number of labs to two to fit the space. As you can see, a relatively complex graph can be created using a few lines of code and the SGPANEL procedure. See Program 5_4 for the full code.

## 5.4.2 Lab Test Panel with Box Plot, Band, and Inset Line Name

The clinical concern levels are included in this graph as a band plot for clarity and easier comparison with the values for the subjects in the study.

**Figure 5.4.2 – Lab Test Panel with Box Plot, Band, and Inset Line Name**

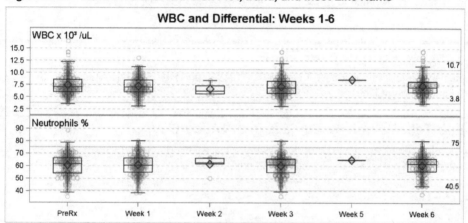

```
title 'WBC and Differential: Weeks 1-6';
proc sgpanel data=labs2 noautolegend;
  panelby line /onepanel uniscale=column layout=rowlattice noheader;
  band x=visitnum lower=numlow upper=numhi / transparency=0.9
        fillattrs=(color=yellow) legendlabel='Limits';
  refline numlow / label noclip lineattrs=(color=cxdfdfdf)
        labelattrs=(size=7);
  refline numhi / label noclip  lineattrs=(color=cxdfdfdf)
        labelattrs=(size=7);
  scatter x=visitnum y=result / transparency=0.9 jitter;
  vbox result / category=visitnum nofill nooutliers;
  inset label / position=topleft nolabel textattrs=(size=9);
  rowaxis display=(nolabel) offsetmax=0.15 grid gridattrs=(pattern=dash);
  colaxis display=(nolabel)  valueattrs=(size=7);
run;
```

This graph shows the lab results for WBC and Differential by visit as described in Section 5.4.1. Different lab values are shown in the panel of rows, with one row for each lab value. In this example, we have displayed the results as a box plot, with overlaid scatter. The scatter plot is "jittered", so that we can see the values spread out over the midpoint range. This allows us to get a better feel for the distribution of the data.

The clinical concern levels are displayed as band plots. The concern level values are still displayed using the REFLINE statements. COLAXIS TYPE=Discrete is not necessary, as the box plot causes the axis to be discrete by default.

Note, the names of each lab test are no longer displayed in a row header on the right side. Such rotated text in the row headers is not optimal for readability. Instead, I have disabled the display of the header entirely by setting the NOHEADER option in the PANELBY statement. . Then, each lab test name is displayed horizontally in the top left corner of each cell using the INSET statement. The result is much more readable.

Some code details are trimmed to fit the page. See Program 5_4 for the full code.

## 5.5  Lab Test for Patient over Time

This graph displays test values for ALAT, ASAT, ALKPH, and BILTOT over study days by subject. The data is simulated.

### 5.5.1  Lab Test Values by Subject over Study Days

The graph is classified by patient ID for three patients as an illustration. All values are plotted from a scale of 0.0-4.0 on the y-axis and by study days on the x-axis.

**Figure 5.5.1 – Lab Test Values by Subject over Study Days**

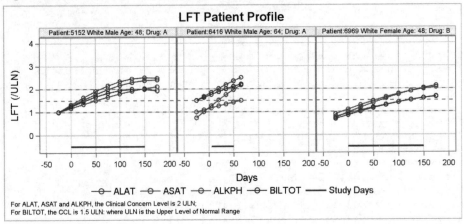

```
ods graphics / reset attrpriority=color;
proc sgpanel data=Safety;
  panelby patient / novarname columns=3 headerattrs=(size=6);
  series x=days y=alat / markers;
  series x=days y=asat / markers;
  series x=days y=alkph / markers;
  series x=days y=biltot / markers;
  series x=days y=dval / lineattrs=graphdatadefault(thickness=2px);
  refline 1 1.5 2 / axis=Y lineattrs=(pattern=shortdash);
```

```
     colaxis min=-50 max= 200 valueattrs=(size=7) labelattrs=(size=9) grid;
     rowaxis max=4 label="LFT (/ULN)" valueattrs=(size=7) grid;
     keylegend / noborder linelength=25;
run;
```

Gridlines are displayed for each axis, along with reference lines for the clinical concern levels of 1.0, 1.5, and 2.0. The duration of the study is indicated using a horizontal line at the bottom of the graph. I have restricted the number of patients to three and set the number of columns to three in order to create a graph that fits in the page.

The number of unique patients does not need to be limited, and the graph will automatically "page" to create multiple graphs with a set number of cells. See Program 5_5 for the full code.

## 5.5.2 Lab Test Values by Subject with Study Days Band

This graph shows the lab test values by patient ID. The study days are indicated by the band.

**Figure 5.5.2 – Lab Test Values by Subject with Study Days Band**

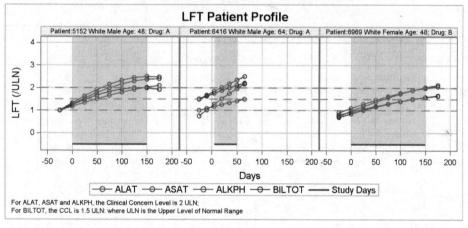

```
ods graphics / reset attrpriority=color;
proc sgpanel data=Safety cycleattrs;
  panelby patient / novarname columns=3 headerattrs=(size=6);
  series x=days y=alat / markers name='a';
  series x=days y=asat / markers name='b';
  series x=days y=alkph / markers name='c';
  series x=days y=biltot / markers name='d';
  series x=days y=dval / lineattrs=graphdatadefault(thickness=2px)
         name='e';
  band x=sdays lower=dval upper=4.5 / transparency=0.6;
  refline 1 1.5 2 / axis=Y lineattrs=(pattern=dash);
  colaxis min=-50 max= 200 valueattrs=(size=7) labelattrs=(size=9) grid;
  rowaxis label="LFT (/ULN)" valueattrs=(size=7)
         labelattrs=(size=9) grid;
  keylegend 'a' 'b' 'c' 'd' 'e' / linelength=25;
run;
```

This graph displays test values for ALAT, ASAT, ALKPH, and BILTOT over study days by Subject as in Section 5.5.1. The data is simulated for illustration of the technique only. All values are plotted from a scale of 0.0-4.0 on the y-axis, and study days on the x-axis. Patient is used as the panel variable, creating a graph with three cells, one for each patient.

Gridlines are displayed for each axis along with reference lines for the clinical concern levels of 1.0, 1.5, and 2.0. The duration of the study is indicated using a horizontal line at the bottom of the graph and also a band extending the height of the graph. This provides for a better view of the data that is within the study duration. See Program 5_5 for the full code.

## 5.6 Vital Statistics for Patient over Time

This graph displays different vital statistics values for a specific subject over time. In this case I have retained systolic and diastolic blood pressure and pulse to fit the graph in the space available. In a real-world use case you can have many unique values for the panel variable. The cells will be automatically split over multiple pages of the graphs, while still retaining uniform axes across pages.

### 5.6.1 Vital Statistics for Patient over Time

Figure 5.6.1 shows as a traditional LATTICE layout with the class values on the right.

**Figure 5.6.1 – Vital Statistics for Patient over Time**

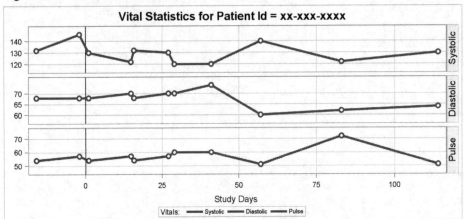

```
ods graphics / attrpriority=color;
title "Vital Statistics for Patient Id = xx-xxx-xxxx";
proc sgpanel data=vss noautolegend nocycleattrs;
  panelby vstest2 / onepanel layout=rowlattice uniscale=column
          novarname spacing=10 sort=data;
  refline 0 / axis=x lineattrs=(thickness=1 color=black);
  series x=vsdy y=vsstresn / group=vstest2 lineattrs=(thickness=3)
          name='bp' markerattrs=(symbol=circlefilled size=11)
          nomissinggroup;
```

```
   scatter x=vsdy y=vsstresn / group=vstest2 markerattrs=(size=11);
   scatter x=vsdy y=vsstresn / group=vstest2 markerattrs=(size=5);
   keylegend 'bp' / title='Vitals:' across=3 linelength=20;
   rowaxis grid display=(nolabel) valueattrs=(size=7) labelattrs=(size=8);
   colaxis grid label='Study Days' valueattrs=(size=7)
           labelattrs=(size=8);
run;
```

The data set is sorted by test value in the order I want, and I have used the SORT=Data option to get the rows in the data order.

The panel variable is VSTEST2, unique values of which are shown in the row headers on the right. Multiple scatter plots are used to render the markers that are shown. ATTRPRIORITY is set to Color, so that all groups of the series plots have a solid pattern. Thus, we can reduce the length of the line in the legend using the LINELENGTH option.

Some options in the code above are trimmed to fit the space.  See Program 5_6 for the full code.

## 5.6.2  Vital Statistics for Patient over Time

In a traditional LATTICE layout, the class values are displayed on the right, rotated vertically. This can often be hard to read or notice.  In this example, the traditional row headers are suppressed, and the class values are displayed inside the cells.

**Figure 5.6.2 – Vital Statistics for Patient over Time**

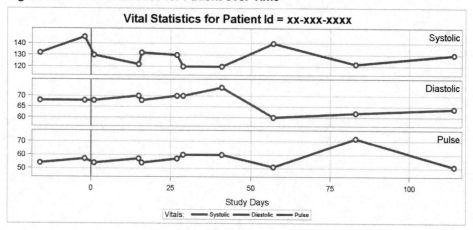

```
ods graphics / attrpriority=color;
title "Vital Statistics for Patient Id = xx-xxx-xxxx";
proc sgpanel data=vss noautolegend nocycleattrs;
  panelby vstest2 / onepanel layout=rowlattice uniscale=column novarname
          spacing=10 noheader sort=data;
  refline 0 / axis=x lineattrs=(thickness=1 color=black);
  series x=vsdy y=vsstresn / group=vstest2 lineattrs=(thickness=3)
          nomissinggroup name='bp';
```

```
    scatter x=vsdy y=vsstresn / group=vstest2
           markerattrs=( circlefilled size=11);
    scatter x=vsdy y=vsstresn / group=vstest2
           markerattrs=(symbol=circlefilled size=5 color=white);
    inset vstest2 / nolabel position=topright textattrs=(size=9);
    keylegend 'bp' / title='Vitals:' across=3 linelength=20;
    rowaxis grid display=(nolabel);
    colaxis grid label='Study Days';
run;
```

Figure 5.6.2 displays different vital statistics values for a specific subject over time, similar to the graph in Section 5.5.1. In this case, I have retained systolic and diastolic blood pressure and pulse to fit the graph in the space available. The data set is sorted by test value in the order I want, and I have used the SORT=Data option to get the rows in the data order.

The panel variable is VSTEST2, unique values of which are shown in the row headers on the right. Multiple scatter plots are used to render the markers that are shown.

Vertically oriented text in the row headers is harder to read, so in this graph I have suppressed the headers using the NOHEADER option and displayed the test values in the top right corner of each cell using the INSET statement.

Some options in the code above are trimmed to fit the space. See Program 5_6 for the full code.

## 5.7 Eye Irritation over Time by Severity and Treatment

This graph shows the percentage of subjects with eye irritation over time by severity and treatment.

### 5.7.1 Eye Irritation over Time by Severity and Treatment

The values are stacked with "None" and "Mild" above the baseline using positive values, and "Moderate", "Severe", "Very Severe", and below the baseline using negative values. The group values are colored to indicate the intensity using the STYLEATTERS option.

**Figure 5.7.1 – Eye Irritation over Time by Severity and Treatment**

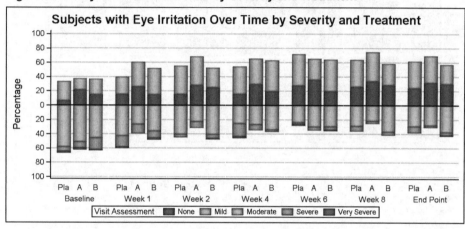

```
title "Subjects with Eye Irritation Over Time by Severity and
Treatment";
proc sgpanel data=eye;
  where param=1;
  format percent abs.;
  panelby time / layout=columnlattice onepanel noborder
          colheaderpos=bottom novarname noheaderborder;
  styleattrs datacolors=(darkgreen lightgreen gold orange red);
  vbar trtgrp / response=percent group=value dataskin=pressed;
  colaxis display=(nolabel noticks);
  rowaxis values=(-100 to 100 by 20) grid offsetmax=0.025;
  keylegend / fillheight=2pct fillaspect=golden;
run;
```

The bars are stacked by severity and clustered by treatment for each visit. We know that a bar chart can support either stacked or clustered grouping, but not both at the same time. A COLUMNLATTICE layout is used to display the graph. Cell headers are displayed at the bottom without header borders so that they look like category (Visit) values. The treatment values are shown above the visit for each bar.

Legend items are made wider for easier viewing using legend options. Some appearance options in the code above are trimmed to fit the space. See Program 5_7 for the full code.

## 5.7.2 Vital Statistics for Patient over Time in Grayscale

This graph shows the percentage of subjects with eye irritation over time by severity and treatment in a grayscale medium using gray shades and fill patterns.

**Figure 5.7.2 – Vital Statistics for Patient over Time in Grayscale**

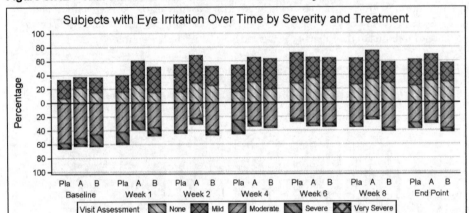

```
ods lisitng style=journal3;
title "Subjects with Eye Irritation Over Time by Severity and Treatment";
proc sgpanel data=eye;
  where param=1;
  format percent abs.;
  panelby time / layout=columnlattice onepanel noborder
          colheaderpos=bottom novarname noheaderborder;
  vbar trtgrp / response=percent group=value dataskin=pressed;
  colaxis display=(nolabel noticks);
  rowaxis values=(-100 to 100 by 20) grid offsetmax=0.025;
  keylegend / fillheight=3pct fillaspect=golden;
run;
```

The values are stacked with "None" and "Mild" above the baseline using positive values, and "Moderate", "Severe", "Very Severe", and below the baseline using negative values. Group values use colors and fill patterns as specified in the Journal3 style.

The bars are stacked by severity and clustered by treatment for each visit.  Again, we know that a bar chart can support either stacked or clustered grouping, but not both at the same time.  A COLUMNLATTICE layout is used to display the graph.  Cell headers are displayed at the bottom without header borders so that they look like category (Visit) values.   The treatment values are shown above the visit value for each bar.

Legend items are made wider for easier viewing using legend options.  Some appearance options in the code above are trimmed to fit the space.  See Program 5_7 for the full code.

## 5.8 Summary

Multi-cell panel graphs by one or more classification variables are very common in the clinical domain. Such graphs can be tedious to create with traditional software, when you must create each cell separately and then replay these together into one gridded layout. It is a challenge to ensure uniformity across all cells.

The SGPANEL procedure does this work for us, based on one or more classification variables. The graph includes a cell for each crossing of the class variables, arranged in a grid. If the grid is large, the procedure automatically breaks up the grid into smaller clusters that are easier to print or handle.

Four different layouts are available, and you can use the one that is most appropriate for your use case.

- PANEL – Supports one or more (N) class variables and creates a cell for each crossing of the class variables that has data. So, if a cell does not contain data, it is skipped entirely. This layout is very useful for "sparse" data sets, where there are many crossings, but not many actual cells.

  Each cell has a cell header at the top that includes the values of each class variable. When there are many class variables, much of the cell space might be taken up by the headers. This can be alleviated by suppressing the headers and adding the information in each cell using the INSET option as described in Section 5.4.2.

- COLUMNLATTICE – Supports one class variable and creates a grid of columns (one row). All cells are retained regardless of whether they have data or not. Each column has a column header that includes the value of the class variable.

- ROWLATTICE – Supports one class variable and creates a grid of rows (one column). All cells are retained regardless of whether they have data or not. Each row has a row header that includes the value of the class variable.

- LATTICE – Supports two class variables, where the first class variable is used for columns and the second for rows. A cell is created for each crossing of the unique values of the class variables, even if they are devoid of data. Each column has a column header, and each row has a row header showing the value of the class variable.

These graphs automatically enforce uniform axes. All y-axes for the rows and all x-axes for the columns have uniform scale. This can be customized as needed by using the UNISCALE option.

However, as we showed in Figure 5.4, when creating a panel of lab results in which each lab has a different scale of data, it is important that such a scale **not** be made uniform.

As can be seen from the various examples in this chapter, it is very easy to create relatively complex multi-cell classification graphs using this procedure.

# Chapter 6: A Brief Review of the Graph Template Language

The Graph Template Language, commonly referred to as GTL, is the syntax that is used to define the structure of a graph in a StatGraph template using the TEMPLATE procedure. We associate the appropriate data with this template to render a graph. This process is used behind the scenes for all procedures and applications that create statistical graphs in SAS, including the SAS analytical procedures, SG procedures, and ODS Graphics Designer.

You, the SAS user, can also use this process to create your own graphs. After a template is created, it can be saved and reused with different data sets--as long as the data types are compatible.

GTL provides you with a structured syntax to define the graph, from simple single-cell graphs like a bar chart or scatter plot to complex, multi-cell layouts and multi-cell classification panels.

## 6.1 Getting Started

Creating a graph using GTL is a two-step process:

1. Define the structure of the graph in the form of the StatGraph template using GTL. The typical syntax is shown below. When you submit this step, the template code is compiled. Grammar syntax errors are written to the log and, if no errors are found, the template is compiled and saved. No graph is created.

```
proc template;
  define statgraph template-name;
    begingraph / <options>;
      <gtl statements to define the graph>
    endgraph;
  end;
run;
```

When the template is successfully compiled, the following note is written to the log:

```
NOTE: STATGRAPH 'template-name' has been saved to: SASUSER.TEMPLAT
```

2. Associate compatible data with the template using the SGRENDER procedure to create the graph.

```
proc sgrender data=data-set-name template=template-name;
  <other optional statements>
run;
```

When the graph is successfully created, the following notes are written to the log:

```
NOTE: There were xx observations read from the data set data-set-
name.
NOTE: PROCEDURE SGRENDER used (Total process time):
real time           x.xx seconds
cpu time            y.yy seconds
```

Variable names can be hard-coded in the template, such as "Height", "Weight", or "Age", as in the SASHELP.CLASS data set. The SGRENDER procedure will validate that variable names that are used in the template are present in the specified data set with compatible types (numeric or character). If everything is in order, a graph will be created. If some issues are found, such as incompatible data or missing data for the whole column, then error or warning messages are written to the log.

When running either of the steps above, it is always a good idea to check the log for compilation or execution errors.

## 6.2 A Simple GTL Graph

Let us start with an example of a commonly used graph to understand the workings of GTL. Here is a graph showing the distribution of Cholesterol for the SASHELP.HEART data set. The code for the template step and the render step is shown on the left in Figure 6.2, and the resulting graph is shown on the right.

**Figure 6.2 – A Simple GTL Graph**

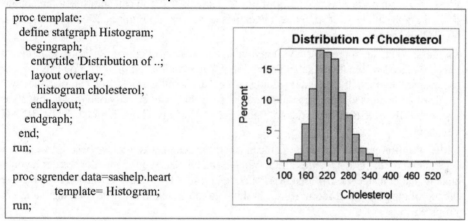

Here are the key parts of the code:

1. The name of the template is "Histogram".
2. The entire GTL code is inside the BEGINGRAPH – ENDGRAPH code block.
3. A title is added using the ENTRYTITLE statement.
4. This graph has one data cell defined by the LAYOUT OVERLAY - ENDLAYOUT block.
5. The cell contains a histogram of the "Cholesterol" variable.

6. The PROC TEMPLATE step compiles and saves the template.

7. The PROC SGRENDER step associates the data with the template in order to create the graph.

The graph shown above is a single-cell graph, with one cell that is defined by the LAYOUT OVERLAY block. GTL enables you to define graphs that range from the simplest single-cell graph shown above to highly complex panels with user-defined layouts as well as classification panels of one or more class variables.

The structure of a GTL graph is defined by placing plot statements within layout statements along with statements for items such as titles, footnotes, entries, legends, and more, as described below.

Here are key GTL components:

1. **Plots:** GTL supports a large variety of plot statements that you can combine to create the desired graph. Plots determine how the data is displayed. In Figure 6.2 we have used one HISTOGRAM statement.

2. **Layouts:** GTL supports a variety of layout statements or containers. All plot statements must be placed within layouts that determine where the plots are drawn. You can use layouts to manage the graph area, creating single-cell or multi-cell graphs. You can nest the layouts inside other layouts to create complex graphs. But there can be only one root layout statement inside the BEGINGRAPH block. In Figure 6.2, we have used one LAYOUT OVERLAY container.

3. **Titles, Footnotes, and Entries:** You can use these statements to place descriptive textual information in the graph. Titles and footnotes can be placed only outside the root layout statement and inside the BEGINGRAPH code block. All titles are automatically displayed at the top of the graph, and footnotes are at the bottom, placed in the order that they are provided.

4. **Axes:** Each cell of the graph can have up to two sets of x- and y-axes. The axes for multi-cell graphs can be independent or uniform. Common row and column axes can be used. Axes are available in different types such as linear, log, time, and category.

5. **Legends:** Your graph can have multiple legends, both discrete and continuous. Legends can be inside the cell data area or outside the data area. Legends can contain contributions from one or more plots in the graph or include predefined LEGENDITEMS statements.

6. **Attribute maps:** Starting with SAS 9.3, you can assign visual attributes for plot elements based on data value. For example, you can define a discrete attribute map specifying which visual attributes are to be assigned for "Drug A". This will be done regardless of its order in the data. Similarly, colors for continuous data ranges can be assigned.

7. **Dynamic variables and macro variables:** You can create templates with hard-coded variable names. In Figure 6.2, we have used the "Cholesterol" variable. You can also use dynamic variables or macro variables instead. These can be assigned at run time to make your template design more flexible.

8. **Expressions and conditional statements:** You can use expressions within the GTL syntax to assign computed data to a plot role. Also, the behavior of the template can be controlled by using conditional statements in the template, often using dynamic variables.

9. **Styles and plot attributes:** Visual attributes for all elements of the graph are derived from the active style for the open destination. Each destination has a default style that has been carefully designed to create an aesthetically pleasing graph. In addition, you can assign custom attributes to all plot elements using options.

10. **Graph:** All GTL statements must be placed inside the BEGINGRAPH – ENDGRAPH block. There can be only one such block in the template.

11. **In-line draw:** Starting with SAS 9.3, you can add arbitrary graphical elements anywhere in the graph using the draw statements. The components can be drawn relative to the origin of any container--including the whole graph.

12. **Annotations:** Starting with SAS 9.4, you can add arbitrary graphical elements anywhere in the graph using the SGAnno data set. This data set contains specific column names for drawing actions, and each observation represents one drawing action.

A GTL graph can be defined by using the above components or statements in countless combinations. Thus, you can define literally any graph.

## 6.3 GTL Graphs and Terminology

It will be useful for us to use a common terminology for referring to various components of a GTL graph listed the following chapters. The terminology applicable to all graphs is shown in Figure 6.3 below. Graphs can be of the following types:

- Single-cell graph
- Multi-cell graph
- Multi-cell classification panel

**Figure 6.3 – GTL Graphs and Terminology**

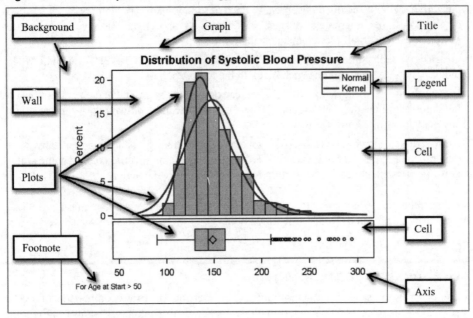

A typical graph has the following components:

- Zero or more titles at the top of the graph.
- Zero or more footnotes at the bottom of the graph.
- One or more data regions called "Cells" for display of the data. The graph in Figure 6.3 has two cells, one for the histogram and one for the box plot.
- One or more plots that are used to display the data in each cell.
- Zero or more legends or insets that can be placed inside or outside the data area.

We refer to every statement that displays the data as a "plot", regardless of whether it is a series plot, scatter plot, bar chart, or histogram.

**Graph:** Refers to the individual output created by the procedure. In most of the common use cases, each execution of the SGRENDER procedure creates one graph output file. Often these procedures produce multiple output files (for BY-variable use or for paging of large panels), each of which is referred to as a "Graph".

**Cell:** Each graph can have one or more data areas to display the data as shown in Figure 6.3. Each one of these is referred to as a "Cell". A cell might or might not have axes.

**Plot statements:** Each plot statement is responsible for drawing only its own data representation. The container tells the plot where the data is to be drawn, and how to scale the data appropriately.

**Layout statements:** The layouts determine how the plot statements are placed in relation to each other. For example, in LAYOUT OVERLAY, all plot statements are stacked in one cell in the order in which they are specified. All plots share the layout axes. In LAYOUT LATTICE, plot statements are placed in individual cells, one per statement.

**Axes:** The axes belong to individual cells. The x- and y-axes are shared by all the plots in the cell. The data range for each axis is determined by the plots in the cell. Each cell can have a second set of axes, called X2 (at the top) and Y2 (on the right). Each plot can specify which axes to use.

**Legends**: A graph can have zero or more legends, and each can be placed in any part of the graph. Each legend can specify the information to be displayed in it.

## 6.4 GTL Plot Statements

GTL supports many plot statements, grouped in six major categories such as basic, categorical, distribution, fit, parametric and other.

### 6.4.1 Basic Plots

These plots display all the observations from the data set in the graph. This could be one marker per observation, or it could be a derived line or band where every observation is represented.

- BANDPLOT
- BLOCKPLOT
- BUBBLEPLOT (SAS 9.3)
- DENDOGRAM (SAS 9.3)
- FRINGEPLOT
- HIGHLOWPLOT (SAS 9.3)
- NEEDLEPLOT
- POLYGONPLOT (SAS 9.4)
- SCATTERPLOT
- SERIESPLOT
- STEPPLOT
- TEXTPLOT (SAS 9.4)
- VECTORPLOT

### 6.4.2 Categorical Plots

These plots display summarized data by category and group.

- BARCHART
- LINECHART (SAS 9.3)
- PIECHART (SAS 9.3)
- WATERFALLCHART (SAS 9.3)

### 6.4.3 Distribution Plots

These plots display the distribution of an analysis variable with or without a classifier.

- BOXPLOT
- DENSITYPLOT
- ELLIPSE
- HISTOGRAM

### 6.4.4 Fit Plots

These plots display a computed fit curve to the detailed data.

- LOESSPLOT
- PBSPLINEPLOT
- REGRESSIOPLOT
- MODELBAND

### 6.4.5 Parametric Plots

These plots are "basic" versions of the categorical or distribution plots, where the user has already computed the display values before using the plot statements.

- BARCHARTPARM
- BOXPLOTPARM
- CONTOURPLOTPARM
- ELLIPSEPARM
- HEATMAPPARM (SAS 9.3)
- HISTOGRAMPARM
- LINEPARM
- MOSAICPLOTPARM (SAS 9.3)

## 6.4.6 3-D Plots

GTL supports two types of 3-D plots that display a response on the vertical z-axis by x-y. These can be used only in the LAYOUT OVERLAY3D container, and can be used alone, or with each other.

- BIHISTOGRAM3DPARM
- SURFACEPLOTPARM

## 6.4.7 Other Plots

These are special plot statements that do not fit into one of the previous categories.

- AXISTABLE (SAS 9.4)
- DROPLINE
- HEATMAP (SAS 9.4)
- REFERENCELINE
- SCATTERPLOTMATRIX

# 6.5 GTL Layout Statements

GTL supports many layout statements or containers to arrange the plots or to manage the area of the graph.

## 6.5.1 The Graph Container

This is the outermost container for every StatGraph template. Every StatGraph template must have one and only one BEGINGRAPH code block that must contain all subsequent statements or code blocks. There can be only a single nested tree of layouts.

## 6.5.2 Single-Cell Layouts

A single-cell graph can be created using one of these layout containers. Alternatively, some of these layouts can be used inside LAYOUT LATTICE or GRIDDED to define a cell that has multiple layers of plot statements.

LAYOUT OVERLAY

This is the workhorse of the GTL layouts. It defines one cell with two or more axes that can contain multiple layers of plots to create a composite plot.

LAYOUT OVERLAYEQUATED

This layout is similar to the LAYOUT OVERLAY, with the special feature that the ranges of the x- and y-axes are equated. This layout ensures that a data range interval (say, 10 units) is represented by the same number of pixels (say, 100) on each x- and y-axis. This ensures that a line of slope=1 is displayed at 45 degrees in the graph, and it ensures that a circle is round.

LAYOUT REGION
> This layout does not have axes. It can contain plots like pie charts and diagrams that do not have external axes. Only one plot can be placed in this layout at a time.

LAYOUT OVERLAY3D
> This layout is for 3-D plots and can contain only the bivariate histogram and surface plot or a combination.

## 6.5.3 Multi-cell Ad Hoc Layouts

These layouts are used to subdivide the graph area into a regular grid of cells. Each cell can then be populated by another nested layout, a plot, or other statements.

LAYOUT GRIDDED
> This layout subdivides the graph region into a regular grid of cells. Each cell can then be populated by a nested layout, a plot, or other statements, or by one of the single-cell layouts.

LAYOUT LATTICE
> This layout subdivides the graph region into a regular grid of cells. Each cell can then be populated by a nested layout, a plot, or other statements. This layout supports use of common external axes and provides additional structures like side bars, and row and column headers to contain other components. This layout provides a very comprehensive set of features to create complex plot panels.

## 6.5.4 Multi-Cell Classification Panels

These layouts support the creation of classification panel graphs, where the graph region is divided into a regular grid of cells based on the number of crossings of the unique values of the classification variables. Each cell of the panel is populated by the same plot types.

LAYOUT DATALATTICE
> This layout can create a rectangular layout of cells based on two classifiers, one for row and one for column. A cell is created for each crossing of the two class variables. Cells are created for crossings that do not have data. However, these cells are empty.

LAYOUT DATAPANEL
> This layout can create a rectangular layout of cells based on crossings of one or more (N) class variables. A cell is created for each crossing of the unique values of the class variables. If some crossings do not have data, those cells are skipped.

LAYOUT PROTOTYPE
> This layout allows the definition of the composite graph that is to be populated into each cell of the data panel or data lattice.

## 6.6  GTL Title, Footnote, and Entry Statements

You can add multiple titles and footnotes to the graph. All titles are displayed at the top of the graph. All footnotes are displayed at the bottom of the graph. Text entries can be added in any cell or in the interior of a graph. Rich text and Unicode characters are supported.

## 6.7  GTL Legend Statements

You can add discrete legends to your graph for interpretation of the group classifiers in the data. Legends can be added inside or outside the data area.

You can also add gradient or continuous color legend for interpretation of the color response information in the graph.

## 6.8  GTL Attribute Maps

Attribute maps enable you to assign specific visual attributes to group levels or to ranges of continuous data. Starting with SAS 9.3, you can use both discrete and range attribute maps to define attributes based on data value. These work in a way that is similar to user-defined formats.

By default, visual attributes for group data such as color, marker symbol, and so on are assigned using the GRAPHDATA1 – GRAPHDATA12 style elements based on their order of occurrence in the data. The assignment of the attributes can change from day to day based on the order or presence of the group values.

A DISCRETEATTRMAP statement can be used to define exactly which attributes are to be used for display of groups by their value. You can use this to ensure that specific group values in the data are represented in the graph with specific colors.

Gradient colors for a color response variable are obtained from the THREECOLORRAMP style element by default. You can use the COLORMODEL option in most plot statements to set the colors to be used. In this case, the data range from the plot is used to map the colors. For full control of the colors and the values, you can use a RANGEATTRMAP statement to ensure that specific data values are represented in the graph with specific colors.

## 6.9  GTL Dynamic Variables and Macro Variables

A GTL template can be defined using hard-coded values for various roles and options. The graph in Figure 6.2 creates a histogram of the variable "Cholesterol". In such a case, the data set that is used to create the graph in the SGRENDER procedure step must contain a column with this name. Similarly, options can be specified as hard-coded values such as DEGREE=2. Such templates are easy and simple to write, but they are not very flexible.

Templates can be made more flexible for use with different column names by using dynamic or macro variables or both for various data roles or options. Macro variables that are used with the standard SAS references are resolved at compile time. Declared macro variables are resolved at run time. Although macro variables are defined and initialized in a DATA step or open code, dynamic variables are defined by the DYNAMIC statement in the SGRENDER procedure.

## 6.10  GTL Expressions and Conditionals

GTL templates can use features of SAS functions inside the template. For example, you can use an ENTRY statement with a value that is evaluated using the N() function as follows:

```
entry halign=left "N = " eval(strip(put(n(cholesterol),12.0)));
```

You can use IF-ELSE-ENDIF syntax to make the template more flexible for use with different data sets. Expressions and conditional statements are used in the examples included in later chapters of this book

## 6.11  GTL Draw Statements

Because all GTL plot statements are data driven, it is easy to create the type of graph that you need without adding custom drawing in the graph. However, often it is necessary to add custom visual elements to a graph that cannot be created using a plot statement. For example, this might be needed to emphasize some feature of the graph.

Starting with SAS 9.3, you can use the draw statements to add custom annotation to the graph. These statements are graphics-centric and not data-centric. They include statements like DRAWLINE, DRAWRECTANGLE, DRAWTEXT, DRAWARROW, and so on.

Drawing the shape can be done in any one of many contexts such as GRAPH, LAYOUT, WALL, or DATA. Drawing dimensions can be done with PIXEL, PERCENT, or DATA.

## 6.12  GTL Annotate

Starting with SAS 9.4, you can add annotations to your graph using the SGAnno data set. This data set contains columns with predefined names that provide information that is needed for drawing the annotation. Each observation provides the data that is needed for one individual annotation. The definition for the SG annotation data set is the same as the one that is used with the SG procedures. For an introduction to SG annotation, see Section 2.9.

## 6.13 Summary

In this chapter we have covered the key components of Graph Template Language syntax that you can use to create your graphs. GTL is a structured language using nested blocks of code. Each template is made of one BEGINGRAPH – ENDGRAPH code block that contains the entire definition of the graph. In addition to titles and footnotes, this code block includes one LAYOUT – ENDLAYOUT block that contains plot statements and other nested layouts.

You can use the TEMPLATE procedure to define a StatGraph template using a combination of various GTL statements. The layouts determine how your graph area is organized, and the plot statements determine how the data is displayed. You can use other statements as needed. You can refer to variables in the data set directly by name, or indirectly using dynamic variables. Dynamic variables, macro variables, and conditional syntax can be used to make your templates flexible and extensible.

After your template is defined and compiled, it is stored in the item store. Templates that are supplied by SAS are in SASHELP.TMPLMAST, and most user-defined templates are in SASUSER.TEMPLAT.

You can change the location where compiled user templates are saved by using the ODS PATH statement. Running the TEMPLATE procedure step only creates the compiled template. No graph is created in this step.

You can associate data with a compiled template to create a graph using the SGRENDER procedure. If your template used dynamic variables, the values for these can be defined in this step. The same template can be reused with different data sets--as long as the variables and types are compatible.

As noted above, GTL can be used to create single-cell graphs, multi-cell classification panels, and multi-cell ad hoc layout panels.

GTL is a large topic, and a full description is beyond the scope of this book. In Chapters 7 and 8, we will use GTL to create many complex clinical graphs. The features and syntax of GTL will become apparent through these examples.

# Chapter 7:  Clinical Graphs Using SAS 9.3 GTL

Many commonly used clinical graphs can be created using the SGPLOT or SGPANEL procedures. Such graphs have a simple single-cell structure with one main data area, two or more axes, and other related items such as insets, legends, and so on. They can be created using the SGPLOT procedure as described in Chapters 3 and 4.  Other graphs have a regular grid of data cells that are determined by the number of unique values of one or more classifier variables. Such graphs can be easily created using the SGPANEL procedure as described in Chapter 5.  These graphs generally cover a majority of the common use cases.

For the remaining cases, we have to go beyond the abilities of the SGPLOT or SGPANEL procedures.  We will need to use GTL to create a graph that requires complex layouts or plot combinations.

The graph in Figure 7.0 shows a multi-cell graph that uses a custom layout that cannot be produced by either the SGPLOT or SGPANEL procedures.

**Figure 7.0 – Multi-Cell Panel Graph**

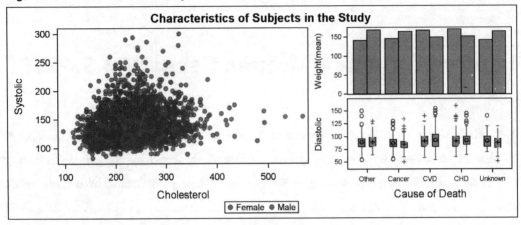

The graph above uses a special layout that shows the distribution of Systolic blood pressure by Cholesterol on the left side of the graph. On the right side, the graph contains two plots that use a common x-axis. The upper plot shows a bar chart of mean Weight by Cause of Death. The lower plot shows a box plot of Diastolic blood pressure by Cause of Death.

The graph above in Figure 7.0 is built using the techniques described in Chapter 6. We have used the TEMPLATE procedure to define a StatGraph template using GTL for this graph. We used nested LAYOUT LATTICE and LAYOUT OVERLAY statements to create this layout, with different plot statements. The graph is rendered using the SGRENDER procedure.

In this chapter, we will create such graphs using SAS 9.3 GTL. In the graph above, note that some of the tick values for "Cause of Death" are shortened to "CVD" and "CHD" to avoid long rotated strings. For full details, see Program 7_0, available from the author's page at http://support.sas.com/matange.

One signature element of many clinical graphs is the inclusion of tables of statistics that are aligned with the x- or y-axis. Often, we will use the SCATTER statement with the MARKERCHAR option to display such information in the graph.

# 7.1 Distribution of ASAT by Time and Treatment

The graph in Figure 7.1.1 displays the distribution of ASAT by time and treatment, along with the number of subjects in the study in the bottom cell, and the number of subjects with a value greater than 2 in the top cell. Data for the graph is shown in Figure 7.1.2.

**Figure 7.1.1 – Distribution of ASAT by Time and Treatment**

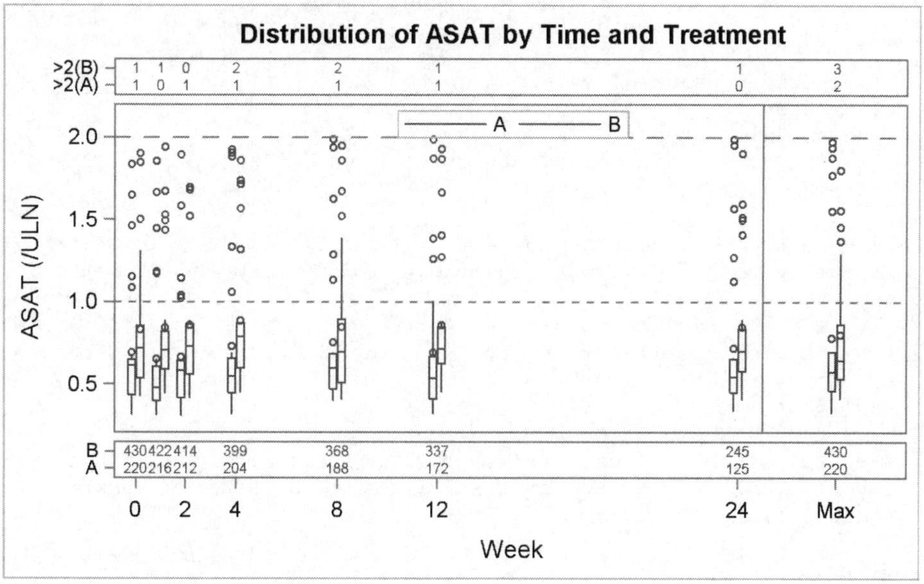

**Figure 7.1.2 – Data for Graph**

| Obs | Week | Drug | ASAT | count | DrugGT | gt2 |
|-----|------|------|---------|-------|--------|-----|
| 1 | 0 | A | 0.44797 | 220 | >2(A) | 1 |
| 2 | 0 | B | 0.79982 | 430 | >2(B) | 1 |
| 3 | 0 | A | 0.63728 | | >2(A) | |
| 4 | 0 | B | 0.44298 | | >2(B) | |
| 5 | 0 | A | 0.33984 | | >2(A) | |

This graph is created using one LAYOUT LATTICE having three rows and one column. Each cell is defined by one LAYOUT OVERLAY – ENDLAYOUT block. The row weights are set to 10%, 80%, and 10%. COLUMNDATARANGE is set to "Union", and one common external x-axis is defined using the COLUMNAXES – ENDCOLUMNAXES block.

The overall structure of the graph is shown below. We use one LAYOUT LATTICE with three LAYOUT OVERLAY blocks.

```
proc template;
  define statgraph Fig_7_1_ASAT_By_Time_and_Trt;
    begingraph;
      entrytitle 'Distributiion of ASAT by Time and Treatment';
      layout lattice / rows=3 columndatarange=union
                       rowweights=(0.1 0.8 0.1) rowgutter=5px;

        /*--Specifiy usage of external column axis--*/
        columnaxes;
          columnaxis / type=linear linearopts=
                       (tickvaluelist=(0 2 4 8 12 24 28) viewmax=30);
        endcolumnaxes;

        /*--The top cell has the subjects with values > 2 by drug--*/
        layout overlay / yaxisopts=(display=(ticks tickvalues line));
        endlayout;

        /*--The middle cell has the Box Plot of ASAT by time and trt--*/
        layout overlay;
        endlayout;

        /*--The bottom cell has the subjects at risk by time and trt--*/
        layout overlay / yaxisopts=(display=(ticks tickvalues line));
        endlayout;

      endlayout;
    endgraph;
  end;
run;
```

The number of subjects with a value greater than 2 for treatments A or B is shown at the top cell. We used a SCATTERPLOT statement with a MARKERCHARACTER option to the display GT2 by Week, also classified (stacked) and colored by DrugGT.

The middle cell displays the box plot of ASAT by Week by Drug with side-by-side groups.

```
/*--The middle cell contains a Box Plot of ASAT by time and treatment--*/
layout overlay / yaxisopts=(offsetmax=0.1) xaxisopts=(type=linear
         linearopts=(tickvaluelist=(0 2 4 8 12 24 28) viewmax=30));
  boxplot x=week y=asat / group=drug name='a' groupdisplay=cluster
         display=(mean median outliers);
  referenceline x=25;
  referenceline y=1 / lineattrs=(pattern=shortdash);
  referenceline y=2 / lineattrs=(pattern=dash);
  discretelegend 'a' /  location=inside halign=center valign=top;
endlayout;
```

One reference line is used to place the vertical divider at X=25, and two reference lines are placed at Y=1 and 2 using different line patterns. A discrete legend is placed inside the graph area at the top center, and space is created by setting OFFSETMAX=0.1 on the YAXISOPTS.

The subjects at risk are placed in bottom cell of the graph using a SCATTERPLOT statement with the MARKERCHARACTER option of Count by Week, classified (stacked) and colored by Drug. The code for the graph is shown below. See the full code in Program 7_1.

```
proc template;
  define statgraph Fig_7_1_ASAT_By_Time_and_Trt;
    begingraph;
      entrytitle 'Distributiion of ASAT by Time and Treatment';
      layout lattice / rows=3 columndatarange=union rowgutter=5px
            rowweights=(0.1 0.8 0.1);

        /*--Specifiy usage of external column axis--*/
        columnaxes;
          columnaxis / type=linear
              linearopts=(tickvaluelist=(0 2 4 8 12 24 28) viewmax=30);
        endcolumnaxes;

        /*--Top cell with number of subjects with values > 2 by drug--*/
        layout overlay / yaxisopts=(display=(ticks tickvalues line))
              xaxisopts=(type=linear
              linearopts=(tickvaluelist=(0 2 4 8 12 24 28) viewmax=30));
          scatterplot x=week y=drugGT / markercharacter=gt2 group=drug;
        endlayout;

        /*--The middle has a Box Plot of ASAT by time and treatment--*/
        layout overlay / yaxisopts=(offsetmax=0.1) xaxisopts=(type=linear
              linearopts=(tickvaluelist=(0 2 4 8 12 24 28) viewmax=30));
          boxplot x=week y=asat / group=drug name='a'
                groupdisplay=cluster display=(mean median outliers);
          referenceline x=25;
          referenceline y=1 / lineattrs=(pattern=shortdash);
          referenceline y=2 / lineattrs=(pattern=dash);
          discretelegend 'a' /  location=inside halign=center valign=top;
        endlayout;

        /*--Bot cell with number of subjects at risk by time and trt--*/
        layout overlay / yaxisopts=(display=(ticks tickvalues line))
                xaxisopts=(type=linear
              linearopts=(tickvaluelist=(0 2 4 8 12 24 28) viewmax=30));
          scatterplot x=week y=drug / markercharacter=count group=drug;
        endlayout;

      endlayout;
    endgraph;
  end;
run;
```

```
/*--Render the Graph--*/
proc sgrender data=asat template=Fig_7_1_ASAT_By_Time_and_Trt;
run;
```

## 7.2  Most Frequent On-Therapy Adverse Events Sorted by Relative Risk

The graph in Figure 7.2.1 displays the incidence of On-Therapy Adverse Events by treatment, sorted by the relative risk of occurrence.

**Figure 7.2.1 – Most Frequent On-Therapy Adverse Events Sorted by Relative Risk**

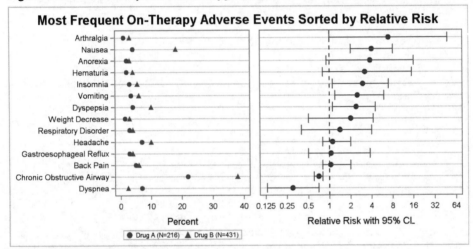

**Figure 7.2.2 – Data for Graph**

| Obs | AE | A | B | Mean | Low | High |
|-----|----|---|---|------|-----|------|
| 1 | Dyspnea | 7 | 2.5 | 0.30 | 0.13 | 0.7 |
| 2 | Chronic Obstructive Airway | 22 | 38.0 | 0.70 | 0.60 | 0.8 |
| 3 | Back Pain | 5 | 6.0 | 1.04 | 0.80 | 2.0 |
| 4 | Gastroesophageal Reflux | 3 | 4.0 | 1.05 | 0.50 | 3.8 |
| 5 | Headache | 7 | 10.0 | 1.10 | 0.80 | 2.0 |

The incidence by treatment is displayed on the left side of the graph, and the relative risks with 95% confidence intervals are displayed on the right. The adverse events are displayed, sorted by the mean of the relative risk.

The data for the graph is shown in Figure 7.2.2 and contains six columns including the AE name, percent incidences for drug A and B, Mean value of the relative risk, and the low and high values for the 95% confidence limits. The data is sorted by Mean. The values are drawn decreasing from the top of the y-axis.

The graph is created using LAYOUT LATTICE with two columns. The weights of the columns are set to 40% and 60% so that the right column is wider. A gutter of 10 pixels is placed between the two cells.

Note, the two cells do not have separate y-axes. Instead, one common y-axis is displayed on the left, and it applies to both cells in the row. This also automatically places the corresponding values with the correct category value for each cell. The plot on the left has a linear x-axis, but the plot on the right has a log (base 2) x-axis.

The structure of the template used to create such a layout is shown below.

1. We use the PROC TEMPLATE statement to define a StatGraph template.
2. The GTL definition is between the BEGINGRAPH and ENDGRAPH statements.
3. An outer LAYOUT LATTICE container is used to create a layout of two columns with 40% and 60 % widths and a common y-axis. A COLUMNGUTTER of 10 pixels is used.
4. The ROWAXES – ENDROWAXES block with one ROWAXIS statement triggers the placement of the single row axis on the left, with grids, ticks, tick values, and line.
5. The first LAYOUT OVERLAY container defines the cell on the left.
6. The second LAYOUT OVERLAY container defines the cell on the right.
7. We finish off the template with the matching ENDLAYOUT, ENDGRAPH, END, and RUN statements.

```
proc template;
   define statgraph Fig_7_2_Most_Frequent_On_Therapy_Adverse_Events;
   begingraph;
      layout lattice / columns=2 columnweights=(0.4 0.6)
                 rowdatarange=union columngutter=10px;

         rowaxes;
           rowaxis / griddisplay=on display=(ticks tickvalues line);
         endrowaxes;

         /*--Left Cell--*/
         layout overlay;
         endlayout;

         /*--Right Cell--*/
         layout overlay;
         endlayout;

      endlayout;
   endgraph;
  end;
run;
```

The definition of the left cell is shown below. Some appearance options are skipped to fit the page.

1. The left cell is defined by the first LAYOUT OVERLAY – ENDLAYOUT block. All the plot statements in this block are layered together and displayed in the left cell.

2. The first SCATTERPLOT statement displays values for drug 'A' by 'AE'. The marker attributes are set to use a filled circle marker using the first group color from the style. This statement has NAME='a', and LEGENDLABEL="Drug A (N=&na)". The string is used for representing this plot in the legend. Note the use of the macro variable "&na".

3. The second SCATTERPLOT statement displays values for drug 'B' by 'AE'. The marker attributes are set to use a filled triangle marker using the second group color from the style. This statement has NAME='b' and LEGENDLABEL="Drug B (N=&nb)". The string is used for representing this plot in the legend. Note the use of the macro variable "&nb".

4. The DISCRETELEGEND statement includes plots 'a' and 'b'. The legend is displayed in the default location outside and below, centered on the x-axis of the graph.

```
/*--Left Cell--*/
layout overlay;
   scatterplot x=a y=ae /
               markerattrs=graphdata1(symbol=circlefilled)
               name='a' legendlabel="Drug A (N=&na)";
   scatterplot x=b y=ae /
               markerattrs=graphdata2(symbol=trianglefilled)
               name='b' legendlabel="Drug B (N=&nb)";
   discretelegend 'a' 'b' / valueattrs=(size=6) border=true;
endlayout;
```

The definition of the right cell is shown below. Some appearance options are skipped to fit the space. See Program 7_2 for the full details.

1. The right cell is defined by the second LAYOUT OVERLAY – ENDLAYOUT block. All the plot statements in this block are displayed in the right cell.

2. A SCATTERPLOT statement displays the 'Mean' occurrence values by 'AE'. The marker attributes are set to a filled circle marker using the first default color from the style.

3. A vertical REFERENCELINE line with a dash pattern is drawn at Y=1.

4. The x-axis is of TYPE log with LOGBASE of 2.

```
/*--Right Cell--*/
layout overlay / xaxisopts=(label='Relative Risk with 95% CL'
        type=log logopts=(base=2 tickintervalstyle=logexpand));
   scatterplot x=mean y=ae / xerrorlower=low xerrorupper=high
               markerattrs=(symbol=circlefilled);
   referenceline x=1 /lineattrs=graphdatadefault(pattern=shortdash);
endlayout;
```

## 7.3 Treatment Emergent Adverse Events with Largest Risk Difference with NNT

The graph in Figure 7.3.1 is a variation on the graph shown in Section 7.2, as created by SAS users Matt Cravets and Jeff Kopicko, using the data set shown below.[1] The difference is the display of the "Numbers Needed to Treat" along the top X2-axis of the right cell, where NNT =1.0 / RiskDiff.

**Figure 7.3.1 – Treatment Emergent Adverse Events with Largest Risk Difference with NNT**

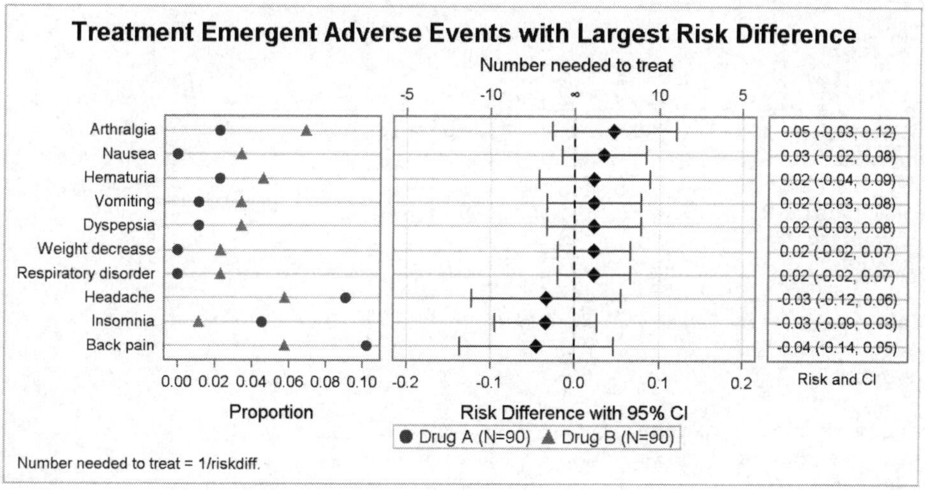

**Figure 7.3.2 – Data for Graph**

| Obs | AEDECOD | PCT0 | PCTR | Risk | LRisk | URisk | RiskCI | NNT | xInset |
|-----|---------|------|------|------|-------|-------|--------|-----|--------|
| 1 | Back pain | 0.10227 | 0.057471 | -0.044801 | -0.13623 | 0.04663 | -0.04 (-0.14, 0.05) | -22.3207 | Risk and CI |
| 2 | Insomnia | 0.04545 | 0.011494 | -0.033960 | -0.09434 | 0.02641 | -0.03 (-0.09, 0.03) | -29.4462 | Risk and CI |
| 3 | Headache | 0.09091 | 0.057471 | -0.033438 | -0.12232 | 0.05545 | -0.03 (-0.12, 0.06) | -29.9063 | Risk and CI |
| 4 | Respiratory disorder | 0.00000 | 0.022989 | 0.022989 | -0.01993 | 0.06591 | 0.02 (-0.02, 0.07) | 43.5000 | Risk and CI |
| 5 | Weight decrease | 0.00000 | 0.022989 | 0.022989 | -0.01993 | 0.06591 | 0.02 (-0.02, 0.07) | 43.5000 | Risk and CI |

Matt wanted to display the NNT axis along the top, matching the RiskDiff axis with inverse values at each tick mark. This means we have an axis that goes from negative small values to negative ∞, and then from positive ∞ to smaller positive values. That means we have two axes at the top.

To do this, we replicate the x-axis as the x2-axis at the top, with the same settings. This ensures that the tick values are aligned, as seen in the very light grid lines. Then, the values on the x2-axis are replaced using the inverse of the values from the x-axis. The inverse of zero is replaced with the Unicode ∞ symbol "221e"x. Note the use of TICKVALUELIST and TICKDISPLAYLIST in the program shown for the details of the "Middle Cell" further below.

For this graph we have used a three-cell layout and used the SCATTERPLOT statement with the MARKERCHARACTER option to display these values in the third cell.

The GTL code for the overall structure of the graph is shown below.

```
/* Define a Lattice layout with two columns and common external y-axis */
layout lattice / columns=3 columnweights=(0.3 0.5 0.2)
                 rowdatarange=union columngutter=10px;
  rowaxes;
    rowaxis;
  endrowaxes;

  /* Left cell with incidence values */
  layout overlay / xaxisopts=(label="Proportion" );
  endlayout;

  /* Middle cell with risk differences and NNT */
  layout overlay;
  endlayout;

  /* Right cell with Risk and CI values */
  layout overlay;
  endlayout;

  /* Bottom-centered sidebar with legend */
  sidebar / align=bottom spacefill=false;
  endsidebar;

endlayout;
```

The left cell displays the proportion values for Drug A and B by adverse event using two scatter plots. Each scatter plot assigns specific marker attributes for each drug. The middle cell displays the risk difference with 95% confidence using a SCATTERPLOT statement with the MARKERCHARACTER option.

The risk difference plot is displayed in the middle cell. The X2 axis displays the values for NNT that are an inverse of the risk values. The inverse of zero is displayed using the Unicode symbol.

```
/* Middle cell with risk differences and NNT */
layout overlay / xaxisopts=(label="Risk Difference with 95% CI"
                    griddisplay=on
                    gridattrs=(color=cxf7f7f7)
                    linearopts=(tickvaluefitpolicy=none
                    viewmin=-0.2 viewmax=0.2
                    tickvaluelist=(-0.20 -0.1  0 0.1 0.20)))
            x2axisopts=(label="Number needed to treat"
                    linearopts=(tickvaluefitpolicy=none
                    viewmin=-0.2 viewmax=0.2
                    tickvaluelist=(-0.20 -0.1  0 0.1 0.20)
                    tickdisplaylist=('-5' '-10'
                    "(*ESC*){unicode '221e'x}"  '10' '5')));
```

```
        scatterplot y=aedecod x=risk / xerrorlower=lrisk xerrorupper=urisk
                 markerattrs=(symbol=diamondfilled color=black);
        scatterplot y=aedecod x=risk / xaxis=x2 datatransparency=1;
        referenceline x=0 / lineattrs=(pattern=shortdash color=black);
    endlayout;
```

The full code is shown below. Some appearance options are trimmed to fit. See Program 7_3 for
the full details.

```
proc template;
    define statgraph Fig_7_3_Most_Frequent_On_Therapy_Adverse_Events_NNT;
    begingraph;
        entrytitle "Treatment Emergent Adverse Events with Largest ...";
        entryfootnote halign=left "Number needed to treat = 1/riskdiff." /;

        /* Define a Lattice layout with two columns and a common y-axis */
        layout lattice / columns=3 columnweights=(0.3 0.5 0.2)
                          rowdatarange=union columngutter=10px;
            rowaxes;
              rowaxis / griddisplay=on
                        display=(tickvalues) tickvalueattrs=(size=7);
            endrowaxes;

            /* Left cell with incidence values */
            layout overlay / xaxisopts=(label="Proportion" );
              scatterplot y=aedecod x=pct0 / legendlabel='Drug A (N=90)'
                  markerattrs=(symbol=circlefilled color=bib) name='drga';
              scatterplot y=aedecod x=pctr / legendlabel='Drug B (N=90)'
                  markerattrs=(symbol=trianglefilled color=red) name='drgb';
            endlayout;

            /* Middle cell with risk differences and NNT */
            layout overlay / xaxisopts=(label="Risk Difference with 95% CI"
                             griddisplay=on gridattrs=(color=cxf7f7f7)
                             linearopts=(tickvaluefitpolicy=none
                                 viewmin=-0.2 viewmax=0.2
                                 tickvaluelist=(-0.20 -0.1  0 0.1 0.20)))
                    x2axisopts=(label="Number needed to treat"
                                 linearopts=(tickvaluefitpolicy=none
                                 viewmin=-0.2 viewmax=0.2
                                 tickvaluelist=(-0.20 -0.1  0 0.1 0.20)
                                 tickdisplaylist=('-5' '-10'
                                     "(*ESC*){unicode '221e'x}"  '10' '5')));
              scatterplot y=aedecod x=risk / xerrorlower=lrisk
                          xerrorupper=urisk
                          markerattrs=(symbol=diamondfilled color=black);
              scatterplot y=aedecod x=risk / xaxis=x2 datatransparency=1;
              referenceline x=0 / lineattrs=(pattern=shortdash color=black);
            endlayout;

            /* Right cell with risk and CI values */
            layout overlay / xaxisopts=(display=(tickvalues)
```

```
                              tickvalueattrs=(size=7));
            scatterplot y=aedecod x=xinset /xaxis=x
                         markercharacter=riskci);
        endlayout;

        /* Bottom-centered sidebar with legend */
        sidebar / align=bottom spacefill=false;
           discretelegend 'drga' 'drgb' / autoitemsize=true
                             valueattrs=(size=8);
        endsidebar;

      endlayout;
    endgraph;
  end;
run;
```

## 7.4 Butterfly Plot of Cancer Deaths by Cause and Gender

The graph in Figure 7.4.1 is the classic butterfly chart showing the incidence of cancer cases by gender along with the deaths for each cause.

**Figure 7.4.1 – Butterfly Plot of Cancer Deaths by Cause and Gender**

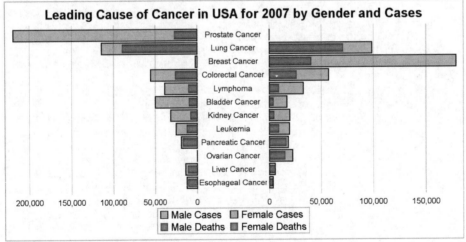

**Figure 7.4.2 – Data for Graph**

| Obs | Cause | MCases | FCases | MDeaths | FDeaths | Cases | x1 | x2 |
|-----|-------|--------|--------|---------|---------|-------|----|----|
| 1 | Prostate Cancer | 218,890 | 0 | 27,050 | 0 | 218890 | 2 | 1 |
| 2 | Lung Cancer | 114,760 | 98,620 | 89,510 | 70,880 | 213380 | 2 | 1 |
| 3 | Breast Cancer | 2,030 | 178,480 | 450 | 40,460 | 180510 | 2 | 1 |
| 4 | Colorectal Cancer | 55,290 | 57,050 | 26,000 | 26,180 | 112340 | 2 | 1 |

The data is shown in Figure 7.4.2, with Cause, Male Cases, Female Cases, Male Deaths and Female Deaths, and total number of Cases, sorted descending by Cases.

```
layout lattice / columns=3 columnweights=(0.425 0.15 0.425)
rowdatarange=union;

  /*--Left cell for male values--*/
  layout overlay;
  endlayout;

  /*--Middle cell for the cancer type label--*/
  layout overlay;
  endlayout;

  /*--Right cell for the female values--*/
  layout overlay;
  endlayout;

endlayout;
```

For this graph we will use the LAYOUT LATTICE to define a three-column layout as shown above in the GTL code snippet. Column weights are set to 42.5% for the left and right cells and 15% for the middle cell. The left and right cells will contain the bar charts of cases and deaths by cause. The middle cell will contain the cause labels, center aligned, and will function as the common axis values.

The left cell is defined by the first LAYOUT OVERLAY – ENDLAYOUT block of the GTL code shown below. Note the following aspects of this code:

1. The x-axis is reversed, and grid lines are displayed.
2. The y-axis is suppressed, and values are reversed so that they are positioned top down.
3. Wall display is suppressed to get a light-weight, modern look.
4. A horizontal bar chart of MCases by Cause is shown, with the name 'mc' and a legend label.

5. A horizontal bar chart of MDeaths by Cause is overlaid with a narrower bar width, with the name 'md', and with skin effect.

```
/*--Left Cell--*/
layout overlay / xaxisopts=(reverse=true label='Males'
                            display=(tickvalues) griddisplay=on)
                 yaxisopts=(display=none reverse=true)
walldisplay=none;
  barchart category=cause response=mcases /
           fillattrs=graphdata1(transparency=0.7) orient=horizontal
           name='mc' legendlabel='Male Cases';
  barchart category=cause response=mdeaths /
           fillattrs=graphdata1(transparency=0.3) orient=horizontal
           name='md' legendlabel='Male Deaths'
           barwidth=0.6 dataskin=pressed;
endlayout;
```

The right cell is defined in a way similar to the left cell using the third LAYOUT OVERLAY – ENDLAYOUT block of the GTL code. The values for female subjects are shown in this cell, and the x-axis is not reversed.

The middle cell is used to create the common axis using a LAYOUT OVERLAY – ENDLAYOUT block. The values are displayed using the SCATTERPLOT statement with the MARKERCHARACTER option. The bar chart with DATATRANSPARENCY=1 is used to ensure correct alignment between the three cells. Wall and axis displays are turned off, with the y-axis being reversed as the other cells.

```
/*--Middle Cell--*/
layout overlay / xaxisopts=(display=none) walldisplay=none
                 yaxisopts=(display=none reverse=true);
  barchart x=cause y=x2 / orient=horizontal datatransparency=1;
  scatterplot x=x1 y=cause / markercharacter=cause;
endlayout;
```

The common discrete legend is placed in the bottom side bar as shown in the code snippet below. The names of each statement that contributes to the legend are listed. The items are positioned in two columns.

```
/*--Bottom Side Bar--*/
sidebar / spacefill=false;
  discretelegend 'mc' 'fc' 'md' 'fd' / across=2;
endsidebar;
```

Alternatively, the data can be sorted descending by total deaths as shown below.

**Figure 7.4.3 – Data for Graph, Sorted Descending by Total Deaths**

| Obs | Cause | MCases | FCases | MDeaths | FDeaths | Deaths | x1 | x2 |
|-----|-------|--------|--------|---------|---------|--------|----|----|
| 1 | Lung Cancer | 114,760 | 98,620 | 89,510 | 70,880 | 160,390 | 2 | 1 |
| 2 | Colorectal Cancer | 55,290 | 57,050 | 26,000 | 26,180 | 52,180 | 2 | 1 |
| 3 | Breast Cancer | 2,030 | 178,480 | 450 | 40,460 | 40,910 | 2 | 1 |
| 4 | Pancreatic Cancer | 18,830 | 18,340 | 16,840 | 16,530 | 33,370 | 2 | 1 |

The full GTL code is shown below. Some appearance options have been trimmed to fit the space. See Program 7_4 for the full details.

```
proc template;
  define statgraph Fig_7_4_Butterfly_Plot_Of_Cancer_Deaths;
    dynamic _title;
    begingraph;

      entrytitle "Leading Cause of Cancer in USA for 2007 by Gender and "
                 _title;
      layout lattice / columns=3 columnweights=(0.425 0.15 0.425)
             rowdatarange=union;

        /*--Left Cell with Male data--*/
        layout overlay / walldisplay=none
                xaxisopts=(reverse=true tickvalueattrs=(size=7)
                    label='Males' display=(tickvalues) griddisplay=on)
                yaxisopts=(display=none reverse=true);
          barchart x=cause y=mcases / orient=horizontal name='mc'
                  fillattrs=graphdata1(transparency=0.7)
                  legendlabel='Male Cases';
          barchart x=cause y=mdeaths / orient=horizontal dataskin=pressed
                  fillattrs=graphdata1(transparency=0.3)
                  barwidth=0.6 name='md' legendlabel='Male Deaths';
        endlayout;

        /*--Middle Cell with case values as axis--*/
        layout overlay / xaxisopts=(display=none) walldisplay=none
                    yaxisopts=(display=none reverse=true);
          barchart x=cause y=x2 / orient=horizontal datatransparency=1;
          scatterplot x=x1 y=cause / markercharacter=cause;
        endlayout;

        /*--Right Cell with Female data--*/
        layout overlay / walldisplay=none
                xaxisopts=(tickvalueattrs=(size=7)   label='Females'
                        display=(tickvalues) griddisplay=on)
                yaxisopts=(display=none reverse=true
                        tickvalueattrs=(size=7));
          barchart x=cause y=fcases / orient=horizontal name='fc'
```

```
                 fillattrs=graphdata2(transparency=0.7)
                 legendlabel='Female Cases';
        barchart x=cause y=fdeaths / orient=horizontal name='fd'
                 fillattrs=graphdata2(transparency=0.3)
                 barwidth=0.6 dataskin=pressed
                 legendlabel='Female Deaths';
      endlayout;

      sidebar / spacefill=false;
        discretelegend 'mc' 'fc' 'md' 'fd' / across=2;
      endsidebar;

    endlayout;
  endgraph;
end;
run;
```

## 7.5 Forest Plot of Impact of Treatment on Mortality by Study

A forest plot is a graphical representation of a meta-analysis of the results of randomized controlled trials.

**Figure 7.5.1 – Forest Plot of Impact of Treatment on Mortality by Study**

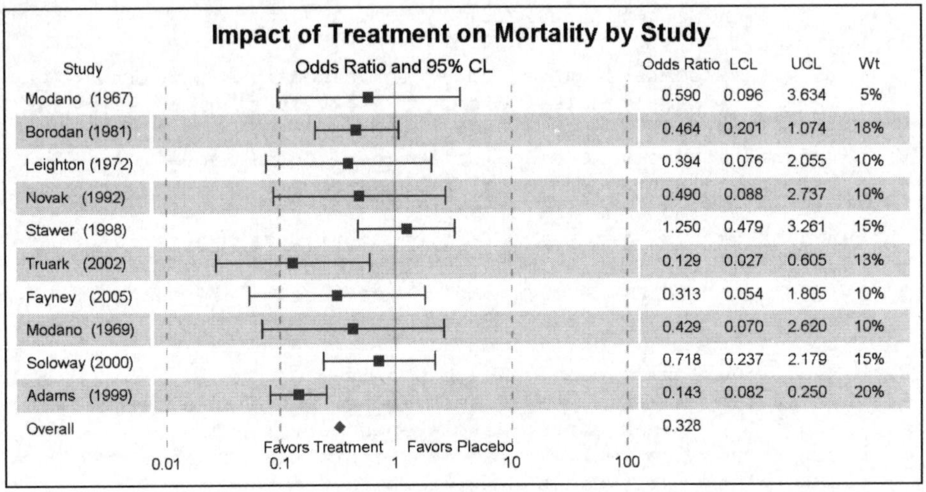
Impact of Treatment on Mortality by Study
Study
Odds Ratio and 95% CL
Odds Ratio
LCL
UCL
Wt
Modano (1967) 0.590 0.096 3.634 5%
Borodan (1981) 0.464 0.201 1.074 18%
Leighton (1972) 0.394 0.076 2.055 10%
Novak (1992) 0.490 0.088 2.737 10%
Stawer (1998) 1.250 0.479 3.261 15%
Truark (2002) 0.129 0.027 0.605 13%
Fayney (2005) 0.313 0.054 1.805 10%
Modano (1969) 0.429 0.070 2.620 10%
Soloway (2000) 0.718 0.237 2.179 15%
Adams (1999) 0.143 0.082 0.250 20%
Overall 0.328
Favors Treatment
Favors Placebo
0.01
0.1
1
10
100

**Figure 7.5.2 – Data for Graph**

| Obs | Study | Grp | OddsRatio | LowerCL | UpperCL | Weight | ORLabel | LCLLabel | UCLLabel | WtLabel | StudyLabel |
|-----|-------|-----|-----------|---------|---------|--------|---------|----------|----------|---------|------------|
| 7 | Fayney (2005) | 1 | 0.313 | 0.054 | 1.805 | 10% | Odds Ratio | LCL | UCL | Wt | Study |
| 8 | Modano (1969) | 1 | 0.429 | 0.070 | 2.620 | 10% | Odds Ratio | LCL | UCL | Wt | Study |
| 9 | Soloway (2000) | 1 | 0.718 | 0.237 | 2.179 | 15% | Odds Ratio | LCL | UCL | Wt | Study |
| 10 | Adams (1999) | 1 | 0.143 | 0.082 | 0.250 | 20% | Odds Ratio | LCL | UCL | Wt | Study |
| 11 | Overall | 2 | 0.328 | . | . | . | Odds Ratio | LCL | UCL | Wt | Study |

The graph in Figure 7.5.1 shows the names of the studies on the left, with a plot of the measure of the effect as an odds ratio of each study and the 95% confidence intervals. Area or width of each marker can be proportional to the weight of each study. The overall meta-analyzed measure of effect is plotted with a diamond-shaped marker. The actual values of the odds ratio, confidence limits, and weight are displayed on the right.

The graph uses a log x-axis, with reference lines at various levels and one at "1", which indicates "no Effect". If the odds ratio and CL overlap the "no effect" line, it demonstrates their effect sizes do not differ from no effect for the individual study at the given level of confidence.

The graph in Figure 7.5.1 is created using a LAYOUT LATTICE container with three columns. The left cell contains the study names, the middle cell contains the odds ratio plot, and the right cell displays a table of four columns of the values.

The overall structure of the GTL template is shown below. The appropriate plot statements with options are added in each layout overlay to populate the items to be displayed. The width of the left cell is 15%, middle cell is 55%, and right cell is 30%.

```
Layout Lattice / columns=3 columnweight=(0.15 0.55 0.3);

   /*--Study Names on the Left--*/
   layout overlay;
   endlayout;

   /*--Odds Ratio plot in the middle--*/
   layout overlay;
   endlayout;

   /*--Table of values on the right--*/
   layout overlay;
   endlayout;

endlayout;
```

In the left cell, we display the study names using the SCATTERPLOT statement with the DATALABEL option and also using DATALABELPOSITION=Right and MARKERATTRS(Size=0). This places the study names on the right of the markers; the markers themselves are not shown. The reason for doing this instead of using the MARKERCHARACTER option is that we want to left-align the study values. A DRAWTEXT is used to display the label "Study" above the study names.

```
layout overlay / yaxisopts=(display=none reverse=true
                            discreteopts=(colorbands=even)
                x2axisopts=(display=none) walldisplay=none;
  scatterplot y=study x=studylabel / xaxis=x2 datalabel=study
              datalabelposition=right markerattrs=(size=0);
  drawtext textattrs=(size=7) 'Study' / x=50 y=101
           xspace=wallpercent yspace=wallpercent anchor=bottom width=50;
endlayout;
```

In the middle cell, we have displayed the odds ratio and confidence limits by the study names using the SCATTERPLOT statement as shown below. The study name column is assigned to the Y role. Reference lines are drawn at 0.01, 0.1, 10, and 100 using the first REFERENCELINE statement.

The X role for reference line accepts either a data column or one data value. So, we could either provide four different REFERENCELINE statements or one statement with X pointing to a column in the data that would contain these four values. We do not have such a column, but in GTL, we can use the COLN() function to generate such a column on the fly. A second REFERENCELINE statement is used to display the value at X=1 using different visual attributes.

The values are displayed in reverse y order, from top to bottom, so that the last value in the data "Overall" is at the bottom. The x-axis line and ticks are suppressed, and the wall fill and outline are suppressed to provide a lightweight, modern look. The x-axis type is set to Log, with min and max values. The axis label "Odds Ratio and 95% CL" is displayed on the secondary x-axis. The study names have been displayed using the left cell, so the entire y-axis is turned off.

```
layout overlay / walldisplay=none
                 yaxisopts=(reverse=true display=none offsetmax=0.05
                            discreteopts=(colorbands=even))
                 xaxisopts=(type=log logopts=(viewmin=0.01 viewmax=100)
                            display=(tickvalues) displaysecondary=(label)
                            label='Odds Ratio and 95% CL'
                            labelattrs=(size=8) tickvalueattrs=(size=7));
  scatterplot y=study x=oddsratio / group=grp
              xerrorlower=lowercl xerrorupper=uppercl;
  referenceline x=eval(coln(0.01, 0.1, 10, 100)) /
                lineattrs=(pattern=shortdash) datatransparency=0.5;
  referenceline x=1 / datatransparency=0.5;
  drawtext textattrs=(size=7) 'Favors Placebo' / x=1.2 y=0
           xspace=datavalue yspace=wallpercent anchor=left width=50;
  drawtext textattrs=(size=7) 'Favors Treatment' / x=0.8 y=0
           xspace=datavalue yspace=wallpercent anchor=right width=50;
endlayout;
```

The last detail is the addition of the labels "Favors Treatment" and "Favors Placebo" to each side of the no-effect line on the x-axis. Normally, an ENTRY statement is used to position text inside a graph area. However, that can be positioned relative only to the container and not to data values. To do that, we have used the DRAWTEXT statement.

Two DRAWTEXT statements are used, one for each label. The labels are placed with XSPACE of DataValue and YSPACE of WallPercent. Therefore, the x position is relative to data, but the y position is relative to the bottom edge of the container. Also, the appropriate ANCHOR is used to position each label. Extra space is created at the bottom of the graph for the labels using the OFFSETMAX option in YAXISOPTS.

The code snippet below describes how we have displayed the table of values in the right cell. Previously, we added four character columns in the data called ORLabel, LCLLabel, UCLLabel, and WtLabel as shown in Figure 7.5.2. All rows for each column contain the string to be displayed at the top.

We can use a SCATTERPLOT statement with the MARKERCHARACTER option to display each column. The Y role is set to Study and the X role is set to one of the four new column names. This causes each column to be drawn with the value in the X role displayed as the tick value on the X2-axis. Four SCATTERPLOT statements are used, one for each column, and the overlay layout automatically arranges them in the table shown in the right cell.

```
layout overlay / yaxisopts=(display=none reverse=true
                           discreteopts=(colorbands=even));
                 x2axisopts=(display=(tickvalues)) walldisplay=none;
   scatterplot y=study x=ORLabel / xaxis=x2 markercharacter=oddsratio;
   scatterplot y=study x=LCLLabel / xaxis=x2 markercharacter=LowerCL;
   scatterplot y=study x=UCLLabel / xaxis=x2 markercharacter= UpperCL;
   scatterplot y=study x=WtLabel / xaxis=x2 markercharacter=Weight;
endlayout;
```

Faint color bands are drawn behind alternate study values to help draw the eye to the study names, odds ratio graph, and the study values across the width of the graph. The full GTL code is shown below. Some appearance options have been trimmed to fit the space. See Program 7_5 for the full details.

```
proc template;
  define statgraph Fig_7_5_Forest_Plot;
    begingraph;
      entrytitle "Impact of Treatment on Mortality by Study";
      layout lattice / columns=3 columnweights=(0.15 0.55 0.3);

         /*--Left cell for study values--*/
         layout overlay / walldisplay=none
                          yaxisopts=(display=none reverse=true
                                    discreteopts=(colorbands=even))
                          x2axisopts=(display=none tickvalueattrs=(size=7)
                          label='Study');
            scatterplot y=study x=studylabel / xaxis=x2 datalabel=study
                     datalabelposition=right markerattrs=(size=0);
            drawtext textattrs=(size=7) 'Study' / x=50 y=101 anchor=bottom
```

```
                        width=50 xspace=wallpercent yspace=wallpercent;
        endlayout;

        /*--Middle cell for display of Odds Ratio plot--*/
        layout overlay / walldisplay=none
                        yaxisopts=(reverse=true display=none
                                offsetmax=0.05
                                discreteopts=(colorbands=even))
                        xaxisopts=(type=log logopts=(viewmin=0.01
                                viewmax=100) display=(tickvalues)
                                displaysecondary=(label)
                                label='Odds Ratio and 95% CL'
                                labelattrs=(size=8)
                                tickvalueattrs=(size=7));
            scatterplot y=study x=oodsratio / group=grp
                    xerrorlower=lowercl xerrorupper=uppercl;
            referenceline x=eval(coln(0.01, 0.1, 10, 100)) /
                    lineattrs=(pattern=shortdash);
            referenceline x=1 / datatransparency=0.5;

            drawtext textattrs=(size=7) 'Favors Placebo' / x=1.2 y=0
                    xspace=datavalue yspace=wallpercent anchor=left
                    width=50;
            drawtext textattrs=(size=7) 'Favors Treatment' / x=0.8 y=0
                    xspace=datavalue yspace=wallpercent anchor=right
                    width=50;
        endlayout;

        /*--Right cell for display of table of values--*/
        layout overlay / walldisplay=none
                        yaxisopts=(display=none reverse=true
                                discreteopts=(colorbands=even))
                        x2axisopts=(display=(tickvalues));
            scatterplot y=study x=ORLabel / xaxis=x2
                    markercharacter=oddsratio;
            scatterplot y=study x=LCLLabel / xaxis=x2
                    markercharacter=LowerCL;
            scatterplot y=study x=UCLLabel / xaxis=x2
                    markercharacter= UpperCL;
            scatterplot y=study x=WtLabel / xaxis=x2
                    markercharacter=Weight;
        endlayout;

    endlayout;
  endgraph;
  end;
run;
```

## 7.6 Forest Plot of Hazard Ratios by Patient Subgroups

The graph in Figure 7.6.1 shows the hazard ratios by patient subgroups. This graph is much like the forest plot shown in Section 7.5, with the added feature of grouping the study values by subgroups. The subgroup labels are displayed with a bold font, but the individual subgroup values are displayed in normal font and indented.

**Figure 7.6.1 – Forest Plot of Hazard Ratios by Patient Subgroups**

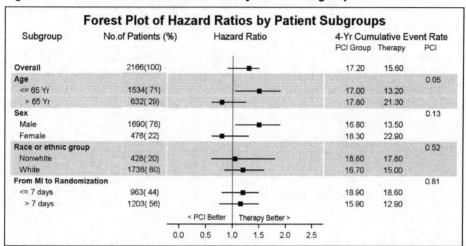

**Figure 7.6.2 – Data for Graph**

| Obs | Indent | Subgroup | Count | Percent | CountPct | Mean | Low | High | PCIGroup | Group | PValue | Ref | Type |
|---|---|---|---|---|---|---|---|---|---|---|---|---|---|
| 1 | 0.0 | Overall | 2166 | 100 | 2166(100) | 1.3 | 0.90 | 1.50 | 17.20 | 15.60 | . | | G |
| 2 | 0.0 | Age | . | . | | . | . | . | . | | 0.05 | Age | G |
| 3 | 1.0 | <= 65 Yr | 1534 | 71 | 1534( 71) | 1.5 | 1.05 | 1.90 | 17.00 | 13.20 | . | <= 65 Yr | |
| 4 | 1.4 | > 65 Yr | 632 | 29 | 632( 29) | 0.8 | 0.60 | 1.25 | 17.80 | 21.30 | . | > 65 Yr | |
| 5 | 0.0 | Sex | . | . | | . | . | . | . | | 0.13 | | G |
| 6 | 1.0 | Male | 1690 | 78 | 1690( 78) | 1.5 | 1.05 | 1.90 | 16.80 | 13.50 | . | | |

To create this graph using SAS 9.3 requires a little bit of extra work to place all the textual columns as shown, along with the text attributes and indention.

Let us examine the features of this graph.

1. The graph consists of five distinct parts:
   a. The column of Subgroup and values on the left.
   b. The column of Patient counts with %.
   c. The hazard ratio graph.

      d.   A table of values with three columns.

      e.   A two-level header for the table.

2.   A key aspect of the graph is that the values are subgrouped into different headings, with multiple values per subgroup.  For example, we have the subgroup heading of "Age", with two values of "<= 65" and "> 65".  The subgroup label "Age" is displayed left-justified, with a bold font.  The subgroup values are indented and displayed with the normal font.

3.   A second column of patient and % data is shown on the left of the hazard ratio plot.

4.   The hazard ratio plot is displayed in the middle, with annotations for effectiveness.

5.   A table of values is shown on the right, made up of three columns.

We will create this graph using a LAYOUT LATTICE of four columns, with varying widths of 25%, 10%, 35%, and 30% for each column.  The overall structure of the graph is as follows.

```
layout lattice / columns=4 columnweights=(0.25 0.10 0.35 0.3)
                 rowdatarange=union;

  /*--Column headers are defined in the top sidebar--*/
  sidebar / align=top;
  endsidebar;

  /*--First column showing Subgroups--*/
  layout overlay;
  endlayout;

  /*--Second column showing Counts--*/
  layout overlay;
  endlayout;

  /*--Third column showing odds ratio graph--*/
  layout overlay;
  endlayout;

  /*--Fourth column showing table of values--*/
  layout overlay;
  endlayout;

endlayout;
```

At the top of the graph, we have the title, followed by the headers for the display below it.  This is created using the SIDEBAR – ENDSIDEBAR block (ALIGN=Top) of the LAYOUT LATTICE. This is essentially a container, and in it we place a nested LAYOUT LATTICE with four columns and one row.  Each cell contains an ENTRY statement defining the header for the cell.

All plot statements in each cell will use "Subgroup" as the Y-variable, thus ensuring that all rows are uniformly aligned.  ROWCOLUMNRANGE=DATA is used.

Note the cell sizing for the header is 22%, 23%, 27%, and 28%. This is not the same as the data columns that we used to allow us to position the header as shown. The code snippet is shown below.

```
/*--Column headers--*/
sidebar / align=top;
  layout lattice / columns=4 columnweights=(0.22 0.23 0.27 0.28);
    entry textattrs=(size=8) halign=left "    Subgroup";
    entry textattrs=(size=8) halign=left " No.of Patients (%)";
    entry textattrs=(size=8) halign=left "Hazard Ratio";
    entry halign=left textattrs=(size=8) "4-Yr Cumulative Event Rate";
  endlayout;
endsidebar;
```

The first cell contains the column of subgroup labels and values. In this column, the subgroups are displayed left-aligned with a bold font. The values are displayed indented with normal font. To achieve this layout, we have used the HIGHLOWPLOT statement.

The HIGHLOWPLOT with Y=Subgroup allows us to place the text of the subgroups with more control over where the text is displayed. If we want text to be left-aligned to a particular location, we use HIGHLABEL option, which places the text immediately to the right of the high value. For right-aligned labels, we use the LOWLABEL option, which places the text immediately to the left of the low value.

Based on the indention column in the data, we have computed two columns, "IndentSub" for the subgroups and "IndentVal" for the values. When one has a value, the other is missing, so we separate the subgroups and values. The first HIGHLOWPLOT statement uses X=IndentSub, which is zero. As a result, the subgroups are displayed with no indention and a bold font. The second HIGHLOWPLOT statement uses X=IndentVal, which is non-zero. As a result, the values are displayed with an indention.

Note the use of the REFERENCELINE statement. This is used in each of the four cells of the graph, and we will address this part of the code later.

```
/*--First column showing Subgroups--*/
layout overlay / xaxisopts=(offsetmin=0 offsetmax=0
                      display=none linearopts=(viewmin=0 viewmax=20))
              yaxisopts=(reverse=true display=none offsetmax=0.1)
              walldisplay=none;
  referenceline y=ref / lineattrs=(thickness=14 color=_color);
  highlowplot y=subgroup low=zero high=indentsub / highlabel=subgroup
            lineattrs=(thickness=0) labelattrs=(weight=bold);
  highlowplot y=subgroup low=zero high=indentval / highlabel=subgroup
            lineattrs=(thickness=0);
endlayout;
```

The Patient count and % are displayed in the second cell. Here, all the values are center-aligned so that we can use the SCATTERPLOT with MARKERCHARACTER option. Once again we use the "Subgroup" variable for the Y role in order to vertically align all the rows in all the cells.

```
/*--Second column showing Counts--*/
layout overlay / walldisplay=none xaxisopts=(display=none)
                 yaxisopts=(reverse=true display=none offsetmax=0.1);
  referenceline y=ref / lineattrs=(thickness=14 color=_color);
  scatterplot y=subgroup x=indent / markercharacter=countpct;
endlayout;
```

The hazard ratio plot is displayed in the third cell. This plot uses the HIGHLOWPLOT statement to draw the confidence limits overlaid with a SCATTERPLOT to draw the mean values. The HIGHLOWPLOT statement is used to display the confidence range without the caps. A REFERENCELINE is displayed at X=1.0.

Note, all the cells use a YOFFSETMAX=0.1. This leaves a 10% blank space at the bottom of the graph because the y-axis is reversed. We have used DRAWTEXT statements to display the "PCI Better" and "Therapy Better" labels in this space. The text strings are aligned to the data value of "1.0" on the x-axis. The first one is placed at x=0.9 with an anchor on the right, and the second one is placed at x=1.1 with an anchor on the left in order to get the placement that we want. The axis label is displayed at the top as a cell header.

```
/*--Third column showing odds ratio graph--*/
layout overlay / xaxisopts=(display=(ticks tickvalues line)
                    linearopts=(tickvaluepriority=true
                       tickvaluelist=(0.0 0.5 1.0 1.5 2.0 2.5)))
                 yaxisopts=(reverse=true display=none offsetmax=0.1)
                 walldisplay=none;
          /*--Draw color Bands--*/
  referenceline y=ref / lineattrs=(thickness=14 color=_color);
  referenceline x=1;

  /*--Draw Hazard Ratios--*/
  highlowplot y=subgroup low=low high=high;
  scatterplot y=subgroup x=mean / markerattrs=(symbol=squarefilled);

  /*--Draw axis labels--*/
  drawtext textattrs=(size=6) '< PCI Better'  / x=0.9 y=1 width=50
           xspace=datavalue yspace=wallpercent anchor=bottomright;
  drawtext textattrs=(size=6) 'Therapy Better >' / x=1.1 y=1 width=50
           xspace=datavalue yspace=wallpercent anchor=bottomleft;
endlayout;
```

The values for the "4-Yr Event Rate" are displayed in the fourth cell. All the values are center-aligned in each column, so we can use the SCATTERPLOT with MARKERCHARACTER option. Here we use the "Subgroup" variable for the Y role to align all the rows in all the cells.

Previously, we have defined three character columns in the data "PCIGrpLbl" with the value "PCI Group" for all observations, "GrpLbl" with the value "Therapy", and "PCILbl" with the value

"PCI". These columns are used as the X role for each of the SCATTERPLOT statements, with X2 as the preferred axis. This displays the values as three columns in the last cell. The tick values for each column are displayed at the top, and they function as the column label for each cell.

```
/*--Fourth column showing table of values--*/
layout overlay / yaxisopts=(reverse=true display=none offsetmax=0.1)
                 x2axisopts=(display=(tickvalues)
tickvalueattrs=(size=7))
                 walldisplay=none;
  referenceline y=ref / lineattrs=(thickness=14 color=_color);
  scatterplot y=subgroup x=PCIGrpLbl / markercharacter=pcigroup xaxis=x2;
  scatterplot y=subgroup x=grpLbl / markercharacter=group xaxis=x2;
  scatterplot y=subgroup x=PCILbl / markercharacter=pvalue xaxis=x2;
endlayout;
```

Lastly, we have used alternating horizontal bands to group the appropriate observations together to make it easier to read. Except for the first "Overall" observation, each subgroup has two individual "Value" observations. So, we have grouped these together using the shaded horizontal bands. This is done by drawing wide REFERENCE lines with Y=ref in each cell as can be seen in the code snippet for each cell. Previously, we computed a new column called "Ref", which has a copy of the Subgroup column for alternating three observations followed by three with missing values.

The full GTL code is shown below. Some appearance options can be trimmed to fit. See Program 7_6 for the full code.

```
/*--Template uses a Layout Lattice of 5 columns--*/
proc template;
  define statgraph Fig_7_6_Forest_Plot_with_Subgroups;
    dynamic _color;
    begingraph;
      entrytitle 'Forest Plot of Hazard Ratios by Patient Subgroups ';

      layout lattice / columns=4 columnweights=(0.25 0.10 0.35 0.3)
                       rowdatarange=union;

        /*--Column headers--*/
        sidebar / align=top;
          layout lattice / columns=4 columnweights=(0.22 0.23 0.27 0.28);
            entry textattrs=(size=8) halign=left "   Subgroup";
            entry textattrs=(size=8) halign=left " No.of Patients (%)";
            entry textattrs=(size=8) halign=left "Hazard Ratio";
            entry halign=left textattrs=(size=8)
               "4-Yr Cumulative Event Rate";
          endlayout;
        endsidebar;
        /*--First column showing Subgroups--*/
        layout overlay / walldisplay=none
                xaxisopts=(offsetmin=0 offsetmax=0
                    display=none linearopts=(viewmin=0 viewmax=20))
                yaxisopts=(reverse=true display=none offsetmax=0.1)
                ;
```

```
      referenceline y=ref / lineattrs=(thickness=14 color=_color);
      highlowplot y=subgroup low=zero high=indentsub /
          highlabel=subgroup
          lineattrs=(thickness=0) labelattrs=(weight=bold);
      highlowplot y=subgroup low=zero high=indentval /
          highlabel=subgroup lineattrs=(thickness=0);
  endlayout;

  /*--Second column showing Counts--*/
  layout overlay / xaxisopts=(display=none) walldisplay=none
                   yaxisopts=(reverse=true display=none
                              offsetmax=0.1);
      referenceline y=ref / lineattrs=(thickness=14 color=_color);
      scatterplot y=subgroup x=indent / markercharacter=countpct;
  endlayout;

  /*--Third column showing odds ratio graph--*/
  layout overlay / xaxisopts=(display=(ticks tickvalues line)
                      linearopts=(tickvaluepriority=true
                      tickvaluelist=(0.0 0.5 1.0 1.5 2.0 2.5)))
                   yaxisopts=(reverse=true display=none
                   offsetmax=0.1)
                   walldisplay=none;
      /*--Draw color Bands--*/
      referenceline y=ref / lineattrs=(thickness=14 color=_color);
      referenceline x=1;

      /*--Draw Hazard Ratios--*/
      highlowplot y=subgroup low=low high=high;
      scatterplot y=subgroup x=mean /
                  markerattrs=(symbol=squarefilled);

      /*--Draw axis labels--*/
      drawtext textattrs=(size=6) '< PCI Better'  / x=0.9 y=1
               width=50 anchor=bottomright
               xspace=datavalue yspace=wallpercent;
      drawtext textattrs=(size=6) 'Therapy Better >' / x=1.1 y=1
               width=50 anchor=bottomleft
               xspace=datavalue yspace=wallpercent;
  endlayout;

  /*--Fourth column showing table of values--*/
  layout overlay / walldisplay=none
               yaxisopts=(reverse=true display=none offsetmax=0.1)
               x2axisopts=(display=(tickvalues));
      referenceline y=ref / lineattrs=(thickness=14 color=_color);
      scatterplot y=subgroup x=PCIGrpLbl /
```

```
markercharacter=pcigroup
                        xaxis=x2;
        scatterplot y=subgroup x=grpLbl / markercharacter=group
                        xaxis=x2;
        scatterplot y=subgroup x=PCILbl / markercharacter=pvalue
                        xaxis=x2;
      endlayout;
    endlayout;
  endgraph;
  end;
run;
```

## 7.7  Product-Limit Survival Estimates

Product-limit survival estimates can be used to measure the lengths of time that patients survive after treatment.

**Figure 7.7.1 – Product-Limit Survival Estimates, Traditional Arrangement**

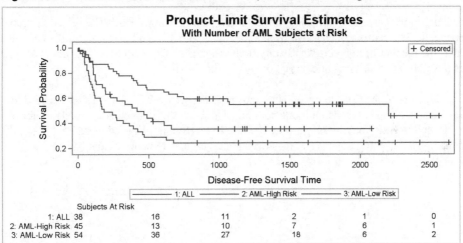

**Figure 7.7.2 – Data for Graph**

| Obs | Time | Survival | AtRisk | Event | Censored | tAtRisk | Stratum | StratumNum |
|-----|------|----------|--------|-------|----------|---------|---------|------------|
| 1 | 0 | 1.00000 | 38 | 0 | . | . | 1: ALL | 1 |
| 2 | 0 | . | 38 | . | . | 0 | 1: ALL | 1 |
| 3 | 1 | 0.97368 | 38 | 1 | . | . | 1: ALL | 1 |
| 4 | 55 | 0.94737 | 37 | 1 | . | . | 1: ALL | 1 |

This product-limit survival estimate graph shown in Figure 7.7.1 can be obtained directly by running the LIFETEST procedure with the sample data SASHELP.BMT. The LIFETEST procedure uses a pre-built GTL template to create this graph. In this section, we will go over how to design such a template so that you can customize the graph to suit your needs.

The first step is to generate the data that is required to create this graph by running the LIFETEST procedure code shown below. The ODS OUTPUT statement is used to write the data to a SAS data set.

```
ods output Survivalplot=SurvivalPlotData;
proc lifetest data=sashelp.BMT plots=survival(atrisk=0 to 2500 by 500);
   time T * Status(0);
   strata Group / test=logrank adjust=sidak;
run;
```

The table above contains multiple observations of the survival probability by time for leukemia stratified by type. The types include Acute Lymphocytic Leukemia (ALL) and two types of Acute Myeloid Leukemia (AML), AML-High Risk and AML Low-Risk.

The key feature of the graph is the display of the survival curves of probability by time and stratum in the upper cell. The censored observations are displayed with a legend inside the cell. The lower cell contains the number of Subjects At-Risk by time and strata. The At-Risk values are displayed by tAtRisk, which is non-missing at every 500 days on the x-axis.

The overall structure of the GTL template is as shown below. A LAYOUT LATTICE is used to split the graph space into two cells with one column. The x-axes of both cells are made uniform using COLUMNDATARANGE=Union. The ROWHEIGHTS option is used to assign 85% of the height to the upper cell for the display of the survival curves, and 15% for the display of the subjects at risk.

```
layout lattice / columns=1 columndatarange=union rowweights=(0.85 0.15);

   /*--Upper Cell--*/
   layout overlay;
   endlayout;

   /*--Lower Cell--*/
   layout overlay / walldisplay=none;
   endlayout;

endlayout;
```

Two cells are defined, one by each of the LAYOUT OVERLAY – ENDLAYOUT blocks. In this case, we want to display only one x-axis. We could use the COLUMNAXES block, but that will place the single x-axis at the bottom. Because we want to display the axis for the upper cell, we did not use the COLUMNAXES block. Instead, we shut off the x-axis for the lower cell. The option COLUMNDATARANGE=Union will ensure that the axes are uniform.

The upper cell is defined below. Some appearance options have been trimmed to fit the space available. The step plot of survival by time with group of stratum draws the survival curves.

```
/*--Survival curves--*/
layout overlay / xaxisopts=(labelattrs=(size=8) tickvalueattrs=(size=7))
                 yaxisopts=(labelattrs=(size=8) tickvalueattrs=(size=7)
                            display=(ticks tickvalues line));
  stepplot x=time y=survival / group=stratum name='s';
  scatterplot x=time y=censored / markerattrs=(symbol=plus) name='c';
  scatterplot x=time y=censored / markerattrs=(symbol=plus)
          group=stratum;
  discretelegend 'c' / location=inside halign=right valign=top;
  discretelegend 's' / valueattrs=(size=7);

  /*--Draw the Y axis label closer to the axis--*/
  drawtext textattrs=(size=8) 'Survival Probability' / x=-6 y=50
          anchor=bottom rotate=90 width=50
          xspace=wallpercent yspace=wallpercent;
endlayout;
```

The scatter plots are used to display the censored observations. The first scatter plot with name 'c' draws the censored observations without a group. So these markers use plus symbols and are drawn with default color. This scatter plot is included in the inner legend. The second scatter plot overplots the censored markers, with group = stratum so that we see the colored markers. A second discrete legend of the three stratum values for the step plot is displayed below the upper cell.

Because we have uniform axes and the lower cell has long label values for each stratum, the y-axis for the upper cell gets pushed out beyond the long label values. To remedy this situation, we have turned off the display of the y-axis label and displayed a y-axis label using the DRAWTEXT statement.

The definition of the lower cell is shown below. The At-Risk values are displayed using the BLOCKPLOT statement of AtRisk by tAtRisk by Stratum. The values for tAtRisk are non-missing only at an interval of 500 days, so the AtRisk values are drawn only at these tick values. CLASS=Stratum stacks the values for each stratum in a table of rows.

```
/*--Subjects at risk--*/
layout overlay / walldisplay=none xaxisopts=(display=none);
  blockplot x=tatrisk block=atrisk / class=stratum
            labelattrs=(size=7) valueattrs=(size=7)
            display=(values label);

  drawtext textattrs=(size=7) 'Subjects At Risk'  / x=1 y=101
          xspace=wallpercent yspace=wallpercent anchor=bottomleft
width=50;
endlayout;
```

The DRAWTEXT statement is used to display the label "Subjects At-Risk" above the table. We have used a DrawSpace of WallPercent for both x and y. The text string is anchored at the bottom left with x=1% and y=101%. This puts the label just above the wall as shown in the graph.

The full program is shown below. Some appearance options are trimmed to fit. Please see the full code in Program 7_7.

```
/*--Define template for Survival Plot--*/
proc template;
  define statgraph Fig_7_7_Survival_plot_out;
    begingraph ;
      entrytitle 'Product-Limit Survival Estimates';
      entrytitle 'With Number of AML Subjects at Risk' /
                  textattrs=(size=8);
        layout lattice / columns=1 columndatarange=union rowgutter=25px
                         rowweights=(0.85 0.15);
        /*--Survival curves--*/
        layout overlay / yaxisopts=(display=(ticks tickvalues line));
          stepplot x=time y=survival / group=stratum name='s';
          scatterplot x=time y=censored / markerattrs=(symbol=plus)
                      name='c';
          scatterplot x=time y=censored / markerattrs=(symbol=plus)
                      group=stratum;
          discretelegend 'c' / location=inside halign=right valign=top;
          discretelegend 's' / valueattrs=(size=7);

          /*--Draw the Y axis label closer to the axis--*/
          drawtext textattrs=(size=8) 'Survival Probability' / x=-6 y=50
                   xspace=wallpercent yspace=wallpercent
                   anchor=bottom rotate=90 width=50;
        endlayout;

        /*--Subjects at risk--*/
        layout overlay / walldisplay=none xaxisopts=(display=none);
          blockplot x=tatrisk block=atrisk / class=stratum
                    display=(values label);
          drawtext textattrs=(size=7) 'Subjects At Risk'  / x=1 y=101
                   width=50 anchor=bottomleft
                   xspace=wallpercent yspace=wallpercent;
        endlayout;
      endlayout;
    endgraph;
  end;
run;
```

The graph in Figure 7.7.1 shows a traditional layout of the product-limit survival plot, where the values of Subjects At-Risk are displayed at the bottom of the graph, below the x-axis values, label, and the legend.

It is possible to place the "Subjects At-Risk" data closer to the survival curves in order to make the data easier to understand. This arrangement is shown in Figure 7.7.3. It reduces the clutter between the curves and the data.

**Figure 7.7.3 – Product-Limit Survival Estimates with Inner Table**

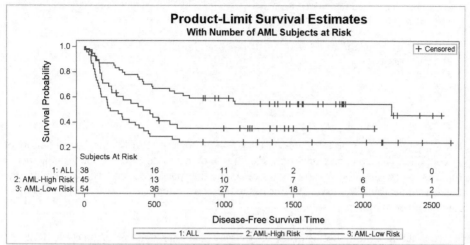

The GTL code for this graph is shown below. We need only one LAYOUT OVERLAY, and both the survival curves and the Subjects At-Risk information can be placed in one container.

```
proc template;
  define statgraph Fig_7_7_Survival_plot_in;
    begingraph;
      entrytitle 'Product-Limit Survival Estimates';
      entrytitle 'With Number of AML Subjects at Risk' /
                 textattrs=(size=8);

      /*--Survival curves--*/
      layout overlay / yaxisopts=(offsetmin=0.1);
        stepplot x=time y=survival / group=stratum  name='s';
        scatterplot x=time y=censored / markerattrs=(symbol=plus)
                    name='c';
        scatterplot x=time y=censored / markerattrs=(symbol=plus)
                    group=stratum;
        discretelegend 'c' / location=inside halign=right valign=top;
        discretelegend 's' / valueattrs=(size=7);
        entry halign=left "Subjects At Risk" / valign=bottom
              textattrs=(size=7);
```

```
            /*--Subjects at risk--*/
            innermargin / align=bottom;
              blockplot x=tatrisk block=atrisk / class=stratum
                        labelattrs=(size=7) valueattrs=(size=7)
                        display=(values label) valuehalign=start;
            endinnermargin;
        endlayout;
      endgraph;
  end;
run;
```

To achieve this layout, we use the INNERMARGIN-ENDINNERMARGIN block at the bottom of
the overlay container. We can place one-dimensional statements in this block. Such statements
span the full axis in one direction (x-axis, in this case) and the space required to draw the plot can
be precisely determined by the software as it is based only on the text attributes. This allows the
graph to size the inner margin precisely.

Using this layout, all the information is inside the overlay container, and the "Subjects At-Risk"
information is placed closer to the survival curves, without any intervening clutter from the x-axis
or the legend. This layout is presented as an alternative to the traditional layout that was presented
earlier.

## 7.8 Bivariate Distribution Plot

The graph shown in Figure 7.8.1 is very useful to view the distribution of data by two variables in any domain, whether clinical, health care, financial, and so on. The graph shows a scatter plot of Systolic by Weight from the data set SASHELP.HEART.

**Figure 7.8.1 – Bivariate Distribution Plot**

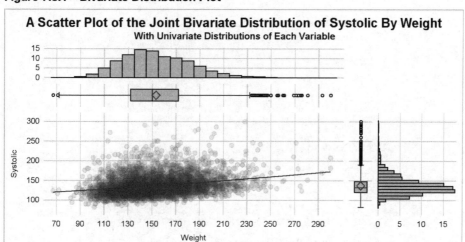

**Figure 7.8.2 – Data for Graph**

| Obs | Weight | Cholesterol | Systolic | Diastolic | Sex |
|-----|--------|-------------|----------|-----------|--------|
| 1 | 140 | . | 124 | 78 | Female |
| 2 | 194 | 181 | 144 | 92 | Female |
| 3 | 132 | 250 | 170 | 90 | Female |
| 4 | 158 | 242 | 128 | 80 | Female |

This graph provides a visual representation of any correlation between these two variables. Solid filled markers are displayed with a high value of transparency, which allows us to view where the dense clusters are in the data. A quadratic regression fit is overlaid.

The graph also shows the univariate distributions of each variable using a histogram and a box plot on each axis. In addition to the scatter plot, this provides us another view of the distribution of the data in each dimension.

The data is shown in Figure 7.8.2.

GTL is the ideal tool to create such a graph. The LAYOUT LATTICE container is used to subdivide the graph space into a 3x3 grid of cells. The row weights are set to 20%, 15%, and 65%, and the column weights are set to 74%, 6%, and 20% to create a layout as shown below.

**Figure 7.8.3 – Layout Schematic for the Graph**

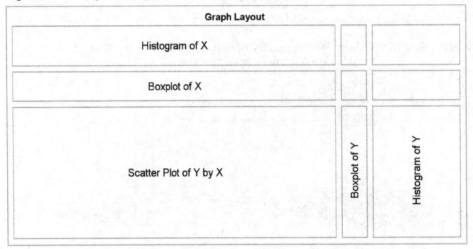

The structure of the graph is created by the following GTL code block.

```
layout lattice / columns=3 columndatarange=union
                rowweights=(0.2 0.15 0.65) rows=3 rowdatarange=union
                columnweights=(0.74 0.06 0.2);

  /*--Define 9 cells using Layout Overlay blocks*/
  layout overlay / <options>;
    < plot statements >
  endlayout;

endlayout;
```

Nine sets of LAYOUT OVERLAY – ENDLAYOUT blocks of code are used to populate each of the nine cells that are defined by the 3 x 3 settings in the LAYOUT LATTICE statement. Each block must contain either a plot statement or an ENTRY statement. In the actual lattice structure for the graph, we do not need cell borders, so individual ENTRY statements can be placeholders for each cell.

There must be a placeholder for each cell, or the arrangement will shift and thus cause alignment problems between axis types. Finally, there must be at least one valid plot type, or else the entire graph layout will be blank. The three cells in the top row are defined as follows.

```
/*--Top Row--*/
layout overlay / walldisplay=none;
  histogram _xvar;
endlayout;

entry ' ';

entry ' ';
```

The individual cells are populated in row major order, from top left to bottom right. Options can be used to reverse the order, if needed. The three cells in the middle row are defined as follows.

```
/*--Middle Row--*/
layout overlay / walldisplay=none;
  boxplot y=_XVar / orient=horizontal boxwidth=0.9;
endlayout;

entry ' ';

entry ' ';
```

Finally, the three cells in the bottom row are defined as follows.

```
/*--Bottom Row--*/
layout overlay / walldisplay=none;
  if (_type = 'heatmap')
    heatmap x=_xvar y=_yvar / xbins=100 ybins=50;
  else
    scatterplot x=_xvar y=_yvar / markerattrs=(symbol=circlefilled)
                datatransparency=0.95;
  endif;
  regressionplot x=_xvar y=_yvar / degree=2 lineattrs=graphdatadefault;
endlayout;

layout overlay / walldisplay=none;
  boxplot y=_YVar / boxwidth=0.9;
endlayout;

layout overlay / walldisplay=none;
  histogram _yvar / orient=horizontal;
endlayout;
```

Note the use of the dynamic variables "_XVar" and "_YVar". These are used to make the template flexible, and they are useful to create multiple graphs with different X- or Y-variables. These dynamic variables can be defined at run time in the PROC SGRENDER step as shown below. Here we have set _XVar='Weight' and _YVar='Systolic' to view the distribution of Systolic x

Weight. The use of dynamic variables allows us to define one template and use it repeatedly with different variable names.

```
proc sgrender data=sashelp.heart
template=Fig_7_8_Bivariate_Distribution_Plot;
   dynamic _XVar='Weight' _YVar='Systolic' _Type='scatter'
        _Title='A Scatter Plot of the Joint Bivariate Distribution of ';
   run;
```

We have also defined other dynamics: "_Type" and "_Title". The "_Type" dynamic is used to control the type of plot that is displayed in the lower-left cell of the graph. In the procedure invocation below, we have specified _Type="heatmap" to get the graph shown in Figure 7.8.4. We have also set the "_Title" dynamic to alter the title accordingly.

To get the "Blue-Yellow-Red" fill colors in the heat map, we have to change the settings for the three color fill ramp that is defined in the style. We have derived a new style called "RampListing" with a parent of Listing, and with the new colors shown below. Then, we have set this new style for the Listing destination. The graph is shown in Figure 7.8.4 below.

```
/*--Define a Style with Blue-Yellow-Red fill ramp--*/
proc template;
   define style RampListing;
      parent = styles.listing;
      style GraphColors from GraphColors /
         'gramp3cend' = cxDF0000
         'gramp3cneutral' = cxEFDF00
         'gramp3cstart' = cx4f7fCF
      ;
   end;
run;

/*--Render graph with Heatmap using RampListing style--*/
ods listing style=RampListing;
proc sgrender data=sashelp.heart
template=Fig_7_8_Bivariate_Distribution_Plot;
   dynamic _XVar='Weight' _YVar='Systolic' _Type='heatmap'
        _Title='A Heat Map of the Joint Bivariate Distribution of ';
   run;
```

**Figure 7.8.4 – Heat Map of the Joint Bivariate Distribution**

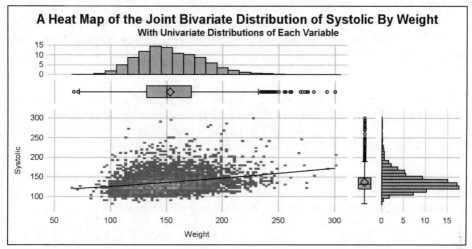

A heat map is a more useful and efficient plot type for display of the distribution of large data. When the number of observations grows large, into the millions or billions of observations, plotting each observation as a marker in a scatter plot becomes inefficient and ineffective.

Such large data sets are likely to reside on cloud servers, and retrieving each observation for plotting is not feasible. Even rendering the scatter plot on the server is not effective, as it is time-consuming, and all we will see is a glob of data. This is true even with the SASHELP.HEART data set, which has only 5400 observations. This can be seen in Figure 7.8.1.

However, creating a heat map provides a faster and more effective solution. Now, we are counting the number of observations in each bin of the plot. The number of bins is constant; they might be 100 x 50 in this case. Each bin is displayed using a color that represents the number of observations in the bin using a three-color model. Now, the areas of high or low density are clearly visible.

A gradient legend could have been included in the display, but I have chosen to skip it because the key here is to see the relative densities, not the actual densities. The full code for the template and graph creation can be seen in Program 7_8.

## 7.9 Summary

SAS 9.3 provides a powerful set of features to create clinical graphs. This includes the HEATMAP and HIGHLOWPLOT statements, and new features such as the Discrete and Range attribute maps. Also included are a set of draw statements to add the display of non-dataset driven shapes and text in the graph.

In this chapter, we have used the HIGHLOWPLOT statement to display confidence intervals. But we have also used it to display the indented rich text in the first column of the subgrouped forest plot as shown in Figure 7.6.1. The DRAWTEXT statement is used in multiple plots to display text labels or the y-axis label where a custom text was needed.

As shown in Chapters 3 and 4, many commonly used clinical graphs can be created using SG procedures. However, often you need a more complex layout of the data. In such cases, you can use GTL, which provides you with more options for the layout of your graph.

---

[1] Matange, Sanjay. "Graphically Speaking." Available at http://blogs.sas.com/content/graphicallyspeaking/. Last updated October 31, 2015. Accessed on February 1, 2016.

# Chapter 8:  Clinical Graphs Using SAS 9.4 GTL

Most commonly used clinical graphs have a simple single-cell structure with one main data area, two or more axes, and other related items such as axis tables that can be configured using the SGPLOT procedure as described in Chapters 3 and 4.  Other graphs have a regular grid of data cells determined by the number of unique values of one or more classifier variables. Such graphs can be easily created using the SGPANEL procedure as described in Chapter 5.  Such graphs generally cover a majority of the common use cases.

That brings us to the remaining cases where we have to go beyond the abilities of the SGPLOT or SGPANEL procedures to create graphs that need a special layout or display.

The graph in Figure 8.0 shows a multi-cell graph that uses a custom layout that cannot be produced by either the SGPLOT or SGPANEL procedures.

**Figure 8.0 – Multi-Cell Panel Graph**

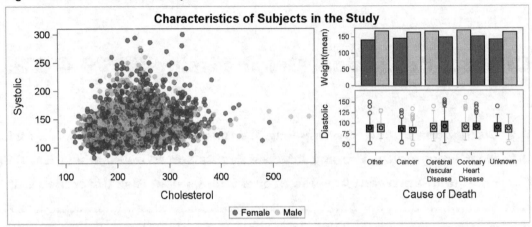

This graph uses a special layout that shows the distribution of Systolic blood pressure by Cholesterol on the left side of the graph. On the right side, the graph contains two plots that use a common x-axis. The upper plot shows a bar chart of mean Weight by Cause of Death. The lower plot shows a box plot of Diastolic blood pressure by Cause of Death.

The graph above in Figure 8.0 is built using the techniques described in Chapter 6. We have used the TEMPLATE procedure to define a StatGraph template using GTL. In this case, we have used nested LAYOUT LATTICE and LAYOUT OVERLAY statements to define the structure of the graph, populated with SCATTERPLOT, BARCHART, and BOXPLOT statements. Then, we have used the SGRENDER procedure to create the graph from the SASHELP.HEART data set. For full details see Program 8_0, available from the author's page at http://support.sas.com/matange.

In this chapter, we will create such graphs using SAS 9.4 GTL. SAS 9.4 includes some useful plot statements such as AXISTABLE that make our task easier. SAS 9.4 also supports features such as tick value splitting that enable you to split long multi-word tick values over multiple lines as shown on the right side of Figure 8.0.

## 8.1 Distribution of ASAT by Time and Treatment

The graph in Figure 8.1.1 displays the distribution of ASAT by time and treatment, along with the number of subjects in the study in the bottom cell, and the number of subjects with a value greater than 2 in the top cell.

**Figure 8.1.1 – Distribution of ASAT by Time and Treatment**

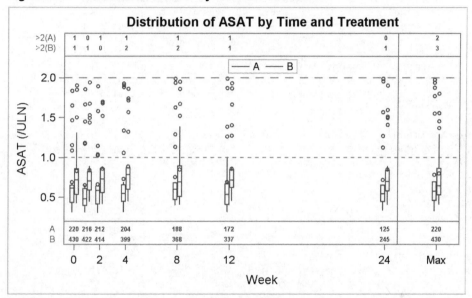

**Figure 8.1.2 – Data for Graph**

| Obs | Week | Drug | ASAT | count | DrugGT | gt2 |
|-----|------|------|---------|-------|--------|-----|
| 1 | 0 | A | 0.44797 | 220 | >2(A) | 1 |
| 2 | 0 | B | 0.79982 | 430 | >2(B) | 1 |
| 3 | 0 | A | 0.63728 | | >2(A) | |
| 4 | 0 | B | 0.44298 | | >2(B) | |
| 5 | 0 | A | 0.33984 | | >2(A) | |

With the advent of the AXISTABLE statement in SAS 9.4, it is possible to create this graph using a single LAYOUT OVERLAY container. The main body of the graph displays the ASAT value by treatment. Inner margins are used to display the number of subjects in the study and the number of subjects with ASAT values greater than 2 by treatment.

```
/*--Define the Template--*/
proc template;
  define statgraph Fig_8_1_ASAT_By_Time_and_Trt;
    begingraph;
```

```
         entrytitle 'Distributiion of ASAT by Time and Treatment';
      layout overlay / yaxisopts=(offsetmax=0.1)
                       xaxisopts=(type=linear
            linearopts=(tickvaluelist=(0 2 4 8 12 24 28) viewmax=29));
         boxplot x=week y=asat / group=drug name='a' groupdisplay=cluster
               display=(mean median outliers);
         referenceline x=25;
         referenceline y=1 / lineattrs=(pattern=shortdash);
         referenceline y=2 / lineattrs=(pattern=dash);
         discretelegend 'a' / itemsize=(linelength=20) location=inside
                             halign=center valign=top;

         innermargin / separator=true;
            axistable x=week value=count / class=drug colorgroup=drug
                  valueattrs=(size=5 weight=bold) labelattrs=(size=7);
         endinnermargin;

         innermargin / separator=true align=top;
            axistable x=week value=gt2 / class=drugGT colorgroup=drugGT
                  valueattrs=(size=5 weight=bold) labelattrs=(size=7);
         endinnermargin;
      endlayout;
   endgraph;
 end;
run;

/*--Render the Graph--*/
proc sgrender data=asat template=Fig_8_1_ASAT_By_Time_and_Trt;
run;
```

The graph uses one LAYOUT OVERLAY for the entire graph. The reason for this is that we are placing the upper and lower numbers inside the graph using INNERMARGIN statements.

The Overlay container contains one grouped box plot of ASAT by Week by Drug. Groups are displayed side-by-side. One reference line is used to place the vertical divider at X=25, and two reference lines are placed at Y=1 and 2 using different line patterns. A discrete legend is placed inside the graph area at the top center, and space is created by setting OFFSETMAX=0.1 on the YAXISOPTS.

The Subjects At-Risk are placed in the bottom inner margin region of the graph using an AXISTABLE of Count by Week classified (stacked) and colored by Drug. The number of subjects with values greater than 2 for A or B are shown at the top inner margin region using an AXISTABLE of GT2 by Week, also classified (stacked) and colored by DrugGT. Note, the data values that are shown in Figure 8.1.2 are simulated and might not match the data. For full details, see Program 8_1.

## 8.2 Most Frequent On-Therapy Adverse Events Sorted by Relative Risk

This graph displays the incidence of On-Therapy Adverse Events by Treatment, sorted by the relative risk of occurrence.

**Figure 8.2.1 – Most Frequent On-Therapy Adverse Events Sorted by Relative Risk**

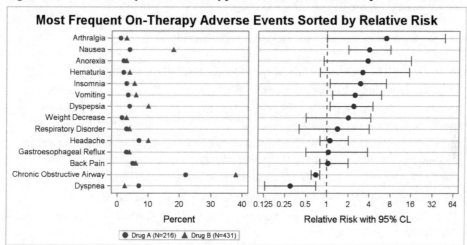

**Figure 8.2.2 – Data for Graph**

| Obs | AE | A | B | Mean | Low | High |
|---|---|---|---|---|---|---|
| 1 | Dyspnea | 7 | 2.5 | 0.30 | 0.13 | 0.7 |
| 2 | Chronic Obstructive Airway | 22 | 38.0 | 0.70 | 0.60 | 0.8 |
| 3 | Back Pain | 5 | 6.0 | 1.04 | 0.80 | 2.0 |
| 4 | Gastroesophageal Reflux | 3 | 4.0 | 1.05 | 0.50 | 3.8 |
| 5 | Headache | 7 | 10.0 | 1.10 | 0.80 | 2.0 |

The incidence of Adverse Events by Treatment is displayed on the left side of the graph, and the relative risks with 95% confidence intervals are displayed on the right. The adverse events are displayed, sorted by the mean of the relative risk.

A portion of the data set for the graph is shown in Figure 8.2.2 and contains six columns including the AE name, percent incidences for drug A and B, Mean value of the relative risk, and the low and high values for the 95% confidence limits. The values are drawn decreasing from the top of the y-axis.

The graph is created using LAYOUT LATTICE with two columns. The weights of the columns are set as (0.4, 0.6), so that the left column is narrower, with 40% of the width. The right column is wider, about 60% of the width. A gutter of 10 pixels is placed between the two cells.

Note, the two cells do not have separate y-axes. Instead, one common y-axis is displayed on the left, and it applies to both cells in the row. This also automatically aligns the corresponding values with the correct adverse event name for each cell. The plot on the left has a linear x-axis, but the plot on the right has a log (base 2) x-axis.

The structure of the template to create such a layout is shown below.

1. We use the PROC TEMPLATE statement to define a StatGraph template.
2. The GTL definition is between the BEGINGRAPH and ENDGRAPH statements.
3. An outer LAYOUT LATTICE container is used to create a layout of two columns with 40% and 60 % widths and a common y-axis. A COLUMNGUTTER of 10 pixels is used.
4. The ROWAXES – ENDROWAXES block with one ROWAXIS statement triggers the placement of the single row axis on the left, with grids, ticks, tick values, and line.
5. The first LAYOUT OVERLAY container defines the cell on the left.
6. The second LAYOUT OVERLAY container defines the cell on the right.
7. We finish off the template with the matching ENDLAYOUT, ENDGRAPH, END, and RUN statements.

```
proc template;
    define statgraph Fig_8_2_Most_Frequent_On_Therapy_Adverse_Events;
    begingraph;
        layout lattice / columns=2 columnweights=(0.4 0.6)
                         rowdatarange=union columngutter=10px;
            rowaxes;
              rowaxis / griddisplay=on display=(ticks tickvalues line);
            endrowaxes;

            /*--Left Cell--*/
            layout overlay;
            endlayout;

            /*--Right Cell--*/
            layout overlay;
            endlayout;
        endlayout;
    endgraph;
  end;
run;
```

The definition of the left cell is shown below. Some appearance options are skipped to fit the page.

1. The left cell is defined by the first LAYOUT OVERLAY – ENDLAYOUT block. All the plot statements in this block are layered together and displayed in the left cell.

2. The first SCATTERPLOT statement displays values for drug 'A' by 'AE'. The marker attributes are set to use a filled circle marker using the first group color from the style. This statement has NAME='a' and LEGENDLABEL="Drug A (N=&na)". The string is used for representing this plot in the legend. Note the use of the macro variable "&na".

3. The second SCATTERPLOT statement displays values for drug 'B' by 'AE'. The marker attributes are set to use a filled triangle marker using the second group color from the style. This statement has NAME='b', and LEGENDLABEL="Drug B (N=&nb)". The string is used for representing this plot in the legend. Note the use of the macro variable "&nb".

4. The DISCRETELEGEND statement includes plots 'a' and 'b'. This is drawn in the default location outside and below, centered on the x-axis of the graph.

```
/*--Left Cell--*/
layout overlay;
   scatterplot x=a y=ae / markerattrs=graphdata1(symbol=circlefilled)
               name='a' legendlabel="Drug A (N=&na)";
   scatterplot x=b y=ae /
               markerattrs=graphdata2(symbol=trianglefilled)
               name='b' legendlabel="Drug B (N=&nb)";
   discretelegend 'a' 'b' / valueattrs=(size=6) border=true;
endlayout;
```

The definition of the right cell is shown below. Some appearance options are skipped to fit the space.

1. The right cell is defined by the second LAYOUT OVERLAY – ENDLAYOUT block shown below. All the plot statements in this block are displayed in the right cell.

2. A SCATTERPLOT statement displays the 'Mean' occurrence values for by 'AE'. The marker attributes are set to a filled circle marker using the first default color from the style.

3. A vertical REFERENCELINE line with a dash pattern is drawn at Y=1.

5. The x-axis is of TYPE log with LOGBASE of 2.

```
/*--Right Cell--*/
layout overlay / xaxisopts=(label='Relative Risk with 95% CL'
                            type=log logopts=(base=2
                            tickintervalstyle=logexpand));
   scatterplot x=mean y=ae / xerrorlower=low xerrorupper=high
               markerattrs=(symbol=circlefilled);
   referenceline x=1 /
lineattrs=graphdatadefault(pattern=shortdash);
endlayout;
```

Some option settings for font and marker sizing have been trimmed to fit the code in the available space. See Program 8_2 for the full details.

## 8.3  Treatment Emergent Adverse Events with Largest Risk Difference with NNT

The graph shown in Figure 8.3.1 is a variation on the graph shown in Section 8.2, as created by SAS users Matt Cravets and Jeff Kopicko, using the data set shown in Figure 8.3.2.[1] The difference is the display of the "Numbers Needed to Treat" along the top X2 axis of the right cell, where NNT =1.0 / RiskDiff.

**Figure 8.3.1 – Treatment Emergent Adverse Events with Largest Risk Difference with NNT**

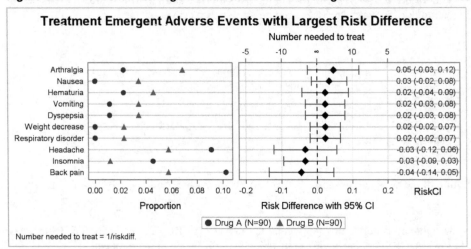

**Figure 8.3.2 – Data for Graph**

| Obs | AEDECOD | PCT0 | PCTR | Risk | LRisk | URisk | RiskCI | NNT |
|---|---|---|---|---|---|---|---|---|
| 1 | Back pain | 0.10227 | 0.057471 | -0.044801 | -0.13623 | 0.04663 | -0.04 (-0.14, 0.05) | -22.3207 |
| 2 | Insomnia | 0.04545 | 0.011494 | -0.033960 | -0.09434 | 0.02641 | -0.03 (-0.09, 0.03) | -29.4462 |
| 3 | Headache | 0.09091 | 0.057471 | -0.033438 | -0.12232 | 0.05545 | -0.03 (-0.12, 0.06) | -29.9063 |
| 4 | Respiratory disorder | 0.00000 | 0.022989 | 0.022989 | -0.01993 | 0.06591 | 0.02 (-0.02, 0.07) | 43.5000 |
| 5 | Weight decrease | 0.00000 | 0.022989 | 0.022989 | -0.01993 | 0.06591 | 0.02 (-0.02, 0.07) | 43.5000 |

Matt wanted to display the NNT axis along the top to match the RiskDiff axis, with inverse values at each tick mark. This means we have an axis that goes from negative small values to negative ∞, and then from positive ∞ to smaller positive values. That means we have two axes at the top.

To do this, we replicate the x-axis as the x2-axis at the top, with exactly the same settings. This ensures that the tick values are aligned, as seen in the very light grid lines. Then, the values on the x2-axis are replaced using the inverse of the values on the x-axis. The inverse of zero is replaced with the Unicode ∞ symbol "221e"x. Note the use of TICKVALUELIST and TICKDISPLAYLIST in the program shown below.

If the Unicode symbol ∞ is too small (as it appears here), we might need to find a better font or replace it using annotation.

```
/*--Define the Template--*/
proc template;
   define statgraph Fig_8_3;
   begingraph;
      entrytitle "Treatment Emergent Adverse Events with Largest ...";
      entryfootnote halign=left "Number needed to treat = 1/riskdiff." /;

      /* Define a Lattice layout with two columns and a common y-axis */
      layout lattice / columns=2 columnweights=(0.4 0.6)
                       rowdatarange=union columngutter=10px;
         rowaxes;
            rowaxis / griddisplay=on  display=(tickvalues)
                tickvalueattrs=(size=7);
         endrowaxes;

         /* Left cell with incidence values */
         layout overlay / xaxisopts=(label="Proportion" );
            scatterplot y=aedecod x=pct0 / name='drga'
                  markerattrs=(symbol=circlefilled color=bib)
                  legendlabel='Drug A (N=90)';
            scatterplot y=aedecod x=pctr / name='drgb'
                  markerattrs=(symbol=trianglefilled color=red)
                  legendlabel='Drug B (N=90)';
         endlayout;

        /* Right cell with risk differences and NNT */
        layout overlay / xaxisopts=(label="Risk Difference with 95% CI"
                            griddisplay=on gridattrs=(color=cxf7f7f7)
                            linearopts=(tickvaluefitpolicy=none
                            viewmin=-0.2 viewmax=0.2
                            tickvaluelist=(-0.20 -0.1  0 0.1 0.20)))
                    x2axisopts=(label="Number needed to treat"
                            linearopts=(tickvaluefitpolicy=none
                            viewmin=-0.2 viewmax=0.2
                            tickvaluelist=(-0.20 -0.1  0 0.1 0.20)
                            tickdisplaylist=('-5' '-10'
                            "(*ESC*){unicode '221e'x}"  '10' '5')));

           scatterplot y=aedecod x=risk / xerrorlower=lrisk
                     xerrorupper=urisk
                     markerattrs=(symbol=diamondfilled color=black);
           scatterplot y=aedecod x=risk / xaxis=x2 datatransparency=1;
           innermargin / align=right;
              axistable y=aedecod value=riskci /
                     class=origin display=(label) labelposition=min);
           endinnermargin;
           referenceline x=0 / lineattrs=(pattern=shortdash color=black);
        endlayout;
```

```
        /* Bottom-centered sidebar with legend */
        sidebar / align=bottom spacefill=false;
          discretelegend 'drga' 'drgb' / autoitemsize=true
                             valueattrs=(size=8);
        endsidebar;

      endlayout;
    endgraph;
  end;
run;
```

Some option settings have been trimmed to fit in the available space. See Program 8_3 for the full details.

## 8.4  Butterfly Plot of Cancer Deaths by Cause and Gender

The graph shown in Figure 8.4.1 is the classic butterfly chart showing the incidence of cancer cases by gender along with the deaths for each cause.

**Figure 8.4.1 – Butterfly Plot of Cancer Deaths by Cause and Gender**

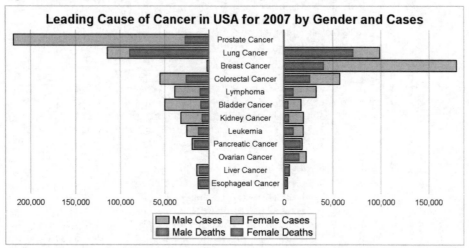

**Figure 8.4.2 – Data for Graph**

| Obs | Cause | MCases | FCases | MDeaths | FDeaths | Cases |
|---|---|---|---|---|---|---|
| 1 | Prostate Cancer | 218,890 | 0 | 27,050 | 0 | 218890 |
| 2 | Lung Cancer | 114,760 | 98,620 | 89,510 | 70,880 | 213380 |
| 3 | Breast Cancer | 2,030 | 178,480 | 450 | 40,460 | 180510 |
| 4 | Colorectal Cancer | 55,290 | 57,050 | 26,000 | 26,180 | 112340 |

The data is shown in Figure 8.4.2, with Cause, Male Cases, Female Cases, Male Deaths and Female Deaths, and total number of Deaths. A LAYOUT LATTICE is used to define the layout of the graph, with two columns as shown below in the GTL code snippet.

```
layout lattice / columns=2 columnweights=(0.45 0.55) rowdatarange=union;
  /*--Left cell--*/
  layout overlay;
  endlayout;
  /*--Right cell--*/
  layout overlay;
  endlayout;
endlayout;
```

Only two cells are defined using the LAYOUT OVERLAY – ENDLAYOUT blocks, so we have only one row. COLUMNWEIGHTS=(0.45 0.55) assigns 45% of the graph space to the left cell and 55% to the right cell. This is made so because the y-axis in the middle of the graph belongs to the right cell, and therefore it needs a bit more space to make the data space for each cell about equal.

The y-axis display for the left cell is suppressed, so the y-axis for the right cell serves as the common axis for both cells. ROWDATARANGE=Union is set to ensure that both cells have uniform y-axes. TICKVALUEHALIGN=Center is used to center-align the values on the y-axis, thus creating the expected appearance of a butterfly chart.

The left cell is defined by the first LAYOUT OVERLAY – ENDLAYOUT block of the GTL code shown below. Note the following aspects of this code:

1. The x-axis is reversed, and grid lines are displayed.
2. The y-axis is suppressed, and values are reversed so that they are positioned top down.
3. Wall display is suppressed to get the lightweight, modern look.
4. A horizontal bar chart of MCases by Cause is shown, with the name 'mc' and a legend label.
5. A horizontal bar chart of MDeaths by Cause is overlaid with a narrower bar width with the name 'md', and with skin effect.

```
/*--Left Cell--*/
layout overlay / xaxisopts=(reverse=true label='Males'
                            display=(tickvalues) griddisplay=on)
                 yaxisopts=(display=none reverse=true) walldisplay=none;
  barchart category=cause response=mcases /
           fillattrs=graphdata1(transparency=0.7) orient=horizontal
           name='mc' legendlabel='Male Cases';
  barchart category=cause response=mdeaths /
           fillattrs=graphdata1(transparency=0.3) orient=horizontal
           name='md' legendlabel='Male Deaths'
           barwidth=0.6 dataskin=pressed;
endlayout;
```

The right cell is defined by the second LAYOUT OVERLAY – ENDLAYOUT block of the GTL code shown below. Note the following aspects of this code:

1. The x-axis grid lines are displayed.
2. The y-axis values are reversed so that they are positioned top down, and the tick values are center-justified. This serves as the common central y-axis for both cells of the graph.
3. A horizontal bar chart of FCases by Cause is shown, with the name 'fc' and a legend label.
4. A horizontal bar chart of FDeaths by Cause is overlaid with a narrower bar width with the name 'fd', and with skin effect.

```
/*--Right Cell--*/
layout overlay / xaxisopts=(reverse=true label='Males'
                            display=(tickvalues) griddisplay=on)
                 yaxisopts=(display=none reverse=true) walldisplay=none;
  barchart category=cause response=mcases /
           fillattrs=graphdata1(transparency=0.7) orient=horizontal
           name='mc' legendlabel='Male Cases';
  barchart category=cause response=mdeaths /
           fillattrs=graphdata1(transparency=0.3) orient=horizontal
           name='md' legendlabel='Male Deaths'
           barwidth=0.6 dataskin=pressed;
endlayout;
```

The common discrete legend is placed in the bottom side bar as shown in the code snippet below. The names of each statement that contributes to the legend are listed. The items are positioned in two columns. The ITEMSIZE option is used to display slightly bigger fill items with the "Golden" aspect ratio. These bigger items are easier to decode.

```
/*--Bottom Side Bar--*/
sidebar / spacefill=false;
  discretelegend 'mc' 'fc' 'md' 'fd' / across=2
                 itemsize=(fillheight=10px fillaspectratio=golden);
endsidebar;
```

Alternatively, the data can be sorted descending by total deaths as shown in Figure 8.4.3.

**Figure 8.4.3 – Data for Graph, Sorted Descending by Total Deaths**

| Obs | Cause | MCases | FCases | MDeaths | FDeaths | Deaths |
|---|---|---|---|---|---|---|
| 1 | Lung Cancer | 114,760 | 98,620 | 89,510 | 70,880 | 160,390 |
| 2 | Colorectal Cancer | 55,290 | 57,050 | 26,000 | 26,180 | 52,180 |
| 3 | Breast Cancer | 2,030 | 178,480 | 450 | 40,460 | 40,910 |
| 4 | Pancreatic Cancer | 18,830 | 18,340 | 16,840 | 16,530 | 33,370 |

The full GTL code is shown below. Some appearance options have been trimmed to fit the space. See Program 8_4 for the full details.

```
proc template;
  define statgraph Fig_8_4_Butterfly_Plot_Of_Cancer_Deaths;
    begingraph;
      entrytitle "Leading Cause of Cancer Deaths in USA for 2007 ...";
      layout lattice / columns=2 columnweights=(0.45 0.55)
            rowdatarange=union;

        /*--Left Cell--*/
        layout overlay / walldisplay=none
                xaxisopts=(reverse=true tickvalueattrs=(size=7)
                    label='Males' display=(tickvalues) griddisplay=on)
                yaxisopts=(display=none reverse=true);
          barchart category=cause response=mcases / orient=horizontal
                fillattrs=graphdata1(transparency=0.7)
                name='mc' legendlabel='Male Cases';
          barchart category=cause response=mdeaths / name='md'
                fillattrs=graphdata1(transparency=0.3) barwidth=0.6
                orient=horizontal dataskin=pressed
                legendlabel='Male Deaths';
        endlayout;

        /*--Right Cell--*/
        layout overlay / walldisplay=none
                  xaxisopts=(tickvalueattrs=(size=7)  label='Females'
                        display=(tickvalues) griddisplay=on)
                  yaxisopts=(tickvaluehalign=center
                        display=(tickvalues line) reverse=true
                        tickvalueattrs=(size=7));
          barchart category=cause response=fcases /
                fillattrs=graphdata2(transparency=0.7)
                orient=horizontal
                name='fc' legendlabel='Female Cases';
          barchart category=cause response=fdeaths / name='fd'
                fillattrs=graphdata2(transparency=0.3)
                orient=horizontal dataskin=pressed
                legendlabel='Female Deaths';
        endlayout;

        /*--Bottom Side Bar--*/
        sidebar / spacefill=false;
          discretelegend 'mc' 'fc' 'md' 'fd' / across=2
                    itemsize=(fillheight=10px fillaspectratio=golden);
        endsidebar;

      endlayout;
    endgraph;
  end;
run;
```

```
ods graphics / reset width=5in height=2.5in
imagename='8_4_Butterfly_Plot';
proc sgrender data=cancerByCases
            template=Fig_8_4_Butterfly_Plot_Of_Cancer_Deaths;
run;
```

## 8.5  Forest Plot of Impact of Treatment on Mortality by Study

A forest plot is a graphical representation of a meta-analysis of the results of randomized controlled trials.

**Figure 8.5.1 – Forest Plot of Impact of Treatment on Mortality by Study**

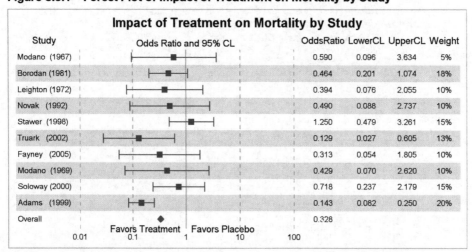

**Figure 8.5.2 – Data for Graph**

| Obs | Study | Grp | OddsRatio | LowerCL | UpperCL | Weight | Q1 | Q3 |
|-----|-------|-----|-----------|---------|---------|--------|-----|-----|
| 7 | Fayney (2005) | 1 | 0.313 | 0.054 | 1.805 | 10% | 0.28 | 0.34 |
| 8 | Modano (1969) | 1 | 0.429 | 0.070 | 2.620 | 10% | 0.39 | 0.47 |
| 9 | Soloway (2000) | 1 | 0.718 | 0.237 | 2.179 | 15% | 0.61 | 0.83 |
| 10 | Adams (1999) | 1 | 0.143 | 0.082 | 0.250 | 20% | 0.11 | 0.17 |
| 11 | Overall | 2 | 0.328 | . | . | . | . | . |

The graph in Figure 8.5.1 shows the names of the studies on the left, with a plot of the measure of the effect as an odds ratio of each study and the 95% confidence intervals.  Area or width of each marker can be proportional to the weight of each study.  The overall meta-analyzed measure of effect is plotted with a diamond-shaped marker.  The actual values of the odds ratio, confidence limits, and weight are displayed on the right.

The graph uses a log x-axis, with reference lines at various levels and one at "1", which indicates "no Effect". If the odds ratio and CL overlap the "no-effect" line, it demonstrates their effect sizes do not differ from no-effect for the individual study at the given level of confidence.

The graph in Figure 8.5.1 can be created using one LAYOUT OVERLAY container with a SCATTERPLOT statement to display the odds ratio and confidence limits. Two inner margin regions are used to plot the textual data, with study names on the left and values on the right.

The overall structure of the GTL template is shown below.

```
layout overlay;
  scatterplot <parameters>;

  /*--Study Names on the Left--*/
  innermargin / align=left;
  endInnerMargin;

  /*--Study values on the Right--*/
  innermargin / align=right;
  endInnerMargin;

endlayout;
```

The odds ratio and confidence limits are plotted by the study names using the SCATTERPLOT statement in the overlay container as shown below. The study name column is assigned to the Y role. Reference lines are drawn at 0.01, 0.1, 10, and 100 using the first REFERENCELINE statement.

The X role for reference line accepts either a data column or one data value. So, we could either provide four different REFERENCELINE statements, or one statement with X pointing to a column in the data that would contain these four values. Here, we have used the COLN() function, which produces a column of the values. Because these values are static, I can use the function with the fixed values inline in the GTL syntax. A second REFERENCELINE statement is used to display the value at X=1 using different visual attributes. Note the use of the DATATRANSPARENCY and PATTERN options.

```
layout overlay / walldisplay=none
                 yaxisopts=(reverse=true display=none offsetmax=0.05
                           discreteopts=(colorbands=even));
                 xaxisopts=(type=log tickvaluepriority=true
                           logopts=(tickvaluelist=(0.01 0.1 1 10 100))
                           display=(tickvalues) displaysecondary=(label)
                           label='Odds Ratio and 95% CL');
  scatterplot y=study x=oddsratio / group=grp
              xerrorlower=lowercl xerrorupper=uppercl;
  referenceline x=eval(coln(0.01, 0.1, 10, 100)) /
              lineattrs=(pattern=shortdash) datatransparency=0.5;
  referenceline x=1 / datatransparency=0.5;
endlayout;
```

The values are displayed in reverse order, from top to bottom, so the last value in the data "Overall" is at the bottom. The x-axis line and ticks are suppressed, and the wall fill and outline are suppressed to provide a lightweight, modern look. The tick values are set to the ones desired, and this also sets the extent of the axis by the use of TICKVALUEPRIORITY. The axis label "Odds Ratio and 95% CL" is displayed on the secondary x-axis.

The study names on the left could be displayed using the y-axis tick values. Normally, axis tick values are right-aligned, but we could fix this using the SAS 9.4 TICKVALUEHALIGN option. However, we also need the label on the top, and we will use a different method. So, the entire y-axis is turned off.

Now, let us examine how we have displayed the study names on the left and the study values on the right. The overlay layout supports inner margins on all four sides of the container. This enables us to insert one-dimensional items in each inner margin. By one-dimensional, we mean items that span the axis in one direction (say, x), but have a well-defined size in the other direction (in this case, y). Usually, these are text-based statements, like axis tables and block plots.

The code snippet below describes the addition of the study labels on the left. We have used an inner margin that is aligned to the left of the container. We have added an AXISTABLE statement, with Y=Study, the same Y variable used with the scatter plot in the middle of the container. It is important to use either the same variable, or else a matching variable, in order to retain the correct alignment of the values across the graph for each study name. The label (header) for the column is displayed, and the font is customized.

```
innermargin / align=left;
  axistable y=study value=study / display=(label) labelattrs=(size=8);
endinnermargin;
```

The code snippet below describes how we have added the display of the four study values on the right by using an inner margin that is aligned to the right of the container. Four AXISTABLE statements are used, each with Y=Study, assigning VALUE to the appropriate column name in the data. The label for each column is displayed, and the values are center-aligned.

```
innermargin / align=right;
  axistable y=study value=Oddsratio / display=(label) labelattrs=(size=8)
            showmissing=false valuehalign=center;
  axistable y=study value=lowercl / display=(label) labelattrs=(size=8)
            showmissing=false valuehalign=center;
  axistable y=study value=uppercl / display=(label) labelattrs=(size=8)
            showmissing=false  valuehalign=center;
  axistable y=study value=weight / display=(label) labelattrs=(size=8)
            showmissing=false  valuehalign=center;
endinnermargin;
```

The last detail is the addition of the labels "Favors Treatment" and "Favors Placebo" to each side of the no-effect line on the x-axis. Normally, an ENTRY statement is used to position text inside a graph area. However, that can be positioned relative only to the container and not to data values. To do that, we either have to use annotation, or the DRAWTEXT statement.

```
drawtext textattrs=(size=8) 'Favors Placebo' / x=1.2 y=0
         xspace=datavalue yspace=wallpercent anchor=left width=50;
drawtext textattrs=(size=8) 'Favors Treatment' / x=0.8 y=0
             xspace=datavalue yspace=wallpercent anchor=right width=50;
```

If the position of the labels were to change from case to case, then the right way would be to use annotation. However, in this case, the labels are always aligned to the no-effect (x=1) value. So, we can use the DRAWTEXT statement, as shown above.

Two DRAWTEXT statements are used, one for each label. The labels are placed with XSPACE of DataValue and YSPACE of WallPercent. Therefore, the x position is relative to data, but the y position is relative to the bottom edge of the container. Also, the appropriate ANCHOR is used to position each label. Extra space is created at the bottom of the graph for the labels using the OFFSETMAX option in YAXISOPTS.

Faint color bands are drawn behind alternate study values to help draw the eye to the study names, odds ratio graph, and the study values across the width of the graph. The full GTL code is shown below. Some appearance options have been trimmed to fit the space. See Program 8_5 for the full details.

```
proc template;
  define statgraph Fig_8_5_Forest_Plot;
    begingraph / datasymbols=(squarefilled diamondfilled);
      entrytitle "Impact of Treatment on Mortality by Study";
      layout overlay / walldisplay=none
            yaxisopts=(reverse=true display=none offsetmax=0..05
                       discreteopts=(colorbands=even
                          colorbandsattrs=(transparency=0.5)))
            xaxisopts=(type=log logopts=(tickvaluelist=(0.01 0.1 1 10 100)
                       tickvaluepriority=true) display=(tickvalues)
                       displaysecondary=(label)
                       label='Odds Ratio and 95% CL' labelattrs=(size=8)
                       tickvalueattrs=(size=7));
        scatterplot y=study x=oddsratio / group=grp
                    xerrorlower=lowercl xerrorupper=uppercl;
      referenceline x=eval(coln(0.01, 0.1, 10, 100)) /
              lineattrs=(pattern=shortdash);
      referenceline x=1 / datatransparency=0.5;

      innermargin / align=left;
        axistable y=study value=study / display=(label);
      endinnermargin;

      innermargin / align=right;
        axistable y=study value=Oddsratio  / display=(label)
                  showmissing=false;
        axistable y=study value=lowercl    / display=(label)
                  showmissing=false;
        axistable y=study value=uppercl    / display=(label))
                  showmissing=false;
```

```
        axistable y=study value=weight      / display=(label)
                   showmissing=false;
     endinnermargin;

     drawtext textattrs=(size=8) 'Favors Placebo' / x=1.2 y=0
               xspace=datavalue yspace=wallpercent anchor=left
               width=50;
     drawtext textattrs=(size=8) 'Favors Treatment' / x=0.8 y=0
               xspace=datavalue yspace=wallpercent anchor=right
               width=50;

        endlayout;
     endgraph;
  end;
run;

ods graphics / reset attrpriority=none;
proc sgrender data=forest template=Fig_8_5_Forest_Plot;
run;
```

## 8.6  Forest Plot of Hazard Ratios by Patient Subgroups

The graph shown in Figure 8.6.1 shows the hazard ratios by patient subgroups.  This graph is much like the forest plot shown in Section 8.5, with the added feature of grouping the study values by subgroups.  The subgroup labels are displayed with a bold font, but the individual subgroup values are displayed in normal font and indented.

**Figure 8.6.1 – Forest Plot of Hazard Ratios by Patient Subgroups**

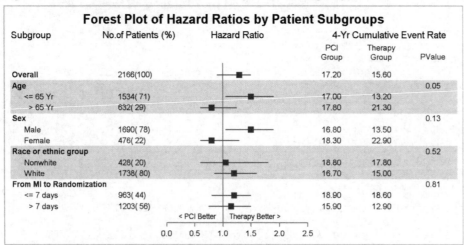

**Figure 8.6.2 – Data for Graph**

| Obs | Indent | Subgroup | Count | Percent | CountPct | Mean | Low | High | PCIGroup | Group | PValue | Ref | Type |
|---|---|---|---|---|---|---|---|---|---|---|---|---|---|
| 1 | 0.0 | Overall | 2166 | 100 | 2166(100) | 1.3 | 0.90 | 1.50 | 17.20 | 15.60 | . | | G |
| 2 | 0.0 | Age | . | . | | . | . | . | . | . | 0.05 | Age | G |
| 3 | 1.0 | <= 65 Yr | 1534 | 71 | 1534( 71) | 1.5 | 1.05 | 1.90 | 17.00 | 13.20 | . | <= 65 Yr | |
| 4 | 1.4 | > 65 Yr | 632 | 29 | 632( 29) | 0.8 | 0.60 | 1.25 | 17.80 | 21.30 | . | > 65 Yr | |
| 5 | 0.0 | Sex | . | . | | . | . | . | . | . | 0.13 | | G |
| 6 | 1.0 | Male | 1690 | 78 | 1690( 78) | 1.5 | 1.05 | 1.90 | 16.80 | 13.50 | . | | |

As noted, the construction of this graph is very similar to the one in Section 8.5, and we have used the AXISTABLE statement to display the textual data by subgroup. A portion of the data set is displayed in Figure 8.6.2. Note the "Indent" column that provides a measure of how much to indent each value. The subgroup labels have zero indention, and the regular values have an indention of 1 unit. Note, for some values, the indention is larger. This is to allow the alignment of the values adjusting for the "<=" or ">" symbols.

The graph above is created using a LAYOUT LATTICE container with one LAYOUT OVERLAY to display the graph and the data columns. A SIDEBAR statement is used to create the multi-level header. The hazard ratio graph is displayed in the middle of the overlay container. One INNERMARGIN statement is placed on the left for the two columns, and one INNERMARGIN statement on the right to display the three columns on the right.

The overall structure of the GTL template is shown below.

```
layout lattice;

  sidebar / align=top;
    layout lattice / columns=4;
    endlayout;
  endsidebar;

  layout overlay;
    scatterplot <parameters>;

    /*--Subgroup Patient Counts on the Left--*/
    innermargin / align=left;
    endInnerMargin;

    /*--Event Rate values on the Right--*/
    innermargin / align=right;
    endInnerMargin;

  endlayout;
endlayout;
```

A LAYOUT LATTICE is used to partition the graph area into the header information at the top and the graph and tables at the bottom. A SIDEBAR statement is used at the top of the lattice. This contains a nested LAYOUT LATTICE with four columns. The COLUMNWEIGHTS option is used to set the width of each column. ENTRY statements are used to define the column headers.

The graph, along with the subgroup names and values, is displayed in the main overlay container using the LAYOUT OVERLAY. Wall fill and outline are turned off to create a modern, lightweight look. The x-axis label is suppressed, and it is shown in the header on top. A specific tick value list is provided, and the axis data extent is set by the tick list using the TICKVALUEPRIORITY option. Display of the entire y-axis is turned off using DISPLAY=none. Display of the values is reversed, so "Overall" is shown at the top.

```
/*--Column headers--*/
sidebar / align=top;
  layout lattice / columns=4 columnweights=(0.2 0.25 0.25 0.3);
    entry textattrs=(size=8) halign=left "Subgroup";
    entry textattrs=(size=8) halign=left " No.of Patients (%)";
    entry textattrs=(size=8) halign=left "Hazard Ratio";
    entry halign=center textattrs=(size=8) "4-Yr Cumulative Event Rate";
  endlayout;
endsidebar;
```

The hazard ratio graph is a scatter plot of Mean by Subgroup. Confidence limits are displayed using the XERRORLOWER and XERRORUPPER options. Note, the Subgroup values will be displayed using the first AXISTABLE statement by Subgroup. All AXISTABLES will use Y=Subgroup to ensure that all the Subgroup labels and values are correctly aligned with the hazard plot. See the code snippet below.

An INNERMARGIN statement is placed on the left side and contains two axis tables to display the Subgroup values and the Patient counts. The first AXISTABLE statement uses INDENTWEIGHT=Indent to position the values that are indented from the left side. INDENTWEIGHT is a multiplier on the INDENT value, which is 1/8" by default. So, indent weight of zero means no indention. Other values of 1.0 and 1.4 are used to indent the values as needed.

```
/*--Hazard Ratio graph--*/
layout overlay / walldisplay=none
                 xaxisopts=(display=(ticks tickvalues line))
                           linearopts=(tickvaluepriority=true
                                 tickvaluelist=(0.0 0.5 1.0 1.5 2.0 2.5)))
                 yaxisopts=(reverse=true display=none offsetmax=0.1);

  referenceline y=ref / lineattrs=(thickness=14 color=_color);
  referenceline x=1;
  scatterplot y=subgroup x=mean / xerrorlower=low xerrorupper=high
              markerattrs=(symbol=squarefilled) errorbarcapshape=none;

  innermargin / align=left;
    axistable y=subgroup value=subgroup / indentweight=indent
              textgroup=type display=(values) valueattrs=(size=7);
```

```
      axistable y=subgroup value=countpct / display=(values)
              valueattrs=(size=7);
  endinnermargin;

  innermargin / align=right;
    axistable y=subgroup value=PCIGroup / showmissing=false
              valuehalign=center pad=(right=10pct);
    axistable y=subgroup value=group / showmissing=false
              valuehalign=center pad=(right=10pct);
    axistable y=subgroup value=pvalue / showmissing=false
              valuehalign=center pad=(right=5pct);
  endinnermargin;

endlayout;
```

Also note the use of TEXTGROUP=Type. This option is used in conjunction with DISCRETEATTRMAP and DISCRETEATTRVAR to use the bold font for observations that have Type='G'. Display of missing values is suppressed using SHOWMISSING=False, and the columns on the right are padded to fit in the space under the spanning header.

In this graph we have used alternating horizontal bands to group observations together to make the graph easier to read. Except for the first "Overall" observation, three observations including the subgroup and its two values are grouped together using the shaded horizontal bands. This is done by drawing wide reference lines with Y=ref. The column 'Ref' has a copy of the Subgroup column for alternating three observations followed by three with missing values.

The x-axis line will extend from end to end, including the inner margin zone. We can use the option AXISLINEEXTENT=Data to restrict the axis line to the data extent only. The "PCI Better" and "Therapy Better" labels are displayed using the DRAWTEXT statements as shown below. The labels are positioned close to the x=1 reference line, using XSPACE=data and appropriate ANCHOR.

```
drawtext textattrs=(size=6) '< PCI Better'  / x=0.9 y=1
        xspace=datavalue yspace=wallpercent anchor=bottomright width=50;
drawtext textattrs=(size=6) 'Therapy Better >' / x=1.1 y=1
        xspace=datavalue yspace=wallpercent anchor=bottomleft width=50;
```

The full GTL code block is shown below. Some appearance options have been trimmed to fit in the space available. See Program 8_6 for the full details.

```
proc template;
  define statgraph Fig_8_6_Forest_Plot_with_Subgroups;
    dynamic _color;
    begingraph / axislineextent=data;
      entrytitle 'Forest Plot of Hazard Ratios by Patient Subgroups ';
```

```
   discreteAttrmap name='text';
     value 'G' / textattrs=(weight=bold);
     value other;
   endDiscreteAttrmap;
   discreteAttrvar attrvar=type var=type attrmap='text';

   layout lattice / columns=1;

/*--Column headers--*/
   sidebar / align=top;
     layout lattice / columns=4 columnweights=(0.2 0.25 0.25 0.3);
       entry textattrs=(size=8) halign=left "Subgroup";
       entry textattrs=(size=8) halign=left " No.of Patients (%)";
       entry textattrs=(size=8) halign=left "Hazard Ratio";
       entry halign=center "4-Yr Cumulative Event Rate";
     endlayout;
   endsidebar;

   /*--Hazard Ratio graph--*/
   layout overlay / walldisplay=none <xaxisopts> <yaxisopts>;

     /*--Draw color Bands--*/
     referenceline y=ref / lineattrs=(thickness=14 color=_color);
     referenceline x=1;

     /*--Draw Hazard Ratios--*/
     scatterplot y=subgroup x=mean / xerrorlower=low
                 xerrorupper=high errorbarcapshape=none
                 markerattrs=(symbol=squarefilled);

     /*--Draw axis labels--*/
     drawtext textattrs=(size=6) '< PCI Better' / <opts>;
     drawtext textattrs=(size=6) 'Therapy Better >' / <opts>;

     /*--Draw Subgroup and Patient Count columns--*/
     innermargin / align=left;
       axistable y=subgroup value=subgroup / indentweight=indent
                 textgroup=type display=(values);
       axistable y=subgroup value=countpct / display=(values);
     endinnermargin;

     /*--Draw Subgroup Values--*/
     innermargin / align=right;
       axistable y=subgroup value=PCIGroup / showmissing=false
                 valuehalign=center pad=(right=10pct);
       axistable y=subgroup value=group / showmissing=false
                 valuehalign=center pad=(right=10pct);
       axistable y=subgroup value=pvalue / showmissing=false
                 valuehalign=center pad=(right=5pct);
     endinnermargin;

   endlayout;
 endlayout;
```

```
      endgraph;
    end;
run;

ods graphics / reset attrpriority=none;
proc sgrender data=forestWithSubgroups2
              template=Fig_8_6_Forest_Plot_with_Subgroups;
    dynamic _color='cxf0f0f0';
run;
```

## 8.7 Product-Limit Survival Estimates

Product-limit survival estimates can be used to measure the lengths of time that patients survive after treatment.

**Figure 8.7.1 – Product-Limit Survival Estimates**

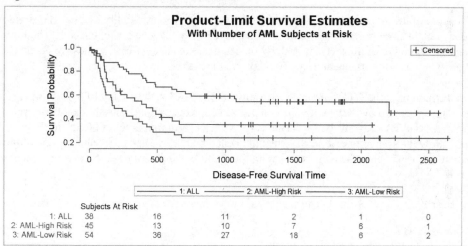

**Figure 8.7.2 – Data for Graph**

| Obs | Time | Survival | AtRisk | Event | Censored | tAtRisk | Stratum | StratumNum |
|-----|------|----------|--------|-------|----------|---------|---------|------------|
| 1 | 0 | 1.00000 | 38 | 0 | . | . | 1: ALL | 1 |
| 2 | 0 | . | 38 | . | . | 0 | 1: ALL | 1 |
| 3 | 1 | 0.97368 | 38 | 1 | . | . | 1: ALL | 1 |
| 4 | 55 | 0.94737 | 37 | 1 | . | . | 1: ALL | 1 |

This product-limit survival estimate graph shown in Figure 8.7.1 can be obtained directly by running the LIFETEST procedure with the sample data SASHELP.BMT. The LIFETEST procedure uses a pre-built GTL template to create this graph. In this section, we will go over how to design such a template so that you can customize the graph to suit your needs.

The first step is to generate the data that is required to create this graph. We can do that by running the LIFETEST procedure code shown below. The ODS OUTPUT statement is used to write the data.

```
ods output Survivalplot=SurvivalPlotData;
proc lifetest data=sashelp.BMT plots=survival(atrisk=0 to 2500 by 500);
   time T * Status(0);
   strata Group / test=logrank adjust=sidak;
run;
```

The table above contains multiple observations of the survival probability by time for leukemia stratified by type. The types include the Acute Lymphocytic Leukemia (ALL) and two types of Acute Myeloid Leukemia (AML), AML-High Risk and AML Low-Risk.

The key feature of the graph is the display of the survival curves of probability by time and stratum in the upper cell. The censored observations are displayed with a legend inside the cell. The lower cell contains the number of Subjects At-Risk by time and strata. The At-Risk values are displayed by tAtRisk, which is non-missing at every 500 days on the x-axis.

The overall structure of the GTL template is as shown below. A LAYOUT LATTICE is used to split the graph space into two cells with one column. The x-axes of both cells are made uniform using COLUMNDATARANGE=Union. The ROWWEIGHTS option is set to PREFERRED, which will allow the system to compute the height needed by the At-Risk table, and the rest of the graph height is given over to the upper cell. With this feature, we do not need to provide the height of each cell.

```
layout lattice / columns=1 columndatarange=union rowweights=preferred;

  /*--Upper Cell--*/
  layout overlay / walldisplay=none
  endlayout;

  /*--Lower Cell--*/
  layout overlay / walldisplay=none xaxisopts=(display=none);
  endlayout;

endlayout;
```

Two cells are defined, one by each of the LAYOUT OVERLAY – ENDLAYOUT blocks. In this case, we want to display only one x-axis. We could use the COLUMNAXES construct, but that will place the single x-axis at the bottom. Since we want to display the axis for the upper cell, we did not use the COLUMNAXES construct. Instead, we shut off the x-axis for the lower cell. The option COLUMNDATARANGE=Union will ensure that the axes are uniform.

The details of the upper cell are shown below. Some appearance options have been trimmed to fit the space available. The step plot of survival by time with group of stratum draws the survival curves.

```
/*--Upper Cell--*/
layout overlay / walldisplay=none
                 yaxisopts=(display=(ticks tickvalues line));

  stepplot x=time y=survival / group=stratum name='s';
  scatterplot x=time y=censored / markerattrs=(symbol=plus) name='c';
  scatterplot x=time y=censored / markerattrs=(symbol=plus)
              group=stratum;
  discretelegend 'c' / location=inside halign=right valign=top;
  discretelegend 's' / valueattrs=(size=7);

  /*--Draw the Y axis label closer to the axis--*/
  drawtext textattrs=(size=8) 'Survival Probability' / x=-6 y=50
           anchor=bottom xspace=wallpercent yspace=wallpercent
           rotate=90 width=50;
endlayout;
```

The scatter plots are used to display the censored observations. The first scatter plot with name 'c' draws the censored observations without a group. So, these markers use plus symbols and are drawn with default color. This scatter plot is included in the inner legend. The second scatter plot overplots the censored markers, with group = stratum so that we see the colored markers. A second discrete legend of the three stratum values for the step plot is displayed below the upper cell.

Because we have uniform axes, and the lower cell has long label values for each stratum, the y-axis for the upper cell gets pushed out beyond the long label values. To remedy this situation, we have turned off the display of the y-axis label and displayed the label using the DRAWTEXT statement.

The details of the lower cell are shown below. The At-Risk values are displayed using the AXISTABLE statement of AtRisk by tAtRisk by Stratum. The values for tAtRisk are non-missing only at an interval of 500 days, so the At-Risk values are drawn only at these tick values. CLASS=Stratum stacks the values for each stratum in a table of rows. COLORGROUP=stratum draws the values using the same color as the survival curves, thus making it easier to associate the numbers with the curves.

```
/*--Lower Cell for Subjects At-Risk--*/
layout overlay / walldisplay=none xaxisopts=(display=none);
  axistable x=tatrisk value=atrisk / class=stratum colorgroup=stratum
            title='Subjects At Risk' titleattrs=(size=7);
endlayout;
```

The full program is shown below. Some appearance options are trimmed to fit. Please see the full code in Program_8_7.

```
proc template;
  define statgraph Fig_8_7_Survival_plot_out;
```

```
   begingraph  / axislineextent=data;
     entrytitle 'Product-Limit Survival Estimates';
     entrytitle 'With Number of AML Subjects at Risk' /
                 textattrs=(size=8);
       layout lattice / columns=1 columndatarange=union
                         rowweights=preferred rowgutter=10px;
         /*--Upper cell--*/
         layout overlay / walldisplay=none;
                          yaxisopts=(display=(ticks tickvalues line));
           stepplot x=time y=survival / group=stratum name='s';
           scatterplot x=time y=censored /
                       markerattrs=(symbol=plus) name='c';
           scatterplot x=time y=censored /
                       markerattrs=(symbol=plus) GROUP=stratum;
           discretelegend 'c' / location=inside
                       halign=right valign=top valueattrs=(size=7);
           discretelegend 's' / valueattrs=(size=7);

           /*--Draw the Y axis label closer to the axis--*/
           drawtext textattrs=(size=8) 'Survival Probability' /
                    x=-6 y=50 rotate=90 width=50
                    anchor=bottom xspace=wallpercent yspace=wallpercent;
         endlayout;

         /*--Lower cell--*/
         layout overlay / walldisplay=none xaxisopts=(display=none);
          /*--Subjects at risk--*/
          axistable x=tatrisk value=atrisk /
                    class=stratum colorgroup=stratum
                    labelattrs=(size=7) valueattrs=(size=7)
                    title='Subjects At Risk' titleattrs=(size=7);
         endlayout;

       endlayout;
     endgraph;
   end;
run;

proc sgrender data=SurvivalPlotData template=Fig_8_7_Survival_plot_out;
   run;
```

The graph that is shown at the beginning of this section shows a traditional layout of the product-limit survival plot, where the values of Subjects At-Risk are displayed at the bottom of the graph, below the x-axis values, label, and the legend. This places a considerable distance between these related parts of the graph, making it harder to decipher the graph.

It is possible to improve the layout of the graph, placing the survival curves and the "Subjects At-Risk" data closer for easier understanding of the data. This arrangement is shown below.

**Figure 8.7.3 – Product-Limit Survival Estimates with Inner Table**

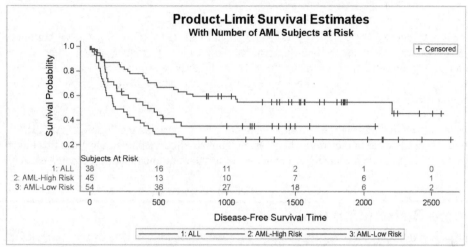

The GTL code for this graph is shown below. We need only one LAYOUT OVERLAY, and both the survival curves and the Subjects At-Risk information can be placed in one container.

```
proc template;
   define statgraph Fig_8_7_Survival_plot_in;
      begingraph;
         entrytitle 'Product-Limit Survival Estimates';
         entrytitle 'With Number of AML Subjects at Risk' /
                    textattrs=(size=8);
         layout overlay / walldisplay=none
                  xaxisopts=(labelattrs=(size=8) tickvalueattrs=(size=7))
                  yaxisopts=(labelattrs=(size=8) tickvalueattrs=(size=7));
            stepplot x=time y=survival / group=stratum  name='s';
            scatterplot x=time y=censored / markerattrs=(symbol=plus)
                     name='c';
            scatterplot x=time y=censored / markerattrs=(symbol=plus)
                     group=stratum;
            discretelegend 'c' / location=inside halign=right valign=top
                     valueattrs=(size=7);
            discretelegend 's' / valueattrs=(size=7);

            /*--Subjects at risk--*/
            innermargin / align=bottom;
               axistable x=tatrisk value=atrisk / class=stratum
                        colorgroup=stratum
                        title='Subjects At Risk' titleattrs=(size=7);
            endinnermargin;
         endlayout;
      endgraph;
   end;
run;
```

```
proc sgrender data=SurvivalPlotData template=Fig_8_7_Survival_plot_in;
  run;
```

To achieve this layout, we use the INNERMARGIN-ENDINNERMARGIN block at the bottom of the overlay container. We can place one-dimensional statements in this block. Such statements span the full axis in one direction (x-axis, in this case) and the space required to draw the plot can be precisely determined as it is based only on the text attributes. This allows the graph to size the inner margin precisely.

Using this layout, all the information is inside the overlay container, and the "Subjects At-Risk" information is placed closer to the survival curves, without any intervening clutter from the x-axis or the legend. This layout is presented as an alternative to the traditional layout presented earlier.

## 8.8 Bivariate Distribution Plot

The graph shown in Figure 8.8.1 is very useful to view the distribution of data by two variables in any domain, whether clinical, health care, financial, and so on. The graph shows a scatter plot of Systolic by Weight from the data set SASHELP.HEART. A few observations from the data set are shown in Figure 8.8.2.

**Figure 8.8.1 – Bivariate Distribution Plot**

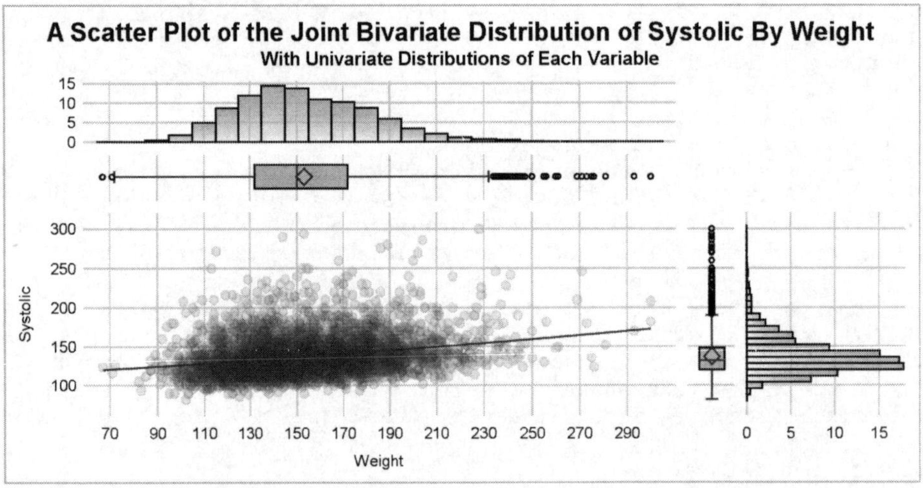

**Figure 8.8.2 – Data for Graph**

| Obs | Weight | Cholesterol | Systolic | Diastolic | Sex |
|-----|--------|-------------|----------|-----------|--------|
| 1 | 140 | . | 124 | 78 | Female |
| 2 | 194 | 181 | 144 | 92 | Female |
| 3 | 132 | 250 | 170 | 90 | Female |
| 4 | 158 | 242 | 128 | 80 | Female |

This graph provides a visual representation of any correlation between these two variables. Solid filled markers are displayed with a high value of transparency, which enables us to view where the dense clusters are in the data. A quadratic regression fit is overlaid.

The graph also shows the univariate distributions of each variable using a histogram and a box plot on each axis. In addition to the scatter plot, this provides us another view of the distribution of the data in each dimension.

GTL is the ideal tool to create such a graph. The LAYOUT LATTICE container is used to apportion the graph space into a 3x3 grid of cells. The row weights are set to 0.2, 0.15, and 0.65 and the column weights are set to 0.74, 0.06, and 0.2 to create a layout as shown in Figure 8.8.3.

**Figure 8.8.3 – Layout Schematic for the Graph**

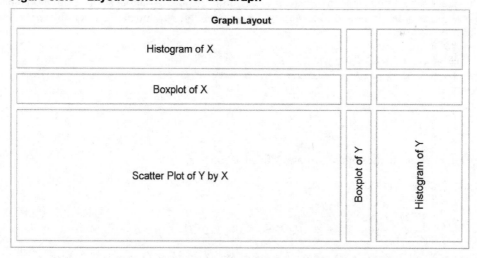

The structure of the graph shown in Figure 8.8.3 is created by the following GTL code block.

```
layout lattice / rows=3 columns=3 columndatarange=union
                rowdatarange=union rowweights=(0.2 0.15 0.65)
                columnweights=(0.74 0.06 0.2);
```

```
/*--Define 9 cells using Layout Overlay blocks*/
layout overlay / <options>;
  < plot statements >
endlayout;
```

```
endlayout;
```

Nine sets of LAYOUT OVERLAY – ENDLAYOUT blocks of code are used to populate each of the nine cells that are defined by the 3 x 3 settings in the LAYOUT LATTICE statement. Each block must contain either a plot statement or an ENTRY statement. In the actual lattice structure for the graph, we do not need cell borders, so individual ENTRY statements can be placeholders for each cell.

There must be a placeholder for each cell, or the arrangement will shift and thus cause other alignment problems between axis types. Finally, there must be at least one valid plot type, or else the entire graph layout will be blank. The three cells in the top row are defined as follows.

```
/*--Top Row--*/
layout overlay / walldisplay=none;
  histogram _xvar / filltype=gradient;
endlayout;
```

```
entry ' ';
entry ' ';
```

The individual cells are populated in row major order, from top left to bottom right. Options can be used to reverse the order, if needed. The three cells in the middle row are defined as follows.

```
/*--Middle Row--*/
layout overlay / walldisplay=none;
  boxplot y=_XVar / orient=horizontal boxwidth=0.9;
endlayout;
```

```
entry ' ';
entry ' ';
```

Finally, the three cells in the bottom row are defined as follows.

```
/*--Bottom Row--*/
layout overlay / walldisplay=none;
  if (_type = 'heatmap')
    heatmap x=_xvar y=_yvar / colormodel=(cx5f7faf gold red);
  else
    scatterplot x=_xvar y=_yvar / markerattrs=(symbol=circlefilled)
                datatransparency=0.95;
  endif;
  regressionplot x=_xvar y=_yvar / degree=2 lineattrs=graphdatadefault;
endlayout;
```

```
layout overlay / walldisplay=none;
  boxplot y=_YVar / boxwidth=0.9;
endlayout;

layout overlay / walldisplay=none;
  histogram _yvar / orient=horizontal filltype=gradient;
endlayout;
```

Note the use of the dynamic variables "_XVar" and "_YVar".  These are used to make the template flexible, and they are useful to create multiple graphs with different X- or Y- variables.  These dynamic variables can be defined at run time in the PROC SGRENDER step as shown below.  Here we have set _XVar='Weight' and _YVar='Systolic' to view the distribution of Systolic x Weight.  The use of dynamic variables enables us to define one template and use it repeatedly with different variable names.

```
proc sgrender data=sashelp.heart
template=Fig_8_8_Bivariate_Distribution_Plot;
  dynamic _XVar='Weight' _YVar='Systolic' _Type='scatter'
        _Title='A Scatter Plot of the Joint Bivariate Distribution of ';
run;
```

We have also defined other dynamics: "_Type" and "_Title".  The "_Type" dynamic is used to control the type of plot that is displayed in the lower left cell of the graph.  In the procedure invocation below, we have specified _Type="heatmap" to get the graph shown in Figure 8.8.4.  We have also set the "_Title" dynamic to alter the title accordingly.

```
proc sgrender data=sashelp.heart
template=Fig_8_8_Bivariate_Distribution_Plot;
  dynamic _XVar='Weight' _YVar='Systolic' _Type='heatmap'
        _Title='A Heat Map of the Joint Bivariate Distribution of ';
run;
```

**Figure 8.8.4 – Heat Map of the Joint Bivariate Distribution**

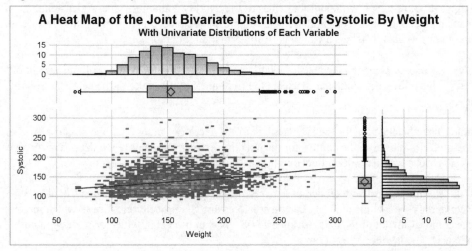

A heat map is a more useful and efficient plot type for display of the distribution of large data. When the number of observations grows large, into the millions or billions of observations, plotting each observation as a marker in a scatter plot becomes inefficient and ineffective.

Such large data sets are likely to reside on cloud servers, and retrieving each observation for plotting is not feasible. Even rendering the scatter plot on the server is not effective, as it is time-consuming, and all we will see is a glob of data. This is true even with SASHELP.HEART data set, which has only 5400 observations. This can be seen in Figure 8.8.1.

However, creating a heat map provides a faster and more effective solution. Now, we are counting the number of observations in each bin of the plot. The number of bins is constant; they might be 100 x 50 in this case. Each bin is displayed using a color that represents the number of observations in the bin using a three-color mode as shown in Figure 8.8.4.

A gradient legend could have been included in the display, but I have chosen to skip it because the key here is to see the relative densities, not the actual densities. The full code for the template and graph creation can be seen in Program 8_8.

## 8.9 Summary

With SAS 9.4, you have a powerful set of features to create clinical graphs. The new AXISTABLE statement was specifically designed to address many different needs to include textual data in the graph. Such data needs to be aligned with the horizontal axis, as in the case of a survival plot, or aligned with the vertical axis, as in the case of a forest plot.

The axis table supports features to assign the text attributes of a row or column for rich text support. Class data can be arranged side by side or stacked. Values can be colored by classifiers. These statements support extensive options for arrangement of the values or labels for the vertical table.

Inner margins are now supported on all four sides of the overlay container. One-dimensional objects can be placed in these regions, and the axis table can be placed in any of the four locations. Multiple columns of an axis tables are automatically arranged into tables.

Axis tables can also be placed in the cells of a lattice container using the row or column weight of "Preferred". This allows the container to assign the right amount of space for the cell based on the font metrics.

New features have been added for the arrangement of the axis tick values and labels. These can be seen in the butterfly plot or in the control for the axis line extent to span only the data. This enables you to create graphs with a modern, lightweight feel.

Many of these features are also included with the SGPLOT procedure. As shown in Chapters 3 and 4, many commonly used clinical graphs can be created using SG procedures. However, often you need more complex layout of the data. In such cases, you can use GTL, which provides you with more options for the layout of your graph.

---

[1] Matange, Sanjay. "Graphically Speaking." Available at http://blogs.sas.com/content/graphicallyspeaking/. Last updated October 31, 2015. Accessed on February 1, 2016.

# Index

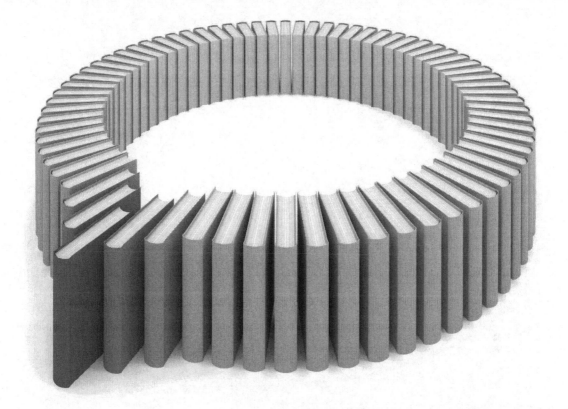

# Gain Greater Insight into Your SAS® Software with SAS Books.

Discover all that you need on your journey to knowledge and empowerment.